Working to Be Someone

of related interest

Shattered Lives
Children Who Live with Courage and Dignity
Camila Batmanghelidjh
ISBN 978 1 84310 434 6

Youth Justice and Child Protection
Edited by Malcolm Hill, Andrew Lockyer and Fred Stone
ISBN 978 1 84310 279 3

The Participation Rights of the Child
Rights and Responsibilities in Family and Society
Målfrid Grude Flekkøy and Natalie Hevener Kaufman
ISBN 978 1 85302 490 0 pb
ISBN 978 1 85302 489 4 hb

Children's Rights and Power
Charging Up for a New Century
Mary John
Children in Charge 9
ISBN 978 1 85302 659 1 pb
ISBN 978 1 85302 658 4 hb

Young Children's Rights
Exploring Beliefs, Principles and Practice
Priscilla Alderson
Forewords by Save the Children and Mary John
Children in Charge 10
ISBN 978 1 85302 880 9

Children Taken Seriously
In Theory, Policy and Practice
Edited by Jan Mason and Toby Fattore
Foreword by Mary John
Children in Charge 12
ISBN 978 1 84310 250 2

Working to Be Someone

Child Focused Research and Practice
with Working Children

*Edited by Beatrice Hungerland, Manfred Liebel,
Brian Milne and Anne Wihstutz*

Jessica Kingsley Publishers
London and Philadelphia

First published in 2007
by Jessica Kingsley Publishers
116 Pentonville Road
London N1 9JB, UK
and
400 Market Street, Suite 400
Philadelphia, PA 19106, USA

www.jkp.com

Library of Congress Cataloging in Publication Data

Working to be someone : child focused research and practice with working children / edited by Beatrice Hungerland ... [et al].
    p. cm.
    Includes bibliographical references and index.
    ISBN-13: 978-1-84310-523-7 (pbk.)
    1. Child labor--Case studies. I. Hungerland, Beatrice, 1962-
    HD6231.W68 2007
    331.3'1--dc22

2007002317

British Library Cataloguing in Publication Data
A CIP catalogue record for this book is available from the British Library

ISBN 978 1 84310 523 7

Printed and bound in Great Britain by
Athenaeum Press, Gateshead, Tyne and Wear

Contents

Part 3: Work and Competence

Part 4: Participation of Working Children

Part 5: Citizenship and Working Children's Movements and Organisations

Part 6: Challenges and Perspectives for Research and Policy

List of boxes

List of figures

List of tables

Introduction

Beatrice Hungerland, Manfred Liebel,
Brian Milne and Anne Wihstutz

With this book we intend to contribute towards giving a new accent to research on children's work, by lending greater weight to the hitherto unheeded experiences, perspectives and voices of working children. And we hope that its contributions will provide an impetus towards more intensive international cooperation on the part of all those for whom child work does not only represent a social problem to be tackled, but for whom its focus is on the working children themselves as social and economic subjects who are to be taken seriously in all conceivable aspects of their lives.

As academic research workers we deem it indispensable to liberate ourselves from ideological biases that have chiefly originated in Europe concerning a supposedly ideal childhood, and which unfortunately have continued up to the present to leave their mark on a good deal of research work, and to a large extent also on programmes and measures to combat child labour propagated by the International Labour Organization (ILO) and partly also by UNICEF (United Nations Children's Fund). Current slogans such as 'Stop child labour – school is the best place to work' or 'School instead of work' may at first sight appear plausible and have the children's best interest in mind, but on closer inspection they can be seen to obscure our view of the multifarious cultural patterns of childhood existing around the globe, in which work and learning or work and play are not irreconcilable opposites, and in which children play an integrated, respected and even influential part in social life.

What is even more problematic, the attitude behind such slogans discriminates against and marginalises all manifestations of childhood that do not correspond to the accustomed western pattern. In our view, this is seen by no-one more clearly than by working children themselves, as is clearly expressed in the autonomous movements of these children that have emerged in the past two decades in many countries in Latin America, Africa and Asia.

Most of the contributions to this book are based on papers presented at an international symposium, which was organised by the editors between 12 and 17 April 2004 in Berlin, Germany, with support of the German Research Association (DFG). We had given this symposium the motto 'What does work mean to children?', intending to provide a counter-accent to the mainstream of research, which enquires predominantly into the causes and effects of child work. Important as these enquiries are, they run the danger of losing sight of the subjective aspects of children's work and of children as social subjects. The search for causes proceeds from a view of child work that sees it exclusively as a social or economic problem, but not as an open field marked by widely differing forms and conditions, and which involves multifarious experiences for the children. In studies of the effects, working children appear as objects of processes over which they have no influence, and even where the work of children is considered in a more differentiated way, the effects of work are almost exclusively deduced from the conditions of the work itself. Little account is taken of the socio-cultural context or of the personal environment and the individual and collective resources of the children, although it is clear to what an extent children's perception and their ways of dealing with difficult and burdensome conditions is marked by them.

In dealing with the question as to the effects of child work on children, it is also still usual for researchers to claim absolute objectivity of judgement, using criteria that they themselves have set up, or which have even been prescribed to them by organisations that commission their work. And even when children are questioned as to their 'opinions', these are commonly subordinated to preconceived schemes of interpretation, and relativised as 'merely subjective'. Finally, working children are denied the competence to judge their own situation.

We suppose that every research concerning children's work has to be guided by ethic maxims like ethical symmetry. Above all it should contribute to the improvement of the working children's living and working conditions, enforce the children's rights and respect children as sensitive, thinking and acting subjects. Moreover research should emphasise that work experiences of children are not in all cases disadvantageous. Rather according to varying conditions and cultural contexts, these experiences also can enable the strengthening of their social responsibility and their social commitment. In this sense, children should gain legal access to interesting and self-determined work. Ideas of education should be extended in a way that work is also viewed as an important learning experience. The educational value of work should be accounted for in educational systems.

A frequently underestimated problem also lies in the concepts, notions or terms used in writings in this field. Of course, concepts are indispensable both in everyday communication and in academic research, as they help us to order and understand social reality. However, inasmuch as they are abstractions, there is always a tension between the assumed social reality and that which we express with the aid of our concepts. This fact, which is unfortunately all too often overlooked, is commonly expressed by the notion of 'social representations'. Once introduced, concepts take on a life of their own, which we research workers are not able to elude. In this connection, the French philosopher Michel Foucault has spoken of 'discourses' and attributed to them a considerable significance in the justification of power (not only in interpretation).

This is particularly evident in the case of the term 'child labour'. It sets off negative associations, and thus in itself characterises to a fair extent the perception of the working children's reality that we label with this notion and attempt to understand with it. Concerning this we point out the necessity to take into account the multitude of sectors, forms and conditions of work. Domestic work and care work is generally ignored. We are also emphasising the need to put more attention to the meaning of the work for children. Perhaps we ought to resolve in future not to refer to research into 'child labour' or 'child work' (whatever term we may use for it), but to research into and with 'working children'.

As the editors of this book, a particular focus of our attention is the 'significance' of children's work. With regard to this question, in our view two aspects need to be distinguished:

- the question of children's own interpretations of their experience
- the question as to the changes in social status that are expressed in children's work and result from it.

The first question has to do not only with the children's 'opinions'; the question arises how a well-considered interpretation of their experience of work is to be worked out (together with the children), and formulated in theoretical terms. In doing so, however, the fact must be taken account of that the children do not exist aside from the society that surrounds them, with the ideologies that predominate in it, and that the children's interpretation of their experience is influenced by these, while at the same time they are able to arrive, by developing their own ideas (in common with others), at an autonomous assessment. We should be particularly interested in this context by the commonly concealed or disregarded knowledge of the children, guided by their interests, and their interpretation of their own reality and the role of work within it.

The second question is concerned with whether the involvement of children in working processes brings with it changes in the children's social status. As we know, where children are reduced to functions of their labour power and its exploitation, and have hardly any chance to make decisions of their own, their subjection can take on extreme forms, going as far as being life-threatening. However, inclusion in the working process can also result in social recognition and a boost to the children's self-awareness, from which not seldom results a reinforcement of their demands for a hearing, and for respect and participation in socio-political matters. This applies not only to the societies of the South (majority world), but is becoming increasingly evident in the countries of the North (minority world). What is involved is not only a change in the relations of dependence and authority with regard to adults, but in the place of children and childhood as a whole within the social framework. Here, it also has to be taken into account that the world of work in recent times has been marked by considerable changes in form and content. Many researchers raise the question whether new kinds of access to and perception of the world of work are thus being rendered possible for children.

In the context of research of this kind, the movements and organisations of working children are – at least in countries of the South – of considerable importance, as they contribute to sharpening the children's perception of reality and freeing them from the ideological preconceptions of the society concerned. These movements give the children experience not provided for in the predominant western pattern of childhood. They could be indicators for a new kind of childhood, in which children are not in the first place objects of the benevolence of adults, but active social subjects exerting their own influence. In this sense, a sensitive form of research, conceived in terms of support and participation, can produce far-reaching insights into the conditions of work for children, either in the sense of their self-interpretation, or of their social recognition and status within the power structure of society.

The contributions of the book make clear that children's work is not a phenomenon of minorities. It is part of daily life of most of the children in the South as well as in the North. The reasons and the conditions for their work differ a lot in the various parts of the world. Neo-liberal globalisation evokes new forms of child exploitation, mainly in the South, which are partly extreme and often hidden. The differences in the significance of work for the formation of identity, too, could not be greater. Thus, in contrast to the South, there is hardly a child in the North that would define himself or herself as a 'working child', not to speak of joining together with other working children in an organisation.

On the other hand in the South as well as in the North many children express an increasing desire for rewarding and interesting work. Great as the differences are, some parallels are striking and yet hardly noted. Thus it emerges from a number of studies that many children both in the North and South regard their earnings from work in a similar way to a chance of becoming more independent, getting more social appraisal and to play a more active role in society or to share the insignia of youth culture. Some years ago, the British–Dutch anthropologist Ben White called this finding an indication of the cultural globalisation of child work.

The book makes evident that there are many possibilities of comparative research work on and with working children in the South and North, and thus also in differing social and cultural contexts. To our knowledge, although interesting publications emerged from earlier comparable international conferences of child work experts – for instance, conferences in Trondheim (1996), Amsterdam (1998) and Paris (2000) – this did not result in any continuous cooperation in practical research work. The network of specialists installed some years ago by the ILO may be useful in some respects, but it is marked by political and ideological preconceptions, which largely precludes international research precisely on the significance of work to children, particularly with the active participation of working children themselves.

The International Working Group on Child Labour (IWGCL), which was initiated in the mid-1990s by two NGOs (non-governmental organisations), is to be thanked for providing an important impetus during the few years of its existence. Above all, it made a new departure with the question: 'Have we asked the children?' Nevertheless it was precisely over this question that it failed, because this went too far for some of the sponsors.

In order to intensify the collaboration between research teams of different countries, at the international symposium it was proposed to initiate a new 'International Study and Action Group in Support of Working Children'. The group should be led by the vision of a world in which working children are accepted and valued as social actors and be able to act independently enough to tackle questions and topics that have so far been taboo. In our view, this should include not only consulting working children, but including them as active partners in practical research. For this reason, it is important that we do not limit our self-awareness as researchers to the academic field, but try to recruit the help of the activists of children's rights and in children's aid organisations who are interested in the same questions. In the book, there will be found contributions of both groups.

We believe that the book presents some lines of orientation for future cooperation as researchers who also feel an emotional bond with working children, and wish with their research work to contribute to the children (sometimes called as those 'out-of-place') instead of being excluded, being able to find a voice and to play their part in influencing the course of events in the world. For this, in view of the mainstream of research into child work hitherto, a change of perspective is inevitable, and we think there is plenty of potential for this.

The book is divided into six main parts. Part 1 presents different perspectives reflecting on the question of how to approach theoretically the social reality of working children, their changing places and roles in different societies and cultures. Part 2 is dedicated to the often neglected and underestimated care and domestic work of girls and boys. In Part 3 the importance of work for gaining socially relevant knowledge and competences is discussed based on empirical research in both 'poor' and 'affluent' societies. Prevailing myths and hidden aspects of children's work are analysed. Part 4 focuses on the question of how children's work contributes to more participation of children in their communities and societies. Particularly for Africa and Asia some inside views concerning the development and different stakes and forms of working children's participation and citizenship are discussed in Part 5, pointing out the relevance and limits of the articles in the United Nations (UN) Convention on the Rights of the Child on participation for such processes. The book ends with reflections about the challenges and perspectives for research and policy in the field of child work and working children (Part 6).

Part 1

Theoretical Approaches

Chapter 1

A Feminist Economist's Approach to Children's Work

Deborah Levison

Statisticians and economists have had an influential role in discussions of child labor, yet much of this role has been hidden from view. This role has come about via international definitions and standards used to construct national accounts, for the end purpose of measuring countries' gross national products and so forth, but used for many other purposes along the way. In this short essay, I use examples to demonstrate the influence of definitions and common practices in collecting and analyzing data on how child work is conceptualized, and on what aspects of child work are given attention or neglected.

My perspective is that of an empirical economist – someone who analyzes microdata (computerized information about individuals) from surveys to better understand child work – and a feminist. Feminist economists have, among other things, studied and theorized about gendered dimensions of work, and many of these discussions are applicable to children's work. My first example draws upon writings by feminist economists about unpaid household work. Standard definitions of work used for producing statistics ignore much of the work done by women and by children, because of the way 'work' has been defined.

Reproductive work

Marilyn Waring (1988, p.2) relates the history of how the United Nations System of National Accounts (UNSNA) came to define the boundaries of 'productive activity.' She critiques its systematic exclusion of women's 'reproductive work' – that is, tasks necessary to maintain and 'reproduce' the labor force by bearing, caring for and training children (future workers), and feeding, clothing, and caring for adults, often men (current workers). Waring points out that a wide variety of policy measures are based on an understanding of economic statistics – but 'from the outset, the figures are rigged' due to the omission of these tasks, so fundamental to life and to the ability to work. Diana Strassman (1993, p.60) writes, 'While economists have given lip service to women's work in the home as one of those "unfortunate" exclusions from the national income accounts, gendered conceptualizations of what counts as work matter greatly for public policy.'

Many feminist economists are concerned about taking reproductive work seriously because ignoring it renders much of women's work invisible, and their contributions to society are thus undervalued. The same argument can be made with respect to children. Children often work under the direction of women doing 'chores,'[1] and such responsibilities take many hours of girls' time, especially in the global South. Boys also spend considerable amounts of time on chores in many cultures, although this seems to diminish in adolescence (e.g., Mensch *et al.* 2000).

Policies and programs to address issues related to children's work are often informed and directed by statistics about the presence, number, and activities of child workers. While in many cases, decision-makers would be better served to read some recent qualitative studies, instead they look at a table or two of statistics. Most tables of this sort show statistics that were produced using definitions and methods that fit nicely into current definitions of economic activity, but which are arguably very far from summary measures based on a child's perspective of children's work. To a great extent, this is because most measures of children's work systematically exclude unpaid, 'reproductive' work done in a child's own home or for the child's own family. By definition, standard measures ignore the many hours of work done predominantly by girls (and by women) as they cook, clean, care for children and the elderly, and undertake other household 'chores.'

Most children engaged in such tasks know that they are working; this is clear from Pamela Reynolds' (1991) path-breaking study, among others. Moreover, some 'chores' may be hazardous – think of small children cooking, for example. Sometimes they interfere with the possibility of school to a greater extent than does labor force work – for instance, when girls take on household responsibilities of women who are now doing labor force work (e.g., Benería 1992).

Even more hidden is the caring labor that children perform for ill, disabled, and old adults. The responsibilities that children have when their parents are alcoholic or drug-addicted must be among the most burdensome, although they are also the most secret, so we know little of these cases.

Intermittent child work

Even numbers that aim to measure children's labor force work – a narrower goal than measuring all kinds of children's work – are distorted by assumptions that underlie survey questionnaires. The assumption that I highlight in my second example concerns the regularity or intermittency of children's work. Surveys that implicitly treat child workers as small versions of adult workers have become standard practice, and the resulting statistics thus do not allow us to consider other possibilities.

Case studies in some contexts – and certainly in urban Brazil, the location of one of my studies (Levison *et al.* 2003) – show that children who do labor force work often do not follow adult employment patterns. They may work long hours one week, then be out of work the next week – because the job was done, or they quit, or they were fired. These children move in and out of labor force work at a much higher rate than do adults. Field work often reports children's labor force involvement as sporadic, opportunistic, quick-to-change, and mainly informal.

Thus, it should not come as a surprise that surveys designed to capture adults' labor force employment and unemployment produce statistics that do not correctly distinguish between children who are usually or often 'workers' and children who are rarely or never labor force workers. These surveys are not designed to capture intermittent work patterns. In most cases, what they do is identify which children were labor force workers *last week*.

This would not be so much of a problem if these numbers were not used regularly for policy and programmatic purposes, with an implicit suggestion that the estimate accurately reflects the prevalence of all child workers in the population. Yet the *last week* estimates can differ enormously from estimates generated by in-depth studies with children, asking about or observing their activities. My collaborators and I have shown that, in urban Brazil, even a fairly limited attempt to capture intermittency can double the employment rates for 10–12-year-olds (Levison *et al.* 2003).

Ignoring children's perspectives

My third example is about 'voice.' Feminists have noted the many situations in which women have been silenced – not given a chance to speak for themselves. Often those in a position of power (usually men) have assumed that they know what women would say, what women would want. Alternatively, those in authority have felt that they know better than women themselves what women *should* want. Adults have acted similarly with respect to children. Children's perspectives on work have been neglected by the expert information-gatherers and statistics-producers, and children have been silenced. One example of this behavior follows.

Bureaucrats at the International Labour Office (ILO)[2] in Geneva are in the process of attempting to standardize how 'child labor' – which they take to mean 'abusive child work' – should be defined and measured. The ILO's child labor group, the International Programme for the Elimination of Child Labour (IPEC), has a very large programmatic division, funded by international donors, to create interventions that remove children from work. IPEC also has a smaller research division, known by its acronym, SIMPOC.[3] This, too, is funded by international donors. Among other activities, SIMPOC has been heavily involved in funding surveys intended to count numbers of child workers in many developing countries, and to collect a variety of other information about them as well. It has developed a 'model' questionnaire for this purpose; countries that partner with the ILO to field a child labor survey are encouraged to use this model questionnaire as a starting point for country-specific surveys.

A review of recent work by Edith De Leeuw and collaborators (e.g. De Leeuw, Borgers and Strijbos-Smits 2002) reveals some of the many downfalls of taking survey methods designed for adults and applying them to children without serious adaptation. Yet this is exactly what has been done in the case of the survey questionnaire recommended by SIMPOC (2002). The child labor surveys undertaken, which are addressed to both parents and children, have not been systematically designed to use language that is developmentally appropriate, that the younger children might understand. For example, children aged 5 to 17 are supposed to be able to answer a variation on a standard labor force question: 'For each day worked during the reference week, how many hours did you actually work?' Another question for 5–17-year-olds asks, 'How often were you injured or ill in the last 12 months?' It seems unlikely that many adults could answer this question with accuracy. Five-year-olds have a hard time reporting events of the past few days, and have no concept of the time encompassed by a year.

The fundamental implication is that children's 'voice' – children's ability to give meaningful input into decisions (Budd 2004) – is not important enough to be taken seriously; if children cannot answer a question, an adult can speak for them. It is this assumption that adults know what children would say, or know what children *should* say, that is problematic. But this is the message being sent by the child labor research unit of the international organization with the greatest influence and authority on the subject of child work.

Many adults, on hearing arguments that children should be given a voice, think that this means that children should make all their own decisions. Yet any parent knows that this would be ridiculous. Children develop different capabilities at different ages, and it is inappropriate to expect them to assume the responsibility of making all their own choices when they are not developmentally prepared to do so. Having a voice does not necessarily mean making a decision. Having a voice means the ability to express an opinion; for example, to give input to a family decision about who will do what tasks. Children may not know when chemicals are harming their bodies, but they can tell us when they are tired, when they hurt, and what they would like to learn how to do. As adults, we should take their preferences into account when exercising the authority of parents, teachers, and employers – and expert information-gatherers.

Do definitions matter?

Statistical definitions may not be of much interest to scholars and activists who interact directly with child workers, conducting case studies and related qualitative research. Do definitions matter, or do concerns about them reflect a misled emphasis on quantitative measures?

While not discounting the value of qualitative scholarship, feminist economists also argue that definitions matter enormously. Definitions and methodologies affect who is counted, recognized, protected, and given alternatives. They affect the allocation of programmatic funds, and they affect what laws are thought to be necessary.

It is convenient for adults not to take seriously many activities that children view as work, or bother about child-specific patterns of work; this 'oversight' is possible because of power differentials between the generations. Feminists are particularly sensitive to how power differentials affect the allocation of resources and tasks along gender lines – and the perceptions of these assignments. When it is performed in and around their own homes, children's work is hidden by the definitions in much the same way that women's work is hidden.

Children's work is obscured by the power that adults have over them. Their own fathers and mothers do not count many of children's 'chores' as work (Reynolds 1991). As I have argued elsewhere, the belief that it is acceptable to exclude children from paid (labor force) work, but reasonable to require them to undertake unpaid work for their families, is a reflection of children's relative lack of power. It is not a result of systematic evidence about how best to promote children's well-being (Levison 2000, pp.125–6).

It is, for example, self-serving for those who make the rules to decide that work done by children in family enterprises is acceptable even at young ages, while work under the supervision of non-family members is unacceptable at many ages. Economic rhetoric reinforces the unstated assumption that parents are best able to judge how to take care of their own children – just as they are granted the right to dispose of their own property. Yet the family violence literature finds unequivocally that children are at greatest risk of verbal, physical, and sexual abuse from fathers and close relatives. We know that children living on the street have often fled from violence perpetrated by family members (e.g., Green 1998). When case studies tell us that many children prefer to work outside the home, these signals should be taken seriously by those adults with the power to influence quantitative definitions and measures.

My main point is that relative power is fundamental in determining how societies and authorities view – and measure – children's work, how parents view children's work, and even how children view their own work. And if we do not often hear children's voices, let us not be misled that children do not have opinions to offer. As Bina Agarwal (1997, p.25) writes, compliance with the established social order 'need not imply complicity.' Measuring work and workers via definitions and measures that take children seriously will require fundamental changes in current practices.

Notes

1. It is notable that, in English, 'chores' is a word that is often understood to have a mildly derogatory implication – it refers to tasks that have to be done, but are not really very important. For example, *Webster's New World Dictionary*'s first definition of chore is 'a small routine task, as of a housekeeper or farmer' (1976, p.252).

2. The International Labour Office exists to carry out the decisions of the International Labour Organization.

3. SIMPOC stands for Statistical Information and Monitoring Programme on Child Labour.

Chapter 2

Working Children and the Cultural Perception of Childhood

Zandra Pedraza-Gómez

To support the historical and constructed character of the modern notion of childhood, in which children are considered individuals with specific and unique characteristics which make them subjects of protection, and whose main occupations should be play and school attendance, results from considering European history since the sixteenth century. The work of Philippe Ariès (1997), despite its limitations and the critiques it has received, is still canonical and an obligatory reference for knowing the development of ideas concerning childhood since the Renaissance. The conceptualisation of childhood as an age of physical and emotional vulnerability and psychological and intellectual incompleteness has been basic to the advancement of the perspective in which the child needs a certain kind of protection that mainly excludes him from productive activities and culminated in the Convention on the Rights of the Child in 1989.

The evolution of this vision of childhood and of the concomitant social and public policy principles, which protect those changes, is part of a wider process, mainly described and analysed in concern with European societies. Elements of this transformation are *The Making of the Modern Family* (Shorter 1975), the rise of the individual, the universalisation of formal (e.g. school) education as one capital resource for socialisation and child time use, and the specialisation of knowledge, that is, the development of expert knowledge concerning, in this case, the child. Pedagogy, paediatrics, child and developmental psychology and psychoanalysis are the most visible disciplines sustaining the modern conception, description and knowledge of childhood. As a result of those processes, human rights evolved in such a way that children deserved a special version of them, one which finally realises the Convention on the Rights of the Child. This Convention principally exposes the cultural perception of childhood made possible by the above mentioned phenomena. It is not possible to isolate this evolution from the fact that expert knowledge about childhood has seriously influenced it. But this knowledge, as the most known and cited authors recognise, refers to the so-called western industrial society, which mainly comprises western European countries, and North America excluding Mexico (Ariès 1987; De Mause 1974; Delgado 1998; Giddens 1991; Gurevich 1994). However, the Convention is conceived to express and guarantee children's rights with independence of family structure, labour conditions, education opportunities and public policies which are to be found in different countries and societies or between different social groups or classes.

The world adherence to the Convention illustrates the reach of the official approval of this perception of childhood. This global and official consensus draws a veil upon the way in which the understanding of childhood has been produced, in so far as the essentialist nature that coats it is in turn a result of that global consensus. This same global character and consensus supports the discussion about the eradication of child labour or, as this book proposes, the debate about the meaning of work for children.

However, this debate has to be held taking into account the diverse cultural and social facts which historically led to the perception of childhood currently represented by the Convention on the Rights of the Child, and recognising that modern and contemporary childhood, as the Convention declares it, is possible mainly under specific social, educational, labour and familiar conditions which are far from being universal. The Rights of the Child are the ultimate expression and the culmination of the way of life and the conceptions of the bourgeois family and the capitalist society as they have been experienced in the western industrial societies.

The interest in proposing to review the concept of childhood focuses on a non-Eurocentric perspective centred on the possibility of thinking about the development and characteristics of children, not in terms of the core European history understood as world history, but in the context of the modern/colonial world system and in a perspective such as that suggested by the concepts of coloniality of power (Quijano 2000) and colonial difference.

Dussel (2000) underlines the need to think about world history in terms of the constitution of the world in the sixteenth century, as a result of the construction of the European history as a lineal diachronic ideological construct which rises in Greece and Rome to become the core of the world history, outside which every society and history is non-political and non-human. This vision is based upon and continually reinforces a racist view of the world. The auto-proclamation of Europe as modern and enlightened obscures the fact that a modern, global world was possible for the first time with the expansion of Europe through colonization, and due to the subordination of all non-European territories based on the supposed sub-human character of their population and nature. Modernity, so Dussel states, emerges not with the accomplishment of the maturity proclaimed by Kant, but as a world characteristic in 1492. At that moment a fundamental determination of the modern world was created – the emergence of a world history in which the central European states, armies, economy and philosophy became the core of the world history and the colonial world was organised so that its victims could be pragmatically and economically made profitable (Quijano 2000).

In this colonial/modern world, colonialism is to be understood as the dark side, a constitutive one, and not as a mere consequence. The colonial/modern world rests on a power pattern sustained by the idea of race and by Eurocentrism. One of its main features is the lasting, after colonialism itself, of a character of coloniality expressed in the form of power. Based on a proclaimed different biological structure made evident by physiognomic features and skin colour, race became the main element for Europe to explain and classify world population. At the same time, all historical forms of work control, resources and products were articulated around capital and world market. This means that the exploitation of human force, for example Indians and slaves, was possible because of the proclaimed superiority of the white race. Control over work, resources and product was made possible in the frame of colonial/modern, for example racial, relations of production.

Race and its subsequent division of labour became structurally associated, and mutually reinforced and produced a racial division of work (Quijano 2000, p.204) which lasted during the colonial period as a fundamental feature of the colonial/ modern capitalism. The racial character of production relation made it possible to interpret body and reproduction as part of this relation. This means that as a way to dominate/exploit the population, children were part of the power pattern and subject to exploitation until the beginning of the nineteenth century.

To produce a reinterpretation of the concept of childhood attending to the modern/colonial condition of the world history, it is important to start by pointing out that the origin of the tendency towards rendering particular consideration and attention to childhood, and the strengthening of an awareness of care and affect for children, which tended to release them from the cycle of production, is contemporary to the colonial character of the world economy and to European expansion policy since the sixteenth century.

Although during this time children in Europe gradually became the object of a growing pedagogical and medical attention and of family and school care, children in European colonies, converted like their parents in subordinates, entered into the productive circuits of servitude and slavery. While European children were gradually liberated from work and European families grew to bourgeois families, education became compulsory and hygiene and basic medical services were slowly available for working classes, children under colonial regimes were part of the working resources of a racially subordinated world population.

In this sense it is necessary to underline the character of the international organisation of labour constituted in the sixteenth century, which ended in a hierarchical ordering of the world population according mainly to the notion of race and its feminisation (Quijano 2000; Mignolo 1998, 2000). This locates the colonised inhabitants, the Indians of the peoples of Americas, in a subordinate condition, and Africans in a slavery relationship with a total loss of liberty and control over the reproduction and education of their children, as well as inhibits in all of them access to forms of labour organised around the wage–work relationship which began to consolidate in Europe, and which has as a condition of existence the liberation of the individual labour force from communal and familiar production.

This situation extended in America over three centuries. Meanwhile, childhood in Europe became an age in need of protection and an object of specialised forms of knowledge. The European struggle and the debate to eradicate child labour, in particular in the industrial sector during the nineteenth century, should also be interpreted in relation to the European loss of direct access to the valuable natural resources of America, that ought to have induced the temporary need to recruit a child labour force before consolidating economic forms that equilibrated the wage–work relationship between the workers.

This phenomenon never developed quite in that way in Latin America, nor did it indeed probably in Africa and Asia. The postcolonial condition of Latin American republics since 1820, and the unbalanced economic relations established with European countries and with the United States, oriented economic production towards extractive forms, to monocultures and towards a handcrafted, and less dynamic, subsidiary production. In such a context, production relationships never transformed in a way that allowed the development of work relationships based on wages and available for the workers; relationships that would have allowed growth and enrichment capable of weakening the participation of children in production so that specialisation of knowledge and labour force could take place.

An important face of the condition of modernity which extends itself after independence is the coloniality of power. This condition drives the white bourgeoisie as ruler and elite of the new nation states, to perceive its interests as the same ones of the former European white rulers and to characterise the national population by the same racial principle the Europeans used to classify the world population after the constitution of the modern world system. This renewed ideological use did also renew the colonial character of the new nations and established social mechanisms to reproduce those differences. One of the most important was the whole educational system, as well as the labour market. The educational system has had in many countries enormous difficulties in guaranteeing a compulsory, free and universal education. On the other side, the coloniality of power hinders the inclusion of a considerable percentage of the labour force in capitalist-waged relations and so excludes them, including their families and children, from the social security system. Many children of low-income families, who have access nonetheless to formal education, don't attend schools which guarantee them an equal legitimate knowledge and labour opportunities which will allow them to enter into stable and fair waged relationships. Under such circumstances, work appears to be a logical and, sometimes, the only possible activity for children.

Since independence in the nineteenth century, the organisation of work in the countries of the region has subsisted on the basis of non-formal and unequal work relationships and the active and necessary participation of children in the economic reproduction of the domestic unit as well as of society. The condition of children as economically exploited agents is characteristic of the subsidiary economies of the world system, just as non-formal work and unfavourable wage conditions are for adults. It is not easy to imagine how, in economies with over 60 to 70 per cent of non-formal labour with daily incomes under US$1 per capita, it should ever be possible to consider the eradication of child work. The condition of the children as economic agents sheds light on the economically subordinate relationships that rule the world system, the racial character of labour relations and the colonial condition intrinsic to subordinate economies, which does not allow the access of workers in the Third World to waged relations and social benefits.

It is true that this situation offends the sensibilities that have emerged in societies whose economies were able to develop inclusive waged forms for the majority of the population as well as robust social protection apparatuses, but this should not be an obstacle to recognising that these economies have been able to become stronger in so far as they are founded on unequal international relations that allowed accelerated capital accumulation, which prevents (on the other side of the scale, the dark side of modernity) even access to basic waged forms for workers of the Third World.

Also, of course, the sensibility of social groups in Third World countries is offended, which have dominant positions, and obviously the sensibility of those who as members of governments, national and international agencies, and non-governmental organisations (NGOs), as well as citizens, would like to see this situation transformed. Nevertheless, they usually consider it isolated from the general work conditions of the children's families and from the subordinate conditions of the social groups (farmers, non-formal workers) to which they belong.

Considering this racial and international division of labour, the conditions of possibility for a modern notion of childhood to take root in the countries of the Third World, and particularly in the non-formal sectors of the economy, between farmers and indigenes is put into question. While most of the children of European workers were outdrawn from factories in the span of half a century and were protected by the scholastic and social system, the children of Indians, slaves and mestizos in America, Africa and Asia continued to participate in the forms of production that are part of the periphery of the world system, which are informality, servitude, slavery and non-industrial manufacture. Even if increases in school attendance, literacy and basic health attention rates are reported, those numbers don't have to obscure the fact that the permanent advance in the degree of knowledge specialisation doesn't guarantee that the formal education to which most of the working children have access will acquire a legitimate enough form to allow them, as adults, to enter a more or less stable labour market. In fact, it has often happened that their parents didn't manage to do it or were expelled from it.

To these forms of economic and social organisation belongs a set of elements that concede to peripheral economies, and concretely to the non-formal ones, characteristics of their own. In the same way as in these economic forms children usually are part of familiar and non-formal kinds of work, they are not inscribed in the school system as the privileged way of obtaining knowledge and maturity. In contexts where learning is not reduced to or concentrated principally in schools, the acquisition of writing and reading skills is not the only way to gain access to knowledge; in those places where forms of knowledge are transmitted orally as vital and functional means to obtain social recognition, the socialisation of children and their paths to adulthood follow other routes.

At the same time and as a result of the colonial condition of power that characterises societies in Latin America, this situation has favoured the strengthening of a modern sensibility towards childhood between the waged sector, and middle and upper classes, which represent less than 40 per cent of the workers in the region. In the framework of this internal division we have to understand that the discussion about children's work and its eradication is led by organisations and persons that operate in a circle where capital-waged relations have been generalised and where the labour force has been freed from informality, as well as where children have been withdrawn from production to being situated exclusively in consumption. This condition as public servants, as well as that of the staff of many NGOs and international agencies, tends to neutralise the condition of informality in which almost all the working children of the region do their work.

These agents often do isolate the child from their social environment, as usually happens with the social intervention forms in which the person is thought of and treated as an individual. However, one often finds that working children are part of familiar and productive nets, where strictly individual considerations and future projection are not the rule. On the contrary, one faces social and cultural conditions where support, common well-being, kinship ties and subsistence in the present prevail.

Taking into account these considerations, it follows to face the question about the condition of the child as productive agent: is childhood possible if children are productive agents, or are only those children inserted as consumers in the economy?

These questions bring us to the problem of the criteria and resources that have been used to model the modern social order and to the fact that questioning most of them shows us the path that has thrown down or at least brought to light the semantic power with which they act to impose a particular order. It is worth remembering that the modern social order is itself structured and based on at least four elements that together play a central role in the symbolic and practical organisation of society following an unequal and hierarchical distribution of power: gender, race, class and age. Critiques of racial and ethnic notions, as well as class and gender, are welcomed – and they have been the object of profound discussions. It is evident for the social sciences, and in many cases for society, that the cultural efforts made over the centuries to order individuals and groups symbolically and practically according to these criteria have turned pale and have lost their argumentative power.

There is a consensus about the constructed character of these notions and about the way they were rhetorically used during modernity, according to specific interests. The work of the feminist and gender theory has been particularly enlightening in making efforts to show the patriarchal and oppressive character of the definitions concerning feminine and masculine essences, as well as the critique of racial arguments.

In this sense a current consensus is growing which puts into question the historical, capitalist and constructed character of the idea of childhood. I am not aware of any work that studies in detail the symbolic and practical processes by which the modern notion of childhood not only defines the possibilities and limitations of children with respect to play and formal education, but also delineates the relationships between parents and children; teachers and pupils; society, the state and the social apparatus; and, in general, profiles romantically the course of childhood around the idea of happiness and the absence of duty and conflict.

Although psychoanalysis showed from its beginning that this is not a real situation, the Convention on the Rights of the Child is a fundamental guide for today's design and comprehension of childhood, is based on these principles, and has reproduced based on the notion of protection the hierarchical principles of the adult world about the world of children, in the same way that sixteenth-century arguments centred on the limited rational capacity of American Indians and the subsequent need for their control by others, or like eighteenth-century discussions of the existence or absence of female judgement to prescribe the need of women to be protected and directed by male rationality and intelligence, due to their childish nature. In both cases the judge able to decide is male and also adult, which declares itself owner of inquestionable maturity, of true knowledge concerning the future and the way to attain it, and uses the notion of infancy to produce that Other par excellence, the child.

The cultural perception of childhood as a stage of preparation for adulthood, as a way to acquire the knowledge that belongs to the adult, his skills and abilities, lacks any kind of emic approach and shows itself insensible towards the possibilities of cognitive change, of the different kind of potentialities in and through which the child lives. The psychology of development is based on a typology oriented to the achievement of maturity understood as adulthood, as if we were somehow clear about what being adult means, as if this notion were not imbued with the absence of criteria, of responsibility, of knowledge, of maturity, ignorance, irrationality, despair and uncertainty. The same developmental psychology shows also that adult life is signified by stages that remain in the growth of the individual and see him walking along a path of mistakes, misinterpretations and crises that are supposed to be overcome in order to achieve growth.

Nevertheless, we should consider that being immature doesn't suppose that individuals are not judicious and rational beings, i.e. adults.

Finally, the similitude between child work and domestic work is astonishing in many senses. On the one side, domestic work was, in many cases, made invisible under the argument that it doesn't produce wealth for the household and the nation. In the same way, the economic meaning of child work is often minimised, arguing low productivity. The measurement of both of them would transform in an important way our understanding of the micro-economic dynamic of national economies. To make an effort to include both in the national accounting would be an useful attempt to situate correctly the economic importance of these activities.

In another sense, and in relation with these ideas, there is the issue of the social and symbolic recognition of child work. As far as its social utility and its economic productivity are denied, by arguing its negative effect on the child and the need for children to spend their childhood playing and attending school, the children's identity is devaluated in the same way as the domestic work of the housewife is devaluated when its contribution to social reproduction is ignored.

The fact that this kind of work is not included in the national accounts diminishes the sense of agency to the individuals who do it. It is in a good part because of these claims that women's movements and, nowadays, children's movements exist. Children work, and the claims of working children oblige societies to face the traditional model of childhood and to think of alternatives that make real the world of childhood, focusing primarily on skills, motivations, experiences and knowledge acquired, instead of concentrating on a deficient character of childhood.

While the discussions about the historical character of gender and youth have permitted us to illuminate the possibilities of women, men and young people, the discussion concerning childhood should allow children to develop outside the essentialist frames that tend to limit their life possibilities to a western adulthood – which is not available for them due to the colonial character of the world-system.

Those interested in questioning the abolitionist goal of eradicating child work have to discuss the notion of childhood. Though there is a consensus about its historical and constructionist character, the same does not happen when the economic and social conditions are considered which make possible the disappearance of forms of exploitation in child work. Organisations interested in eradicating child work usually ignore the structural conditions surrounding child work in Third World countries. They promote social policies and programmes specifically designed to retire children from the work without considering the familiar, social and cultural conditions around these activities.

These attitudes focus on school and play as activities defining childhood and have strong connection with the Convention on the Rights of the Child, where the rights of parents and families are not considered as making part of childhood in the western sense. The condition of the child as an economic agent, and as a productive one in particular, is a figure that does not fit into this Convention and this fact radically puts into question one of the main power relationships which is at the base of the modern organisation: that between state, family and child.

Chapter 3

Harmed by Work or Developing Through Work?: Issues in the Study of Psychosocial Impacts[1]

Martin Woodhead

Children working in hazardous situations have been a target of international action for nearly a century, and a matter of concern for many more decades than that. Eighty years on from the first child labour convention (1919), international commitment was encapsulated within United National Convention on the Rights of the Child [UNCRC] Article 32:

> States Parties recognise the right of the child to be protected from economic exploitation and from performing any work that is likely to be hazardous or to interfere with the child's education, or to be harmful to the child's health or physical, mental, spiritual, moral or social development. (UNCRC 1989)

Article 32 became a catalyst for debate around definitions of hazardous and harmful work, leading to greater awareness of the limitations of simplistic distinctions between more benign 'child work' and more damaging 'child labour' (White 1996). Child work – it became clear – covers a vast range of activities and situations affecting girls and boys in diverse socio-economic and cultural contexts, from earliest childhood through to 18 (UNICEF 1997). For many children, initiation into work begins in infancy, often as an extension of simple domestic tasks. Work is viewed as part of everyday life, a way of learning skills and responsibility, as well as being essential to family survival. For other children, work may not begin until middle or later childhood, and it may be part time, short term and incidental to the major activities shaping their prospects, notably school.

Generalisations about harmful impacts of child labour gave way to more qualified views, in which potential work hazards were considered in the wider context of children's lives, and took account of a variety of perspectives, including from working children themselves (Boyden, Ling and Myers 1998; Woodhead 2001).

Recognition of the diverse realities of working children's lives has important policy implications. Universal, single strategy solutions have increasingly been challenged in favour of more localised, child-centred strategies within which both risks and benefits are considered and 'the best interests of the child' translated into a range of appropriate interventions (Boyden *et al.* 1998; Lieten and White 2001).

A more focused approach to international action was also emerging, of 'targeting the intolerable' (International Labour Organization (ILO), 1996), formalised through ILO Convention 182 (1999) on the elimination of the worst forms of child labour. Two categories of worst forms are identified in ILO Convention 182, which have been described as the 'unconditional' and the 'unresolved' (Ennew, Myers and Plateau 2003, p.14). The 'unconditional' are specific worst forms outlawed in Article 3 as violations of basic human rights, including all forms of bondage, trafficking and use of children in prostitution and illicit activities. The 'unresolved' are encompassed by a more general statement about worst forms: 'work which, by its nature or the circumstances in which it is carried out, is likely to *harm* the health, safety or morals of children' (ILO 1999, Convention 182, Article 3d, my emphasis). These 'unresolved' worst forms are more 'conditional'. They are defined not by the nature and circumstances of children's work *per se*, but according to the probability that harm will result.

The two different bases for identifying worst forms have important implications. Whereas 'unconditional worst forms' invite action targeted on particular forms of child labour, 'conditional (unresolved) worst forms' require action targeted towards children at risk, irrespective of which sectors they work in. The extent to which work constitutes a risk to children's well-being is conditional on a whole range of circumstances, not just on the nature of the work itself, encapsulated in the following question: 'Which children – in which kinds of work – and in which situations – are most at risk of being harmed by their work?'

Considerable progress has been made in identifying hazards that put children's physical health at risk (e.g. Forastieri 1997; Graitcer and Lerer 1998). Rather less progress has been made in the area of psychosocial hazards. Yet Boyden *et al.* argue: '…often children are at greater psychological or social risk than physical. This is because they lack authority and physical power, because their work is not always valued as a productive activity, and because they usually have the lowest status of all workers' (Boyden *et al.* 1998, p.81).

This short paper summarises issues surrounding the psychosocial impact of child work (see Woodhead 2004 for a more detailed analysis). I argue that exclusive attention to hazards can be misleading. Focusing on hazards perpetuates the dominant perception that work is inherently damaging to children's well-being. Children's multifold contributions to family, economy and social life are thereby overlooked, as are the positive functions that moderate levels of work can play in children's lives. For example, it is estimated that over 70 per cent of working children are engaged in family-based work, notably in rural economies (O'Donnell, van Doorslaer and Rosati 2002, p.8). Even when faced with situations that would generally be regarded as child labour, 'hazard assessments' may be an unreliable predictor of psychosocial risk unless such assessments also take account of psychosocial and economic rewards from working, which children (and families) may perceive as crucial to their welfare (Woodhead 1998).

First, I summarise some challenges for the study of psychosocial impacts of child work. Starting with a list of challenges is not a counsel of despair. Recognising these complexities is the starting point for constructing more appropriate frameworks that can inform research, monitoring and intervention.

Defining psychosocial well-being

The term 'psychosocial' is frequently used as a catch-all for aspects of children's psychological development and social adjustment, but equally often disguises competing understandings about the boundaries of the concept. In the study of child work, a distinction is often made between 'physical', 'educational' and 'psychosocial' impacts. Physical impacts refer to environmental hazards and associated ill-health, injuries or disease. Educational impacts are about access to schooling and effects on achievement in literacy, numeracy, etc. Psychosocial impacts can appear to cover pretty much everything else! In terms of UNCRC Article 32, psychosocial might thus be taken to cover '...mental, spiritual, moral or social development'.

Elsewhere, I have proposed five broad domains most relevant to assessing psychosocial impacts of child work:

- cognitive abilities and cultural competencies (e.g. intelligence, communication skills, technical skills)

- personal security, social integration and social competence (e.g. secure attachments, positive adult/peer relations, social confidence, sense of belonging)

- personal identity and valuation (e.g. self-concept, self-esteem, feeling valued and respected)

- sense of personal agency (e.g. self-efficacy, internal locus of control, positive outlook)

- emotional and somatic expressions of well-being (e.g. stress levels, sleeping and eating patterns, general health) (Woodhead 2004).

These domains are not just concerned with children's inner psychological state. They are also about children's relationships and social integration, with their peers as well as adults. Some concepts are based on specific theories and research (e.g. locus of control). Others are more widely understood (e.g. self-esteem), although indicators relevant to these concepts are based on more precise technical definition.

Caution is needed in assuming these broad domains will necessarily translate meaningfully to child work situations in diverse cultural settings. Local concepts of psychological development and local expectations for personal and social adjustment can strongly mediate the impact of work.

Identifying 'impacts' on psychosocial well-being

Framing the issue as being about the 'impact' of child work, and about potential 'harm' to psychosocial well-being, suggests work is an external force, something that happens to children, directly affecting their well-being, equivalent to being injured by a reckless car driver. Children themselves appear relatively passive in this process. This is an oversimplification. Working children are also social actors, trying to cope with their situation, negotiating with parents and peers, employers and customers, and making the best of oppressive, exploitative and difficult circumstances. Children shape their working life to some degree at least, at the same time as being shaped by it. Judgements made by an observer about possible risks or benefits of work may not coincide with how children receive those influences. To some extent at least, children define what affects them through processes of selective attention and interpretation (Woodhead 1999b).

Recognising children as social actors is closely linked to another key concept, which is about respecting children's agency in relation to their work. A sense of personal agency is one of the five domains of psychosocial functioning outlined above. Some repressive situations deny children the ability to make even the most basic day-to-day personal choices (e.g. where their needs and rights are not respected and/or where their day-to-day lives are strongly regulated by an employer). By contrast, some situations demand that children exercise high levels of personal responsibility, for example working semi-autonomously on the streets. Recognition that children are social actors and social agents draws attention to the limitations of simple cause–effect models when assessing the impact of work.

Work in children's development

Talking about 'impact' of work also suggests working involves a specific event at a particular point in time, whereas an individual child's work can involve:

- a range of different activities
- a range of work relationships – e.g. with employers, clients, parents and peers
- several different settings
- an extended time-frame.

For some young people, work is an occasional and relatively peripheral activity. For others, working is a core experience of childhood. Many children aren't so much affected by work as developing through their work. Taking account of the age children begin working and the intensity of their engagement with work become important. Equally important is the place of work in children's life course (e.g. whether the work they undertake as children is a short-term necessity or a long-term vocation).

Focusing on the individual child in isolation – on the ways their work impacts on their well-being – also has limitations. It may be appropriate for some types of work, such as where children are isolated or working alone, for example, as domestic workers. But most types of work do not impact on a lone child, but on children as part of a work group a family group, a peer group etc. These wider groupings can be important in providing a shared source of identity and support, buffering the impact of difficult circumstances (as studies of risk and protective factors reveal, e.g. Luthar 2003).

The nature of work and the circumstances of work

Demonstrating how work impacts on children's well-being is not straightforward, even where relatively tangible indicators of physical health and well-being are the major focus. For example, an 18-country study of health hazards failed to find consistent evidence of a link between work and ill-health (O'Donnell *et al.* 2002, p.4). This study draws attention to the limitations of 'broad brush' approaches to monitoring and evaluation: that aggregate different types and intensities of economic activity irrespective of context; that rely on relatively global indicators of health; and that are insensitive to the various causal pathways between work and health in children's lives (Hesketh, Gamlin and Woodhead in press).

For some sectors it is also possible to identify psychosocial risks specifically associated with the work itself, such as trauma following mining accidents, or low self-esteem among sex workers. But for many children, the activities of work may not be the most significant indicator of psychosocial hazard. This was signalled in ILO Convention 182 by the phrase '...work which, by its nature or the *circumstances in which it is carried out...*' (Article 3d, my emphasis). Children's working environment, their conditions of work, and especially their treatment by employers is a major influence on their well-being, but highly variable in potential to harm (or to benefit) children, even where children's work is broadly similar in nature. Consequently, the extent to which children are at psychosocial risk may vary significantly within sectors, as well as between sectors.

Most children engaged in hazardous work are also among the most impoverished and marginalised groups within their society, making it difficult to isolate effects of work per se, even within quasi-experimental research designs. For many children living in extreme poverty, the opportunity to work – even in a hazardous sector – may be one of the few assets that contributes to their (and their families') psychosocial well-being, at least in the short term (Boyden *et al.* 1998). These complexities draw attention to the limitations of a sector-by-sector approach to assessing the impact of work, and further endorse the case for a more child-centred and context-centred approach.

The diversity of children's response to child work is illustrated by local, qualitative studies (Woodhead 1998). Gender is especially important. It shapes children's experiences of and responses to work, with girls often working longer hours, very often in domestic activities that are barely recognised as work, often without social power and often without receiving direct payment (e.g. Cohen 2001; Nieuwenhuys 1994). The implication is that focused, localised assessments based around multiple negative and positive indicators are most likely to reveal which combinations of *Children + Activities + Situations + Contexts* are at greatest risk (and which are more benign or even beneficial for children's well-being).

Cultural expectations and the impact of work

Another layer of complexity is about how well-being is locally understood by those most responsible for shaping children's experiences – employers, parents and children themselves. The psychosocial impact of child work is embedded in social relationships and practices, and it is mediated by cultural beliefs and values of parents, employers and children themselves (e.g. Bey 2003; Blanchet 1996; Nieuwenhuys 1994; Reynolds 1991). These beliefs and values include:

- how children develop and should be socialised
- what is in their best interests
- what contributes to their integration within their families and community
- what puts them 'at risk' and constitutes 'hazard' or 'harm'.

Beliefs and practice are often strongly differentiated according to children's gender as well as their age, with many activities almost exclusively the province of boys versus girls, and with a status hierarchy associated with specific occupations (e.g. Nieuwenhuys 1994; Punch 2001; Reynolds 1991; Woodhead 1998).

Working children are frequently confronted by competing expectations about what is in their best interests. For example, self-esteem is an important indicator of psychosocial well-being. Children acquire positive self-esteem through feeling competent in what they do and feeling their activities are valued. Positive self-esteem may be centred on their work, schooling, family and peer relations or some combination of all of these. Where children's work is valued and respected, their feelings of self-worth are likely to be enhanced. Conversely, their work may constitute a psychosocial hazard if it is devalued as mundane; or inappropriate to their age, social status or gender; or where they see no future prospects; or where they are stigmatised for what they do:

> For age groups where economic activity is *valued*, being unable to work challenges core human needs for identity, role and value. For age groups where economic activity is *devalued*, the impact of being required to work may in some respects be similar. If children feel ashamed of having to work. this may be one of the harmful effects of work. (Woodhead 1999b, p.49)

In short, we need to ask how far psychosocial hazards associated with work relate to children's age, developmental stage and greater psychological vulnerability at this formative period in their lives. But we also need to ask how far hazard is about children's relative powerlessness, their limited awareness of the consequences of their work, their vulnerability to abuse, and their limited capacity to protect themselves. Finally, we need to ask how far hazard is about children's working lives being viewed as inappropriate for adjustment to modern societies. Each involves a rather different basis for judging the impact of work, and for prescribing appropriate interventions.

Visibility and 'psychosocial toxins'

In recent years, attention has begun to focus on the most invisible and isolated groups of working children, notably girls working as domestic servants (Black 1997) and girls or boys working at or around their homes. These children are least accessible to monitoring. The boundaries on their duties are least clearly defined, with the result that they may be working excessive hours, without any significant breaks and without opportunities for play or education.

A second visibility issue relates to the identification of a hazard. It is relatively straightforward to identify some of the major physical hazards in children's work environment (e.g. handling dangerous substances, lack of ventilation, lack of protective clothing, risk of accidents). Many psychosocial impacts are much less visible. To begin with, they are about subjective experiences as much as about observable processes. For example, children are strongly affected by how far they feel valued and appreciated for their work, and proud of what they do. Conversely, feeling humiliated or ashamed by work can undermine children's self-confidence, self-esteem and self-worth.

Of course, children can be asked how they feel, and they may speak openly about their feelings. But they may be reluctant to speak out about feeling humiliated by their employers, as well as fearful of the consequences of sharing those feelings. Others may not even recognise how much they are being affected. In this respect, it is tempting to draw a parallel with the way undetected toxins in children's working environment can have devastating consequences for long-term well-being. The challenge is to identify what might be described as the 'psychosocial toxins' embedded in everyday social and psychological processes. Their detection may be even more elusive, because maltreatment of children can be much more readily disguised than is practical for dangerous chemicals or machinery.

Research into children's psychosocial development

Finally, progress in this field is hampered by the imbalances in research into children's psychosocial development. While a good deal of policy work and field experience is available, drawing attention to potential hazards (as well as benefits) of child work, systematic research on these issues has until recently been surprisingly rare, especially in view of the millions of children whose lives are dominated by working (Alaraudanjoki 2000; Boyden 1990; Boyden et al. 1998; Fyfe 1989; Marcus and Harper 1996; Myers 1991; Stegmann 2003; Woodhead 1999c). By contrast, many hundreds of studies are carried out each year into children's psychosocial development in settings other than work (notably in homes, schools and playgrounds), and reported in dozens of specialist journals. This imbalance presents difficulties for the study of working children's psychosocial development because of the uncertainties surrounding generalisations between very different situations. Theories of child development, like indicators of psychosocial well-being, have been constructed mainly within affluent western societies, whereas most hazardous child work is in least affluent, non-western societies

(Burman 1996; Woodhead 1999c). Individualistic theories and concepts about children's psychosocial well-being and development do not translate readily to other societies, where expectations about the development of identity, personal agency and autonomy may be quite different.

The discussion so far points towards three major principles:

1. *Development*: recognising the place of work in children's lives within a long-term perspective, from their initiation into work, through various phases of childhood and beyond.

2. *Context*: recognising that the circumstances and context of work may be as important as the work itself in determining how far the impacts are beneficial or harmful.

3. *Mediation*: recognising that cultural beliefs and expectations surrounding the value of children's work, goals for their development and indicators of well-being will strongly mediate children's perspectives on and experiences of work, and in turn its positive or negative impact on their lives.

These principles help guard against overly simplistic conclusions about cause and effect in favour of a more complex and holistic understanding. They draw attention to the different points in children's life/work cycle when hazards and their impacts can be assessed, and indicators identified.

Hazards, risks and harm

The priority for future research is to trace longer-term impacts which have greater potential to inform policy. However, the findings from longitudinal studies are by definition a long time coming, and they are not necessarily conclusive. Studies of immediate impacts also play an important role. For example, take situations where a child is engaging in – or is forced to submit to – situations, activities and relationships which constitute neglect, maltreatment or abuse. The child's situation is itself an indicator of potential threat to that child's psychosocial well-being – whether or not the experience has repercussions for their medium or long-term psychological and social adjustment (Boyden *et al.* 1998). On the other hand, children encounter all kinds of hazards throughout their daily lives, even in the most protected environment. For example, exposure to a virus does not mean children are necessarily at risk; they may have already built up resistance. And even where they are at risk, this does not mean they will necessarily succumb to disease. So too with psychosocial impacts – it may be helpful to distinguish:

*   the presence of a 'hazard'
*   the level of 'risk' that children will be affected by the hazard
*   whether they are actually 'harmed'.

Transitions and child work careers

These considerations open the way to the assessment of psychosocial impact at different points in working children's 'career', and beyond:

- *Initiation into work*: at this point children may experience a significant shift in their social world. Indicators include the demands made on children, the ways they are treated by employers and their reactions to the experience, including evidence of heightened stress or distress.

- *Working lives*: at this point children may have been working for some months or even years, and they are likely to be familiar with expectations of employers, working practices and skills etc. Indicators at this point may be based on observations and reports on their working environment, as well as on employers' relationships with children. Children's feelings about various aspects of their work can be assessed, along with more standardised indicators of psychosocial well-being.

- *End of childhood*: at this point children may have stopped working, moved onto other work, or still be doing the same work, but in the context of adult responsibilities. The main focus at this point would be on indicators of the young person's psychosocial well-being, their reflection on their experiences as a working child and their understanding of their present situation and future prospects.

Ecologies of work

Taking account of 'context' and 'mediation' is important, especially in helping to understand how children (peers, parents and others) feel about their work and the place it holds in their personal development. It warns against the expectation that a universal set of indicators of psychosocial hazard can be applied 'across the board', to the full range of children, sectors and situations. It also draws attention to the interdependencies between different areas of children's lives, notably between work, family and schooling. The combination of these influences shapes the opportunities available to them, and the developmental pathways they follow. This 'ecological' principle (Bronfenbrenner 1979) is well recognised in studies of psychosocial risk and adversity (e.g. Belsky 1980; Cicchetti and Lynch 1993). It can also be applied in studies of the ecology of work. Work can be seen as one micro-system in a child's life, alongside other micro-systems, centred around home and family, school, community activities, etc. (see also Mortimer and Finch 1996). Taking account of the wider context of children's lives, and recognising the multiple pressures that they face, can help explain why children may be eager to continue hazardous work as the most adaptive solution to difficult circumstances. Taking account of these pressures and the alternatives available to children – or lack of them – is a prerequisite of appropriate intervention, as field experience has shown (Tolfree 1998).

Working children's perspectives

Recognising the subjective meaning and cultural value children attach to their work has implications for research and policy development. It resonates with the principles outlined above: that children are social actors trying to make sense of their experiences; and that these experiences are strongly mediated by cultural understanding and values about children's status, needs and development. From an early age they begin to develop an understanding of their and their family's circumstances, and they develop a strong sense of justice, including whether adults' behaviour towards them is 'fair'. These narratives about what is normal, fair and reasonable are co-constructed through conversations with other children, as part of everyday living, and especially through what they are told by parents, teachers, employers and others, as well as through religious teachings, popular culture, children's rights, etc.

Children's perspectives extend to the work they are expected to do and the ways they are treated by others, including whether the work they do is excessive or reasonable and whether punishments they receive are justified or abusive. For example: 'The worst work is weaving as there is a lot of physical and verbal abuse...but the best work is also weaving because we are...learning a skill which will give us more money than other occupations' – 'In the garment factory there are times when you are scolded. But that is to help you learn the skill. Whereas in domestic helping they beat us...not for our own good' (Woodhead 1998, 1999a).

Consulting with children is respectful of their participatory rights. But it is also important for any assessment of psychosocial impact. When children feel their work is a normal thing to do, that they are doing something valued by their families, and they are treated fairly, these feelings can serve as a coping mechanism that helps their resilience. When they feel stigmatised or ashamed or unjustly treated this can add to their vulnerability, and distress. For example: 'I feel terrible when visitors (come to employer's house)...because we are poor (employer) is always saying, "Stand away from (her). Don't touch (her) clothes." As if my body is smeared with filth' (Woodhead 1998, 1999a).

Hazards and functions of work

Finally, questions need to be asked about the functions that work plays in children's lives – in the present, as well as in the past, and especially in the future. By way of conclusion, I tentatively identify six theoretically distinct functions of child work:

1. *Subjugation*: long-term labour where children feel little power to improve their situation (e.g. bonded labour).

2. *Survival*: children recognise long-term necessity of their work to ensure the well-being of their family and see no realistic alternative (e.g. much family-based farm work, domestic work, unskilled manual work in subsistence economies).

3. *Vocation*: children value their early initiation into a skill that has long prospects (e.g. apprenticeship to a trade).

4. *Distraction*: children treat hardships of work as short-term necessity, to support family and perhaps pay for schooling (e.g. street vending and other 'child occupations').

5. *Socialisation*: short-term opportunity to acquire valued adult skills, such as responsibility, communication skills and team work (e.g. work experience schemes).

6. *Instrumental*: mundane, casual work as means to greater autonomy and consumer power, but with no long-term significance (e.g. fast-food work among affluent students).

Seeking to understand these and other diverse functions of work in children's lives is I believe a more promising starting point for research and intervention than many more simplistic studies of hazard and harms (Woodhead 2004). Even so, the picture is a great deal more complex, with children aware of multiple discourses surrounding the function of work in their lives. For example, there is evidence that children distinguish their personal valuation of their work from their parents' expectations of their work, for example where they gain self-esteem from their schooling, but feel their parents are more interested in their economic contribution (Woodhead 2001).

Note

1. This chapter is a short version of a paper prepared for the joint World Bank/ILO/ UNICEF project 'Understanding Children's Work' and published in full as: 'Psychosocial Impacts of Child Work: A Framework for Research, Monitoring and Intervention.' *International Journal of Children's Rights 12*, 4, 321–377.

Chapter 4

The Reintegration of Children into the Adult World of Work: Ominous Sign or Cause for Optimism?

Dieter Kirchhöfer

The history, contemporary situation and the future of working children are all inextricably linked with the history of labour and the history of the division of human labour. The development of human labour hauled children into the world of work and spat them out again. Changes in the social context of labour have both opened up possibilities for children to engage in work as well as closing them down again. The establishment of the factory system involved children in the adult world of work in a new way, since physical strength was no longer a criterion and enabled the use of 'workers without muscular strength or of immature physical development' (Marx 1979, p.416).

This system so developed the specialisation of tasks that only the 'speed and flexibility of the limbs were required'. The body of the child too became integrated into the mechanical activity and carried out standardised piece work and ultimately became a fundamental part of the machine system. 'Female and child labour were therefore the primary element in the capitalist application of machine technology' (Marx 1979, p.416). As 'large-scale industry' developed, following on from technical and technological developments it was not only piece work that was mechanised even further, but the diversely connected piece-work elements were combined in structured machine systems within an automatised production process which could manufacture with a degree of ease, precision and speed that the experienced hands of even the most skilled craftsmen could not match. The eye for detail of the individual, emptied machine labourer vanished as a 'tiny irrelevance in the face of science, immense natural powers and the social mass of labour, all of which are embodied in the machine system and which, with it, form the power of the master' (Marx 1979, p.446).

The work of the 'master' in large-scale industry only called for adults now, just as earlier the simple labour of the 'hands' or feeders (who provide the machines with the material to be worked) had absorbed children. In addition, in many manufacturing areas industrial mass production reduced the amount of domestic work in which, traditionally, all family members had been part of the workforce and thus liberated children from these tasks. Such a process was accompanied by a further intellectualisation of much industrial work and the extension of more complicated tasks. This process has continued up to the present day, and has been further intensified with the shift to the information economy, keeping children at one remove from the world of work. Immediate manufacture not only no longer requires children, but also no longer the active participation of adults.

A historical perspective on the development of child labour however also forces us to consider the fact that children need not permanently be excluded from the adult world of work, and that the manifest changes in labour society could possibly reintegrate children into the adult world of work. There is much evidence that the present segregation of children from the adult world of work in Central Europe is only one portion of the long history of child labour and that the transformed division of labour and the creation of new fields of work will place in question the divisions of work and school, learning and working, and childhood and adulthood which up to now have been dominant. The structures of an information- and service-led society will bring about a new evaluation, distribution and organisation of the possibilities of integrating children into the world of work as a whole.

The fragmentation of labour

If we reduce the discussion on the future of work and society to a kernel of ideas which relate to the situation of children, then the following lines of argument emerge: work as income-generating labour, in the breakdown of traditional divisions, abandons its traditional spatial, temporal, mediated and social frameworks, which were characterised by separate work spaces, shift patterns of work and hierarchised manufacturing and performance structures (Erpenbeck 1997).

The main principle of the qualitatively new social organisation of labour increasingly moves away from the densest possible control of the options available for carrying out activities aimed at detailed processes and ends, but rather the opposite: the organisation of diffuse spheres of activity whose structuring processes are clearly much less externally determined; these processes now have to be brought about by workers with their own responsibility for the performance (Voß 1998, p.477).

The breakdown of traditional divisions leads to the fact that economic interests are increasingly directed to areas outside those of traditional industrial labour. With this fragmentation, the way such activities are shaped by the market and the possibilities for their professionalisation are connected to specialised communicative, cognitive and social competencies which the workers possess.

Such processes are accompanied by similar processes of lifestyle fragmentation. From the perspective of current or potential income-generating activity these lifestyles unshackle themselves in the sense that they are directed on an everyday level towards income generation and an efficient organisation of daily activities. The achievement and securing of paid work colonises all other areas of life. The erosion of everyday life that is connected with this leads to a merging of work and private life and relativises the boundaries between work and leisure. Tendencies that can be identified in this process are the trend towards the dissolution of normal work relationships, the decoupling of professional training and future professional activity, the dissolution of a life-long connection to a profession and the ending of a life-story connected to one's profession or also the movement of labour away from one fixed site of production, the extension of new independencies and growing barriers to access to the labour market.

The breakdown of labour patterns also increasingly encompasses the places, times and organisational forms of learning (see Table 4.1). The organisation of learning which up to this point has been institutionally and principally school-structured will have to produce new forms of learning. Those competencies which were gained outside the activity undertaken or the training to which they were supposed to relate will become more important for earning money; it will at least become clear that those competencies that were gained through institutional training will not be sufficient to ensure a job for life.

In the process, precisely those preconditions for the division of labour disappear, which, with the growth of large-scale industry, had caused children to disappear from the adult world of work.

The fragmentation opens up new forms of work for children as well, or annexes children's activities as a site of work. Wherever work manifests itself – household, neighbourly relations, family, community, leisure, sport, the environment – we find children. The worlds of work, play and learning become blended, mutually take on each other's characteristics; they lose their monolithic character and their generational exclusivity.

In the literature on the topic, the new type of work is described as non-Fordist (Hengst 2000; Kudera 1995). Table 4.2 lists the differences between traditional Fordist and non-Fordist types of work, whereby this typology represents an ideal construction which in reality manifests itself in manifold overlappings and intermediate forms between the categories.

What is so scientifically interesting about the present situation is that no-one can yet say for certain how the world of work is going to develop and what forms of labour society there will be. Without doubt even the transition from Fordist to post-Fordist labour which I have predicted and described will not be the only future developmental trend.

From what has been said so far, it can be fairly clearly deduced that the fragmentation of labour will also change children's relationship to the adult world of work, and that new possibilities will open up for children to integrate into that world of work. These extended possibilities for integration, which appear both as a result and as a constituent element of the fragmentation, are in actual fact a reintegration. The historically transitory phase of the exclusion of children from the world of work is reversed.

Table 4.1 The dimensions of the fragmentation of work and learning (cf. also Kirchhöfer 2004a)

Element of the work and learning process	Fragmentation of work	Fragmentation of learning
Time	Flexibilisation and pluralisation of forms of working hours in terms of length, biographical situation and regulation	Extension to life-long learning, learning carried on in concert with other activities
Space	Fragmentation of local structures and regional connections	Dissolution of established connections to specific learning environments, extension of learning environments
Means	Growing interchangeability, compatibility and individual availability	Information technology (IT) used for the variable construction of learning arrangements and learning networks
Social form	Dissolution of established cooperative connections	Individually determined and organised social forms
Form of organisation	Reduction of institutional regulations and normatively acting structures; autonomy of the actors	Institutional change, increase in self-organisation
Content	Securing of capability of work self-initiative, flexibility and adaptability	Restructuring and flexibilisation of specific learning arrangements
Biography	A reduction in the number of standard professional careers	Disappearance of biographically fixed times for learning
Establishment of meaning	Self-determined setting of goals as opposed to workplace connections which externally impose such goals	Active autonomous cultivation of self-directed setting of goals as part of an individual learning culture

For the acceptance of such a historical tendency, the following arguments can be adduced.

The labour market is fragmenting into virtual and media-related spheres of work, which are subject in different degrees to commodity formation, such as in

Table 4.2 Traditional and fragmented (non-Fordist) types of work

Element of the labour process	Traditional type of work (Fordist, Taylorist)	Non-Fordist type of work
Labour outcome	Objectification	Virtuality
Labour experience	Sensual	Discursive
Experience of self	Via the product	Via acceptance
Cooperation	Division of labour, externally organised	Individualised; self-organised
Time	Economy based on living and reified labour	Economy based on immediate need
	Time as a definitive disciplinary power	Time as a flexible element
Rationale	Rationality directed towards the ends required: planning and programmed direction of manufacture	Planning of punctual arrangements – innovative capacity to respond to situations – trial and error
Ascription of meaning; value rationale	Social integration	Egotism
	Future	Present
Learning culture	Externally directed	Self-determined

advertising, show-business, event organisation, web-page design, information research or trend-setting and trend analysis, in which children participate alongside adults, using their generational advantages in each case. Tele-working demands, for example, 'online competence' which, depending on the age of the worker, 'only' demands the:

> capacity to orientate oneself in virtual networks and to be able to think and act in virtual network connections, the capacity to work in a goal-directed fashion in virtual networks in a team environment which makes high demands on social skills; or the capacity to use new online forms of learning independently. (Schröter 2004)

Work fragments into areas of what is often referred to as the social environment, which, as it constitutes component parts of the service sector such as social services, domestic work and ecological tasks, is traditionally occupied by children.

Work takes on aspects of childhood such as the aforementioned freedom from regulation, the reduction of fixed shift patterns or of the demands of financial prudence, the changing uses of activities, flexibly moving from one activity to another, imagination/intuition in taking on and carrying out activities whereby the possibilities for the spontaneous shaping of the task increase. This aspect of closeness to the world of children is due less to a possible simplification of the tasks involved and more explicable by the establishment of a new type of work which we had designated as post-Fordist.

No sooner has one asserted the expectation of a reintegration of children into the labour market than one has to relativise it. This reintegration will come to maturity as a historically long-term, contradictory process with delays and reactions. It will turn out to be a complicated balance between objective economic-technological demands, social role-models and a general will to shape it on the behalf of civil society. It will become reality in a field of complex tensions which may produce solutions that have not yet been thought of. In addition, the dominant property and power relationships will lead both to phenomena of alienation which push this process in one particular direction and to market interests leading these developments into the least opportune of directions.

The limits of fragmentation

As varied as the opinions on the contemporary labour market may be, they are also insightful. As with the current reforms of the labour market a process is being completed which furthers the fragmentation of labour and at the same time creates the limits of fragmentation. The administrators of the labour market are forced by the reform package to think of areas of activity, which, as so-called 'one-Euro jobs' or 'work opportunities with expense compensation', demand, indeed presume, a broad understanding of the concept of work. The Berlin Senate, in a letter to the labour agencies (*Berliner Zeitung*, 8 December 2004), defines fields of work for the following areas: social care; health; youth and family; women; ecology, environment and nature conservation; culture and science; sport; *standort* support; and names, for example, for the area of social care/health activities such as the following (**bold** indicates activities carried out by children; *italics* those potentially to be carried out by children):

- **shopping for and care of the elderly**
- socio-pedagogical care in clubs and locations for the elderly
- renovation of meeting places
- **organisation and carrying out of neighbourhood services and meetings**
- mobile care on offer to families
- **travel accompaniment for the disabled**
- *reading services for the blind*
- help in dealing with the authorities

- additional care and communicative assistance in old-people's homes and care homes
- general social advice for the disabled
- help and advice in defusing conflict situations in the family
- *care of the elderly in migrant communities*
- *advice and assistance to single parent migrants*
- *leisure time care within migrant families*
- *integrated group work with senior citizens of different nationalities*
- *integration of single women with physical and mental disabilities*
- *support of soup kitchens for the homeless.*

For the area of youth and family/women, the following tasks were named:

- courses on preventing violence for schoolchildren, teachers and parents
- **orientation of young people for jobs in IT and the media**
- **supervision of children and adolescents using PCs (personal computers)**
- **advice, supervision and educative activity in multicultural areas**
- assistance for families with addiction-related problems
- **supervision of children of single mothers and fathers**
- *the shaping of natural free space and the creative shaping of play spaces in children's and adolescent institutions*
- *support of traffic awareness initiatives*
- enlightenment about racism and right-wing violence
- pedagogical supervision of computer games
- *analysis of the need, and initiation of the provision of sports opportunities for disabled children and adolescents*
- *media assistance for disabled children and adolescents*
- *instruction in domestic activities.*

For the areas of ecology, environment and nature conservation, the following tasks were named:

- advice on rubbish disposal in schools
- *production of visual material on environmental education*
- **environmentally-friendly recycling of raw materials**
- **nature protection measures in urban areas**
- *PR (public relations) work in nature and environmental conservation*

- *recording of buildings containing nests of endangered species*
- *updating of the arboreal register and the land contamination register at district level*
- *investigating and removing illegal rubbish disposal*
- composting of biological refuse
- recording of suspected areas of contamination
- ecological cartography.

These activities clearly share a number of characteristics: the designation 'one-Euro jobs' causes one to prick up one's ears. These are no longer professions or life-long activities, but rather transitory opportunities – part-time jobs – which are subsidiary to subsistent money-earning activity. The life-long working activity which is connected to a profession loses the function it had of ordering life and value-systems in society. If the Taylorist form of labour had still striven to assure itself of the result of the labour involved, i.e. 'the production of a certain quantity of commodity or an intended use effect in a given time frame' (Marx 1979, p.499), then the post-Fordist oriented tasks outlined above indicate only the direction of the result; the outcome is no longer conceptually taken for granted. The activities listed above may require in addition a lower level of qualification; even if they need a certain kind of competence, they require no professional qualifications nor additional educational training. They point to an easily recognisable reification- and use-effect and therefore the ascription of meaning and they integrate the individual through participation in the total labour of society within society, or, rather, this integration is itself the task and the precondition of the activity. Here 'labour' is now only understood (Liebel 2001b, p.159) as 'a conscious and goal-oriented human activity which is directed towards change of the conditions outside the individual and which objectifies itself in these changes and in doing so produces a use value' (Kirchhöfer 2004b, p.42). In this way, a conception of labour is applied which whatever happens is necessary in a changing labour market in order to comprehend the fragmenting world of work.

It is doubtless unintentional that several problems of the future labour market and possible tensions in the field of child work become visible in the list of jobs.

Qualification – de-qualification

It could be a fatal error to assume that future work will merely produce highly qualified intellectualised labour tasks. It is also too simple to assert that the amount of mental labour is increasing, the amount of physical labour diminishing (Schröter 2004). The fragmentations dissolve existing structures in all manner of ways and relativise them at the same time through the setting of new boundaries. Alongside the continued existence and the further intensification of highly qualified labour, above all in the IT sector, as well as the continued existence and potential extension of traditional manual labouring activities, the tendency will become evident that working activities take on the character of simple labour, i.e. the 'exploitation of simple labour power which, on average, every ordinary person possesses without any particular training, in his bodily organism' (Marx 1979, p.59): such work will not only require a low level of qualification, but will above all demonstrate a low level of learning.

The negative aspect of such activities is that the workers are not forced to learn while working. The worker does not need to think while working any more and he only thinks outside the work situation; he is not 'at one with himself' while working and only at one with himself when not working – a classic case of alienation. The de-qualification of work takes effect beyond the individual and affects the whole world of work, causing a further lowering of the level of education. It is also the case that even areas where high levels of innovation are expected, as for example those of IT or the media, alongside highly qualified activities, also generate a number of activities, such as sorting, transporting, ordering, which make lower demands.

At the same time activities within the service and leisure industries, which again awaken expectations of innovation, produce new professions with their own qualification demands. It is utterly conceivable that these working activities will legitimate themselves through qualification and become fields of work which require higher levels of qualification. In addition, these activities, which to begin with are seen as simple labour within the service sector requiring low qualifications, may indeed call for certain personal, social or methodical competencies such as high communication competence, empathy or the capacity to follow others' train of thought, the competence flexibly to alter one's own behaviour among other things, all of which require one to identify with the task in hand. The development of a particular 'degenerated', de-qualified and disqualifying type of labour is only one possibility inherent in these activities but it does exist.

It may well be possible to make only one judgement about the future developments of the world of work: that this development will be multidimensional, open-ended and contradictory. The field of working children will not exclusively be located in this realm of simple labour, although the connection may seem obvious. It would be an inauspicious consequence if the division of labour into simple and complicated labour were to become a generational division, as is already the case in terms of the division of society. Children will most definitely be active in what might be considered complicated areas. Branches of the IT-field generate labour activities such as web-surfing design, mailing and chatting, scanning and the administration of data, which are not only accessible to children, but where they can operate in sovereign fashion.

Working for money – non-profit labour

Just a brief glance at the 'working opportunities with coverage of expenses' offered by the Berlin Senate must awaken the impression that we are dealing here with activities which are already frequently carried out by children or which correspond to the characteristics and behavioural patterns which older children, between the ages of 10 and 16, already possess. Society opens up fields of labour and defines through the division of labour spheres of activity which are interesting, attractive and manageable for children. There is clearly an internal dynamic to the social division of labour which produces possibilities for working children and fragments the generational division of labour. This area, however, is a site of debate about the distribution of labour for different actors, among other reasons due to the fact that no specific qualification is required and a 'work-flow' is made possible, and, as a result, the danger arises that struggles could arise over the distribution of work in this area into which children could be drawn.

This so-called tertiary sector of the labour market is primarily a region of non-profit-oriented work. But already we hear above all from small and medium-sized firms talking about genuine competition. In addition, this area is now entered by workers with 'one-Euro jobs' and, on top of this, children claim for themselves important areas of general labour (e.g. babysitting, assistance with shopping, entertaining older people). The segregation of children, which is sought by adults, could increase through the intended repression of competitors for the work which is in short supply. Any solution whereby children could work without being paid, while the adults would be paid for the same work, would cause generational divisions once more and would be of little use in trying to set up models for the future.

Working to earn money and working in the community

From such a perspective these activities belong in important areas of what is known as community service, i.e. unpaid work which is carried out not in order to earn money, and which is done in and for the community. Without doubt community service is of central civil significance as an established part of the regional labour network for the development and stabilisation of communities, for the maintenance of regional infrastructures, for the production of regional identities and regional development. It would however be counterproductive for the development of civil society if, through this so-called 'low wage sector' a form of labour came into existence which was stigmatised in advance. The fact that children were involved in this work would then not only stigmatise the children but also community service itself. It would cause irreparable damage if the equation were to emerge: *community service = cheap labour = simple labour = child labour*. In addition, such an orientation towards areas of community service demands a restructuring of the ways in which children participate in the shaping of social processes, a problem which demands comprehensive social solutions for all members of society and which asks questions of the efficiency of the form of democracy which we have had up to now.

Part 2

Care and Domestic Work

Chapter 5

Child Domestic Workers in Zimbabwe: Children's Perspectives

Michael Bourdillon

Introduction

In considering what domestic employment means for child workers, I draw mainly on what the children themselves have said about it. I thus focus on the children's understanding of their work rather than analyse its effects on their lives through more objective criteria. The children make clear that many of them need help. It is not so clear what form help should take to provide the best chances for children with little material support from their own families (if indeed they have families).

It has been suggested that domestic work should be classified as one of the worst forms of child labour, since it often involves long hours, or work at night, or confining the child to the premises of the employer (Pflug 1995, p.10; UNICEF 1999). In our study of child domestic workers in Zimbabwe, we found evidence that some children are treated badly and need protection: in a few cases, removal from their employment appears the best option. Many children, however, are happy in their work, and, while they have complaints, they do not want this opportunity for earning money taken from them. Two contrasting remarks illustrate the variety of situations.

A 15-year-old girl complained:

> How can I be happy when I get up at four in the morning and go to bed at ten at night and all the work is for me to do?

In contrast, a 12-year-old girl commented:

> Where I work, I am happy because I am bringing in money. I also have enthusiasm for my work. I have days for resting, when I visit relatives and friends. My wish is that you elders help us to ensure that we continue to be treated well where we work.

The second girl works as a live-in domestic, working about four hours a day, washing dishes, sweeping, scrubbing, and polishing the house. This is less work than some children have to do unpaid for their families (for example see Mangoma and Bourdillon 2002, pp.26–9).

My information comes from various sources. Tinashe Pfigu (2003) first conducted three detailed case studies of child domestic workers in different situations. Second, children in clubs formed by the Zimbabwe Domestic and Allied Workers' Union (ZDAWU) helped to formulate a questionnaire returned by 116 children in the children's native languages. Further information was obtained from discussions with the children in their clubs, and with representative children in various workshops. Although the return rate on the questionnaire was uneven and the sample was not random, the responses indicate a range of working conditions and problems faced by the children. Our sample is probably biased towards more benign situations: there are other children under strict control of their employers, who cannot attend group meetings.[1]

Background

Two aspects of the social context are particularly significant for working children in Zimbabwe. The economy of the country is in a state of collapse, with widespread extreme poverty. Second, the HIV/AIDS (human immunodeficiency virus/acquired immune deficiency syndrome) epidemic has devastated families and communities: 20 per cent of children in the country have lost at least one parent. So we have many children who can no longer rely on adults to support them. Although we would like to improve the livelihoods of impoverished communities, and to educate children in a way that allows them to move out of poverty, the majority of working children are likely to remain poor and in poor communities. Idealised models of childhood formulated in vastly different contexts are unlikely to be helpful to families and children in such situations.

Child domestic work operates in the context of widespread patronage in society, in which disadvantaged persons receive access to resources in exchange for loyalty and service. In the idiom of patronage is that the wealthier person bestows favours on the poorer person: this idiom is usually adopted by both sides and often conceals gross exploitation. But exploitation is not necessarily the dominant side of the relationship: patrons can genuinely help clients, help that would be lost in a blanket condemnation of patronage. To understand the complexity of such relations, we need to examine both positive and negative aspects, and to avoid stereotypes that evade consideration of particular situations in which they occur.

Seeking patronage is a strategy for the poor, as is mobility between households. Where families for any reason have difficulty in providing adequate care for their children, they may try to improve the situation by placing children with relatives or other patrons who can provide better care of the children (Van der Waal 1996, pp.43–5). While the patron receives services from the child, the child receives shelter, nourishment, and sometimes care from the patron.[2] In populations devastated by HIV/AIDS, patronage can be the salvation of many orphans. Child domestic work mingles patronage with exploitation in ways that are not easily disentangled. Where the alternatives for the children are likely to be worse than their domestic employment, such patronage is to their advantage, but employers must be persuaded to take responsibility for the well-being and development of the children they employ.

The children

The majority (72 per cent) in our sample were aged 15–18, of whom 67 per cent were girls. Twenty-nine children were under 15, the legal minimum age for employment in Zimbabwe. This younger age group was evenly divided between boys and girls.

We asked the children if they were happy in their work. We need to be cautious about the significance of their replies: these may reflect the current mood of the children, based on recent incidents, as much as their long-term contentment. Nevertheless, the responses indicate that at the time of the survey about half the children were content. The majority (81 per cent) of the younger children said they were happy, as opposed to only 40 per cent of the older children. These older children are likely to be thinking about their futures and many have little chance of improving themselves in domestic service.

More of the older children are girls. More girls (58 per cent) than boys (35 per cent) are unhappy. I am not able definitely to say why, but a possibility is that girls are liable to suffer sexual harassment in the household. Although boys sometimes complain of having to do girls' work, most boys are well able to adapt to the situation.

We asked the children to list what they liked about their work and what they disliked. Fourteen (12 per cent) listed nothing among the dislikes, some commenting that they liked everything about their work. Thirty-six (31 per cent) listed nothing that they liked, again sometimes explicitly commenting that there was nothing. The majority listed items on both sides.

Choice and duress

About two thirds of the children said that they chose to seek employment, as opposed to being compelled to do so by guardians. In some cases, the work gives the children a sense of achievement and pride. Several of the children mentioned specific needs that were fulfilled from their work as reasons for their employment, such as 'I need the money to eat' and 'This is where I can find money to buy clothes'. There was, nevertheless, often an element of duress in this choice. A third of the children were compelled to work, and most of these were unhappy.

A small majority of children (61 per cent) said that they did not want to stop work. The reasons they gave for why they want to continue to work confirm constraints on their choice. The Shona verb *kuda* covers a range of desires, from serious need, through wants and preferences, to mild likes or wishes. When children say they do not want to leave their work, it might be that they are happy, but in some cases it is because work fulfils important needs and they see no alternative. So we find 17 children who are unhappy in the work but do not want to stop, and 13 who are happy but want to stop.

Thus one 17-year-old girl comes from a small-scale farming family. She said that she likes her work and she appears to be happy in her situation. Nevertheless, she said she wants to stop, explaining that she would like to go back to school if she had the means.

A 13-year-old boy explained his predicament:

> I wish I could buy some clothes. For my part I am troubled to find the money that I am working for. I am troubled to get the things that other children get. I would like to have money and become a person who finds things that will help in the future. I want to find work in the open that I can do on my own like some men, not a person who works in the house. If God helps me, I will pass at school and have a respectable life, not being given work that I do in the house with a grievance.

Among children who were unhappy with their work and living conditions and did not want to stop was a 16-year-old girl, working in a high-density Harare suburb for very low wages and finding nothing she liked in her work. She did not like going to bed while she was still hungry, getting up while it was still dark, having to sleep with only one blanket in winter, having no jersey to wear, not being treated like the others in the house. But she did not want to leave her job 'because if I stopped work, I would have nowhere to go'. She explained:

> My parents do not have enough money to send me to school. They do not find enough food... I have younger brothers and sisters at school. I want to help them as well but the money is not enough to do this.

A 17-year-old girl, who has no father, does not like her work because both her employers, husband and wife, make her work hard and scold her often. But she cannot leave her job:

> If I stop working, there is nowhere for me to live, and I will not find money for the things that help me.

Another explained that although she had no free time, received low pay, slept in the kitchen, and was very unhappy, she did not want to leave her job 'because if I stopped working, there is no one who can look after my life'.

Some older children took for granted that they should be working. A 14-year-old boy, living with his father and working around five hours a day, explained why he did not want to leave his job: 'There is no other place where I could find work.' A 17-year-old girl commented that she did not want to be like an unemployed person. Another girl, who was unhappy with her situation, wanted to leave and find better employment. A 16-year-old girl was happy in her work, although she worked around 10–11 hours a day: she commented, 'What will I do if I stop working?' – a sentiment echoed by several children.

Even younger children sometimes like to work for a wage. A 13-year-old girl lives with her father and works for a relative of her mother. She continues to go to school, but complains of being beaten and scolded at work. Nevertheless, she is happy to work because she gets enough to eat, is paid each month, and can buy what she needs.

Education

Education was a high priority in the minds of many of the children. Some sought work precisely to continue their schooling, only to be let down when time, or payments, or employers did not allow them to study.

Four of our sample admitted that they had never been to school. Half the children had reached secondary school. Twenty-three had not completed their primary education and of these only 13 were still in school. Another 17 were in secondary school, making altogether 30 (26 per cent) still in school, 15 per cent of the older children and 42 per cent of those below 15. One other child was being helped by his elder brother to do a sewing course in his spare time. The majority (79 per cent) of those who were still in school were also content in their work.

Of the children who were not in school, most were above 15 years of age. The vast majority of those out of school (over 90 per cent) cited lack of funds as the reason for leaving school. Other reasons could also have been related to money, such as 'My father, who was sending me to school, died.' One child claimed that work left no time for school. Two had completed their schooling. One refused to continue at school (having reached grade 5 in primary school).

Of those who were still in school, many depended on employment for their schooling. A 17-year-old girl works around 6½ hours a day, and her employer pays her fees for secondary school. She likes her work, likes receiving her pay, and likes having her schooling paid for. She does not like the way the employers' children insult her. But she does not want to stop working. She says:

> If I stop, I would not find money for school and would be a trouble to my mother.

A 17-year-old boy explained more fully:

> Where I work, they treat me well because they give me the money I need for school if I fail to find my share. But if I could find money for school, I would prefer not to work. One of my parents died, the one who provided the money I needed for school, and that is why I am working. But I say to other children who are not going to school, 'Look for what you can do to find money that will enable you to go to school.'

Some employers are conscientious in the matter of education. A third of the children still in school (ten cases) had their fees paid by their employers. Three of these were working for relatives, and two for people previously known to the parent: five employers, although previously unknown to the child's family, ensured that the child was educated. Eight of the ten were in the small town of Zvishavane, where the culture cares better for working children than does the drive of big cities.

While employment sometimes makes education possible, it still interferes with school performance. A 17-year-old boy commented in detail:

> I work for my sekuru[3] but the reason for this is poverty. I say that if my father was able to find enough money to send me to school, I would be a person who does better at school because I would have time to read well and do homework and relax my legs and be in our own house. Now things concerning work are tedious because someone is watching to see that you do the work, as if you are prostituting

yourself. The things of school are considered a favour, as if you entered work without the aim of being sent to school.

Work also supports the education of siblings. An 18-year-old boy showed his sense of responsibility to his family. Although he complained of being scolded frequently and being treated like a slave, he said that some things are good. He does not want to leave work 'because this is where the money comes from for my younger brother to go to school'.

Working conditions

Many of the children complained about conditions of employment and living conditions. Complaints included long hours of work: of those whose workloads we were able to estimate, about 30 per cent were doing less than six hours a day, and 42 per cent were doing over eight. Children are aware of the legal maximum of six hours of 'light work' a day for children under 17 years of age. In group discussions, they said this was unrealistic, and proposed instead a maximum of six hours a day for children under 13, eight hours a day for children in the 13 to 14 age group, and ten hours a day for children aged from 15 to 17. They complained of having little time to rest and play, and of inadequate or no leave – many have less leave than the minimum required for adult employees.

Wages varied, but were generally low, usually below the adult minimum wage. Children sometimes complained of deductions from pay for small mistakes, and that payment was sometimes delayed or paid to relatives instead of to the child.

Children also complained of danger from unsanitary conditions, chemicals, or electricity. Some pointed to poor or inadequate food, poor sleeping conditions, being punished and even beaten when they made mistakes.

They complained at being given work and responsibilities inappropriate for their age or gender. Several boys mentioned that they disliked cooking, sweeping, and tidying the house, whereas these jobs were often mentioned as tasks that girls liked. Girls on the other hand disliked having to work in the garden or washing the car, tasks that boys liked. Some tasks, such as laundry and washing plates, were disliked by both girls and boys. A 17-year-old boy complained at having to bathe girl children.

In group discussions on appropriate work, children pointed out that what they think is reasonable differs from what they are expected to do. They noticed that some children are more competent than others at certain tasks, and it is difficult to set definite rules about what children can do at particular ages. Although the children in our discussions were older than 12, some had started work when they were young, and remembered how difficult it was to cope with the work and responsibility.

The groups decided that young children under the age of 13 should be expected to do only the simplest of tasks, like sweeping and washing dishes. They can do their own laundry, but should not be expected to do that of the whole house. They can do other chores that can be fun with other children, like washing cars.

The groups agreed that children aged 13 to 14 can wash plates, cook, and wash and iron clothes (but point out that it is against custom to wash other people's underwear – a cultural taboo sometimes ignored by employers). They learn these things from a young age. They should not be expected to work in the garden, nor to handle poisonous chemicals, such as pesticides, in the house or garden. Children under 15 should not be required to carry heavy loads, since their bodies have not yet built up. We noticed that some children complained at the strain of putting heavy goods on a cart, while others quite liked carrying loads when they earned extra money in this way.

Children aged 15 to 17 can work in the garden, although some girls felt that this was unsuitable for them. They can be sent to sell things and manage a stall, because they have learned the value of money and can handle change. They can be sent on errands, but should not be sent on errands at night, when they can be molested and even robbed.

We were concerned that even young children are left to look after the home while adults are away, sometimes with even younger children of the household in their care. Children suggested that young children under 13 can be left to play with toddlers, provided there is an adult around, but they should not be expected to take care of children. Older children can take care of younger ones, and those aged 15 to 17 can even take care of babies for half a day. The children say that they do not have the experience of a mother, and cannot provide the same kind of care that mothers can give: if they are left for longer, accidents can happen.

Only five (17 per cent) of the younger age groups answered that they are some-times left alone in the house, as did 70 per cent of the older group. Most of the responses indicated that they were alone in the house while the owners were away at work on weekdays. In a couple of cases, when something went wrong during the day, children mentioned being helped by neighbours. Four of the older workers mentioned that they sometimes stay in the house when the owners are away over-night.

Children argued that it was a heavy responsibility for a child to look after a home with no adults present. They pointed out that con-artists may visit the house during the day, and younger children may believe them, so no-one under 15 should be left alone in charge of the house. Older children can look after the house during the day, but they should not be left alone overnight. They will be blamed if thieves rob the house, yet there is nothing they can do.

Lack of respect

Only a third said that they were happy with the way their employers treat them. The children's most common complaint was that they were constantly being scolded. The Shona word for this, *kutukwa*, is sometimes translated as 'to be shouted at', and carries heavy connotations of insult. One child pointed out that if they make a mistake, they can be corrected without shouting.

In the wider society, children are often treated with scant respect and ignored as if they have no opinions worth hearing. The problem is exacerbated when the children are of a lower socio-economic class than are the relevant adults. Indeed, occasionally children complained of being insulted and even beaten by other children of the household.

The lack of respect for working children applies beyond the employers' families. A 15-year-old boy commented:

> For my part, I work well, and accordingly some people give me respect because I am on the road forwards, but others despise me and laugh at me. I do not mind because my affairs go well.

When the children are learning to cope with difficulties, perhaps with the loss of parents, by earning their keep through conscientious work, they deserve respect and appreciation, not further trauma through insulting and degrading treatment.

In a culture in which children are seen as belonging to a family, rather than as individuals in their own right, children without family to protect them are easily despised as children without rights. In one case, a visit by adult relatives of the child was needed to make the employer adhere to agreements about education and care for the child. Sometimes the children themselves adopt such an attitude, complaining of being treated as orphans: 'They treat me like a child without parents; but I do have parents.'

Part of the family

Child domestic workers are in some contexts regarded as members of the family they are working for, and in others as formal employees. To employ an adult domestic worker, a written contract of employment is required by law, stating terms of service, hours of work, leave, and other benefits. Only 29 of the children (25 per cent) said they had formal contracts, and 77 per cent of these said they were happy in their work. In such cases, the hours and work are clearly defined, and the child is treated as an employee with rights.

There may, however, be advantages in less formal treatment. One girl initially had fixed hours of work and was free in the evenings, but she lived on her own in an outhouse on the property. Later, her employer's elderly mother moved into the household and the child worker was given a bed in the old lady's room so as to be always available to see to her needs. She now ate with the family. Although the workload increased and the hours were now undefined, the girl regarded her situation as much improved.

Part of the ideology used to defend child domestic work is that the child is cared for as part of the family.[4] Some of the children explicitly appreciated that they were treated by their employers as if they were the employers' own children. Many of the workers ate, slept, and played with other children in the family. Some older girls spoke with appreciation of how their female employers took on the role of mother or aunt and instructed them on important issues of life, and especially about sex.

Occasionally, children complained of the lack of sympathy of employers when they were sad or homesick. A person who employs a child must take on responsibilities that may not be appropriate in the case of adult employees.

We asked the children about eating arrangements. Those who were included in the family at meals were more likely to be happy in their work. Just under half (46 per cent) ate with the family, and 84 per cent of these were happy in their work. A further 28 per cent said that they ate the same food as the family they worked for, and the majority of these were also happy. Twenty-five per cent were given different food, and only two of these said they were happy, several of them commenting that the food they were given was insufficient and of poor quality. One commented, 'Me, I am given food…the meat is no different from what they give their dog.'

Another girl commented of her employers:

> They do not want me to use their things, not even to drink water from their cup… They say, 'Don't even taste my food or eat my food.' If they leave any food uneaten, they give it to the dog. If I suggest that I might eat the food they have left, they say, 'You are not my relative.'

Apart from meals, some of the children complained that they were not allowed to sit on easy chairs in the living room and they were not allowed to watch television. In an extreme case, one girl claimed that if she used a cup normally used by her employers, they would throw it away. In such cases, employers adopted a model of employment from the old colonial and racial situation, in which black domestic workers were kept at a distance by their white employers, and used separate facilities and utensils. Children felt insulted by such treatment from black employers.

When a child worker falls sick, employers often fail to take on familial responsibilities. Forty of the children said they had at some time been sick while they were at work. Only 15 of these were cared for by members of the employers' households. Eleven who were sick said that no-one helped them and they got better on their own, sometimes mentioning that they had bought medicines. A twelfth child said that no-one helped her with money, but the people she worked for brought water to cool her down. Children pointed out that the wages they earn are not usually enough for medicines. Children also complained that sometimes their employers do not believe them when they do not feel well, and force them to go on working. Alternatively, some employers do not allow the children time off, and suggest that they should do light work while they are not well. Some employers deduct wages for the time that the children are sick and not working.

Conclusion

Domestic work means different things to the children. To some, it means a place to live and provision of necessities of life; to others, it means long hours of unpleasant work for little reward. To some, it means an opportunity to continue schooling; to others, an end to their schooling. For some, it is a first step into the labour market: to others, it offers no future. To some, it is something they have chosen willingly; others work only because they have no alternative. For some, their work is a source of pride; for others, severe humiliation.

Rather than trying to classify domestic work generally as benign or harmful, we should pay attention to the situations and interests of the children involved and consider how these can best be served. In particular, when the children see employment as their best response to their situation, they should be taken seriously. Employers who take children's wishes seriously and offer them wages for work are not for that reason to be condemned.

Employing children is not the same as employing adults. While children become increasingly active agents as they grow, they are still learning. Adults in charge of children have a responsibility to teach and guide. When an adult employs a child, the adult must accept responsibility for the child's continuing development, most clearly seen in the formal education of the child.

Projects in other countries have enabled children to move out of domestic service, by providing alternative sources of income (Groves 2003, p.16). This, however, is unlikely to be a solution for the majority of children in Zimbabwe, given the devastation to families caused by HIV/AIDS, and the severe shortage of resources in a collapsed national economy.

Current legislation is unlikely to help the children. The children in the clubs have learned their rights under current Zimbabwean legislation, but regard these as unrealistic – particularly the minimum age for employment. They do not want to lose their jobs, but they do want to be protected from abuse. Many are not happy with the work that their employers expect them to do. They need, therefore, legislation that will realistically meet the needs of employers, while protecting the children from harm.

Many of the employers see themselves as doing the children a favour, and accept responsibility for the care of needy children. Many of the children see themselves as benefiting from their employers, through having better lives and even education. These views of the children should not be summarily dismissed. Nor is it enough to concede that such employment is permissible. We should acknowledge that when employers take on responsibility for the care and development of disadvantaged children they employ, this is a benefit to children and to be encouraged, even while we try to find other and better ways of helping the children. We should be aware that patronage by outside organisations is not necessarily more sustainable and better for the children in the long term than benevolent patronage within their own communities.

So I am not concerned about how to classify child domestic work. But I am concerned about the way children are sometimes mistreated and abused in domestic work. The children need support and protection within their work.

Notes

1. A fuller account of this research, with recommendations arising from it, can be found in Bourdillon 2006.

2. Employers of child domestic workers in Bangladesh see themselves saviours of poor children, and there are parallels between employment and fostering (Blanchet 1996, pp.102–3).

3. This term refers to male relatives either of the grandparents' generation or of one's mother's lineage.

4. Domestic employment of children in Indonesia is commonly seen in terms of kinship links, and so outside normal labour legislation, although the majority of children were previously unknown to their employers (White and Indrasari 1998, pp.28–9).

Chapter 6

Negotiating Gender Identities: Domestic Work of Indian Children in Britain and in India

Vinod Chandra

Children's domestic work has remained marginalised both in the debate on the division of domestic labour as well as child labour. Commenting on marginalisation, Corsaro (1997) argues that whenever children figure in the debate on domestic labour they have been seen as an object of additional domestic labour rather than sharer of it. The main reason for this is the social-psychological image of children. Children are positioned as dependent and immature in the given family circumstances. This socially constructed image of children thus excludes the possibility of including children as competent contributors to domestic labour.

On the other hand, child labour debate does appear to offer an area where children's work in the family should find a place. However, it so happens that under the concept of acceptable forms of work children's domestic work has been subsumed under the developmental framework. This framework is based on the narrow view of work according to which child work cannot be recognised within the family atmosphere since children are considered completely under the protection of parents (James, Jenks and Prout 1998). Normally, the child labour debate addresses kinds of children's work considered 'unacceptable'. The distinction between 'acceptable' and 'unacceptable' forms of work was endorsed by the socialisation paradigm of understanding children's lives. Most studies before 1990 (e.g. Straus 1962; Thrall 1978; White and Brinkerhoff 1981) focused on children's domestic work as activities in the context of their socialisation. They examined related issues such as the extent and nature of children's domestic work, reasons for choosing housework, impact of that on their development and factors affecting their involvement in housework. With the advent of sociology of childhood in the late 1990s, attempts have been made to highlight the importance of children's domestic work for others. It has been shown that children's domestic work affects all people who live around them and relate to them in any way. For instance, Mayall (1996) has shown that children's domestic activities affect the social order of the family, while Solberg (1997) has found their household activities affect parents' working lives too. Morrow (1992, 1996) also demonstrated how children's domestic work contributes to the domestic economy. The findings of this new research gave impetus to recognising a diverse range of children's household activities as domestic work that are socially meaningful (James *et al.* 1998).

The emergence of the sociology of childhood provided a new orientation toward children's work by challenging the overemphasis of socialisation by developmental psychologists and protectionist sociologists who took children out of the division of labour. By placing them in school and child-care institutions they seem to claim they were helping children to prepare for adulthood. The new perspective, what I call an 'agency perspective',[1] argues that placing children in school is in reality apprenticeship for future work (Qvortrup 1985, 2001). Likewise children's work at home was also seen as a positive contribution to the social order of the family. Qvortrup (1987) argues that children are active social agents and their activities should not be seen as merely training or learning in school and at home. He placed them in the division of labour and suggested work in the family be seen as much an important contribution to domestic work as that of adults. Children's agency was further extended by Morrow (1992, 1996) in her empirical study of children's contribution to domestic economy. She challenged the notion of dependency of children and referred to reciprocal relationships between children and parents especially in providing care and services within their families. She argues that parents are equally dependent on children as children are on them and this inter-dependence can only be understood by recognising children's agency. Noting the ambiguity between 'dependence' and 'independence' of children and adults Brannen (1995) supported Morrow's concept of 'inter-dependence'.

In an attempt to theorise childhood within the scope of the new sociology of childhood, James *et al.* (1998), in their seminal volume *Theorising Childhood*, presented a comprehensive review of ideological and theoretical debates on children's work and labour with regard to the family and the labour market. They emphasised that we needed an understanding of children's experience of their own work and that children's domestic work may be an important issue for studying children's agency in the social construction of their own lives. To understand children's agency in terms of their domestic work I would like to examine their power of negotiation. This exercise first explores what autonomy children gain by their contribution to domestic work and negotiation in the whole affair. With the achieved autonomy and new positions in the power structure of the family how far these children are successful in negotiating their gender identity will be our main focus here.

Gender and work-role responsibility: the case of Indian children

Data used in this chapter were collected by the author for his doctoral study during 1997 and 1998 at the University of Warwick, UK. Both girls and boys between the ages of ten and 15 years from ten families of Indian origin in Coventry (UK) and ten in Lucknow (India) were studied. Altogether 43 children were interviewed. Qualitative methods such as in-depth interviews with open-ended questions and closed observation were adopted for data collection. Children were main informants and their views on domestic work were used as the core of the study. Initially the interviewer did not use the word 'work' and the attempt was to explore the children's concept of work in general and domestic work in particular. During research, it was found that children in both the places were very aware of their work in the maintenance of family social order. Children were asked about the division of household work in families. Children said they were very well aware of the division of domestic work on gender lines. It was found that girls were dissatisfied with gender-bias in domestic work but did not report many instances when they rejected or challenged that work. The similarity in disagreeing with the distribution of domestic work on gender lines and dissimilarity in rejecting or attempting to reject the gender-based division of domestic work in Coventry and Lucknow girls draw our attention toward the comparative importance of socio-cultural contexts. Girls in both locations had similar experiences but, due to different socio-cultural contexts, reactions differed.

Findings referred to earlier show that girls in Lucknow have taken over boys' work but it is very rare. However, there is no evidence to suggest that Lucknow boys also moved into the work area of girls' domestic world. In Coventry boys and girls are found sharing each other's work. The perceptible reason for this difference between Coventry and Lucknow children is that the Coventry Indian children are exposed to the British socio-cultural milieu which is quite different to children in Lucknow. The socio-cultural context of Lucknow children's family is part and parcel of the wider Indian society in which gender is the most powerful structure for the determination of domestic work. Gender emphasis on the domestic work of children is, therefore, more prominent and formidable while the Coventry situation is different. For Coventry children the family's socio-cultural values are still those of Indian society but the social context in which they live is that of British society. Because of different social contexts on these children the force of family socio-cultural values is allayed to some extent.

The conventional view focuses on children's gender-based domestic work as a 'gender-role socialisation' or gender reinforcement. It argues that gender has been perpetuated by encouraging children to take up gender-specific tasks such as caring and cooking (Gill 1998; Thrall 1978). This argument has been developed on the basis of parents' views. In my study, however, children's views on undertaking gender-specific tasks challenge this argument. I find it not true in all circumstances. Particularly, Coventry children feel they involve themselves in gender-specific tasks to keep cultural ties intact and culture alive. For instance, a 14-year-old Coventry girl reported her parents do not allow her to go out in the evening. Although she is not convinced by reasons for not going out then, she has to listen to her parents. On the issue of going out she accepted her parents' will but on the issue of housework in the evening she negotiated her own will. She reported:

> She [mother] says that going out in the evening is not safe for girls. I don't really feel that this is the only reason. Anyway, it's not fair on her part. This is not only what my parents do. I know all Asian parents do the same. They have a bit different rule for us. Boys can go alone and they don't mind where they go and with whom. Parents have got to have an equal treatment for boys and girls, but unfortunately they haven't. But I said to them [parents], if you won't allow me to go out I'll do whatever I wish to do.

> Interviewer: Okay. Did they listen to you?

> Yes they have to. If they don't allow me to go they have to listen to me. I told them that whatever I like, I'll do…and I do whatever I want to. My dad understands me. He's a bit liberal, but my mum isn't.

> Interviewer: Did your brother do the jobs which normally you do?

> Well he didn't want to, but he had to. I said to my dad, if I'm doing these jobs then why can't he, he should also clean the house. And now my dad asks him to do some jobs. Except washing dishes he does everything. But not always… [smile].

This example explains that she is not able to break the gender barrier by going out but quite able to negotiate housework. She attempts to confront the gender-based division of domestic work and, to some extent, is successful. Like this girl, another Coventry girl aged 12 years also admits that in her family her brother receives concessions on housework. However, she appositely describes how she has negotiated her gender-based household tasks:

> My mum always thinks that because you are a girl you have to do housework. She was always favouring Ajay [elder brother]. She wasn't giving any jobs to him. She started depending on me for housework. I also get on with the jobs. What annoys me when I find…he hasn't got responsibility of any job, whereas I've got to do everything. This is really terrible…

> Interviewer: Have you not complained for this?

> Yeah! One day I told my parents that I'm not going to do all this. I'm not getting time for myself, so I won't do [housework] any more. Then my parents realised that he [her brother] should also do some of the jobs… Actually my dad is very sensible, he asked my mum to give some of the jobs to him. Now he does a bit.

> Interviewer: So do you feel comfortable now?

> Yes I do. I wouldn't feel comfortable if I kept silent. Now I'm happy because he does at least something. My dad is of the opinion that everyone should do his jobs…and that's why everybody has some share in the housework in our family.

The above example explains how Coventry girls are aware of gender and how they react to assigned gender-based housework. Examples also show they tried to redefine housework for boys and girls. One girl accepted that her parents treat them differently on the question of going out in the evening but her substantive and pivotal contribution to domestic work makes her an active and assertive member of the family. Through those qualities she deconstructs stereotypical images of gender. Another example demonstrates that the moment she took over housework she realised her position as a girl and started questioning her treatment. To some degree she succeeded in her efforts. She did not deny that her family practises gender bias; nevertheless her active involvement in domestic work reduces it to some extent. In another example girls advocated female responsibility for caring for children in their family. Identifying themselves with femininity they cared for siblings. This is not just submission to gender-based work but reconstruction of gender through domestic work. What is common in these girls is that they are actively involved in deconstruction and reconstruction of gender through domestic work. It is a different matter whether they are fully successful in negotiation of gender roles or whether they reach only a degree of approximation to it. They have expressed discontent and dissatisfaction against parents' expectation for domestic work on gender lines. This is sound proof of interaction between children's agency and structural factors related to gender. Thus, domestic work provides an opportunity for children to exploit agency optimally and to interact with structures in society.

Gender is also prominent in the experience of Coventry boys. Here it is interesting to note that, similar to girls, boys in Coventry have not silently accepted gender-based division of labour but the interactions between their 'gender identities' and the 'nature of work' reflect their personhood. A Coventry boy aged 13 justifies his work by saying:

> I do all that what my dad does. My sister does all that what my mum does in the kitchen.
>
> Interviewer: Why do you do your dad's jobs and why can't she [sister]?
>
> I think I can do them better than her. Actually people say (that) boys are like fathers and girls are like mothers, and I'm a boy so I help my dad... She can't do heavy lifting or so. I think it's me who has to do these jobs after dad. The kitchen work is necessary for her, she must know all that...

Another Coventry boy aged 14 says:

> I don't think it's only me who gets favour. My sister Leena also gets favours. Whatever she wants she gets. My parents always say 'She is doing a lot for us. She has taken over the responsibility of the kitchen'. My mum feels my jobs are less important than my sister. But I feel mine are equally. I did the paint in two bedrooms last week. I help my dad in every task. Even I take them to hospital whenever needed. My work is mine.
>
> Interviewer: How do your parents take your work?

It depends. Sometimes they appreciate and sometimes they take it very casually. Mum always takes the side of Leena. But my dad is neutral. He treats us in the same manner. I think I'm a boy so I have to help my dad and she is a girl so she has to do kitchen work. Why is her work more important than mine? Both of us do equally important jobs. So why are my jobs less than hers? No matter what I do and what she does.

As far as Lucknow children's experience of gender is concerned the study finds interesting and informative instances whereby children react to and interact with gender. For example, a girl stated that in her family boys do not do cleaning, tidying or cooking because of the tradition which prescribes such type of work be done only by girls. Her reaction is limited to the feeling of being 'fed-up'. The cast iron frame of tradition did not offer her opportunity to give voice to her desire for involving boys in indoor housework. The critique of another 15-year-old Lucknow girl is more extensive as she specifically mentions social inhibition. In comparison to others she is more argumentative, saying: 'what's wrong if boys share in housework? We all are equal and if we are cooking or cleaning then why should they be spared'. The girl who says her parents believe in the division of tasks on gender lines also says they do not like her doing outdoor jobs, although she has done so whenever she had a chance. On probing further whether she was dissatisfied with this she explained:

> No. I'm not. But I can't go away. In every family kitchen goes to girls and outside jobs go to boys. For me, every child can do all type of jobs. Look, whenever my papa is out or mummy is sick we all are doing all type of jobs. So, that's not the matter that girls can't do outdoor jobs and boys can't do indoor jobs. All this depends on the family.

This girl's initiative balances the gender distinction in situations where parents are not available to guide or restrict them. It indicates that gender does not affect her work in special circumstances. However, another 13-year-old Lucknow girl negotiates when and how to do gender-specific jobs in the presence of parents. She says:

> I didn't say no to my mum but I did say that I would do the work the way I like.

Interviewer: Could you explain it a bit more?

> Well like my mummy has given me the job of cooking in the evening. I said to my mummy that I will do it but I will not serve it whenever everybody wants. I will prepare the meal and put it on the table. Suppose my Bhaiya [brother] wants to eat any other time then I won't warm it up and serve it to him. If he has to eat he will take by his own. My mummy agreed and now I'm cooking but when to cook and how to cook is my wish.

Interviewer: And how about what to cook?

> Well my mummy tells me sometimes what to cook. But it entirely depends on my convenience. Say...if I have to do other jobs also or I'm tired then I cook dishes which take less time. But if I am free I cook what I am asked to.

In the above series of examining girls' reaction to gender the most interesting instance of utilisation of gender has come to light in a 14-year-old Lucknow girl's experience of a ration shop[2] for collecting a sugar quota every month. She says:

I go to the ration shop to bring sugar every month.

Interviewer: But why do only you go to the ration shop?

You know that the queue of males in ration shops is always very long. Women have a shorter queue and therefore it takes less time in getting sugar. So I do this job.

This example illustrates that it is not a question of gender being a help or constraint for children but strictly speaking the manner in which they react that brings out their character as such. This girl volunteers to do a job that squarely lies in the male category of work and does it just as well.

Insight and initiative reflected in the handling of gender can be gathered from examples quoted above. A girl uses her gender by choosing child care for herself. Another has made use of her gender to do boys' work. Both examples show they have utilised gender to realise wishes and do not give up hope easily in the face of conflicts of interest with parents but have their feet on the ground and forge ahead using all skills to manipulate adults. The result is that they mostly succeed in approximating to their end object: social agency.

Children's negotiation of gender and domestic work: a discussion

Indian children see gender as crucial in their domestic work. The experience of these children in both settings confirms allocation of domestic work is based on gender lines. Parents play an important role in the construction of gender by pushing forward division of domestic work on gender lines. The most important issue here is how children receive and react to gender in domestic work in daily life. As far as children in India (Lucknow) are concerned it is notable they more or less accept prevalent constructions while Indian children in Britain (Coventry) are more critical and assertive receiving them. The activities of Lucknow children are more or less determined by parents on grounds of gender. Sons and daughters usually take after father and mother respectively. Like their fathers, sons normally have to do outdoor tasks which they opt for and have the pick of the indoor tasks if and when they like. However, socio-cultural norms do not permit girls enjoying this privilege. Prevalent cultural norms in India are evident from one girl's words – 'What a family! Girls are sitting and boys are cooking' – whereas the experience of Indian children in Coventry is slightly different. When gender is thrust at them through gender-specific domestic work they do not passively accept it. They have challenged and rejected it. Thus, it may be concluded that gender shapes children's domestic work in Lucknow more than in Coventry because of difference in socio-cultural contexts. Goodnow's ambivalence with respect to gender, 'whether the push for gender comes from the parents or from the children' (Goodnow 1988, p.15), is ascertained in this study. The push comes from both parents and children.

Gill's (1998) view that it is parents who transform gender identities of children needs to be modified. Here evidence shows that children themselves take part in construction of gender. Their agency interacts with existing models of gender in their family. Their experience of domestic work works as an instrument in construction of gender. They are seen as active participants in the process more than merely passive recipients of gender. The evidence of simmering dissatisfaction among some girls and outright challenge by others gives voice to their efforts to construct or reconstruct gender whenever they have the opportunity. By means of justifying domestic work these children effectively legitimise their gender identity. The Coventry girl's preference for looking after siblings instead of work in a shop explicitly demonstrates her involvement in the construction of gender identity on cultural grounds.

These children have gone ahead in this process. They utilise negotiation power in setting and re-setting work roles. For instance, a Lucknow girl undertook her brother's outdoor tasks. Her experience led her to claim that every child can do all types of work. For her, gender should not be a limiting factor. The success of some girls in Lucknow in modifying allotted domestic work is an example of negotiation. Some changed the manner and others altered times for doing domestic work. This evidence amounts to the reconstruction of gender through their contribution to domestic work. Another very significant result of this study referred to earlier is a girl who was very heavily involved in domestic work and was more successful in negotiating her gender and power within the family structure. Children who worked daily for families were more successful in gaining autonomy and freedom that helped them to negotiate gender and other identities.

Finally, it appears that gender is not the limiting factor of domestic work. They neither include nor exclude an area of work but help in showing how the innate agency of children finds ways and means of expressing it through them. This characteristic has been examined in two settings in Lucknow and Coventry. The result is that its presence is perceived all through structural constraints of gender in different socio-cultural surroundings. In fact the determination of constraints including cultural handicaps are seen as social inhibitions that all reinforce the key idea of agency asserting itself against all odds. In this way, Nieuwenhuys' (1994) observation that existing gender inequalities have failed to stifle children's will to act on their own and contain agency which enables them to construct their own childhood has been validated.

Empirical evidence shows that children are competent negotiators in their own right to some extent. The recent work by Punch (2003) also explains how children negotiate their roles and responsibilities in sibling care and other domestic tasks. Her study reveals children's competence in negotiation of child–adult relationships in the family. This study proves that work done by children in family settings is not less than parents' contributions since they free their parents for many other jobs. This is explicitly reflected in children's views of their work. No matter how powerful they are in comparison to adults in the outer world they exercise their power and negotiation skills to achieve desired ends. These children are successful negotiators of their own rights and change the direction of adult–child relationships according to their convenience within the family. This is not to say that they control absolute power as adults have in some circumstances over children. Children who substantially contribute to domestic work enjoy more power through which they negotiate their position and gender identity in the inner world of the family. Examination of children's perspectives also explains that in some cases children's competence and negotiation power is no less than of adults.

Recognition of children's competence is necessary to understand children's social worlds; 'the adult world does not recognize children's praxis, because competence is defined merely in relation to adults' praxis' (Qvortrup 1994, p.4). If we engage children's perspectives to define competence and power in terms of negotiation skills there is no doubt left in arguing that children are social actors in their own right who define and redefine the boundaries of their world, thus children's childhood. Levison (2000) very aptly raises a fundamental question that 'can we accurately consider children's standpoints and agency without placing them in the context of the family?' To answer this it is clear on the basis of theoretical positions and empirical understanding that without listening to children (whether in family, school or peer group) and specific socio-cultural contexts we cannot understand their position in social space. Although attempts have been made to understand children's childhood, we have to take other related issues of children's life within and outside the family into consideration in order to provide a complete picture of children's childhood.

Notes

1. In the last decade many sociological and anthropological studies adopted a children's agency perspective to understand children's work and related issues. Qvortrup *et al.* (1994) undertook a project entitled 'Childhood as a Social Phenomenon' in 10 European countries. European scholars such as Boyden *et al.* (1998), James *et al.* (1998), Knutsson (1997) and Nieuwenhuys (1994, 1996, 1998) have also contributed to the development of the agency perspective. Deborah Levison (2000), a feminist economist, also advocated to engage this perspective in economics too; to understand children as workers.

2. Under the State Public Distribution system for essential goods, the Indian government runs ration shops which provide goods at controlled prices according to a fixed scale of quota to the public. It is common experience that queues of males are much longer than females.

Chapter 7

The Significance of Care and Domestic Work to Children: A German Portrayal[1]

Anne Wihstutz

The chapter draws on the significance which house and care work has for girls and boys working within and outside their respective families in Berlin, Germany. Of particular interest is the relationship of work and status and how children locate themselves within their families and social communities. The approach adopted is child-centred, viewing children as experts in their own right. The findings that are based on semi-structured interviews with 9- to 15-year-old children in Berlin are discussed alongside concepts of participation, social belonging and the implications of their work to children in terms of generational and gender relations.

The German context

Differently to the Scandinavian countries, Great Britain and Ireland there is very little awareness in Germany about children working in wealthy industrialised countries. Even less consideration is received by children working within the 'private sphere'. However, structural economic changes like a continuous high rate of unemployment, the cutting of welfare services and a growing number of women seeking paid employment inevitably influence family relations. The labour force attempts to respond to the increasingly demanding requirements of the labour market (e.g. extending work into the evening and weekend work) by adjusting and fitting their private (family) life. Especially families with members in need of care face a challenge trying to respond to the high demands of the labour market while at the same time the offer of available social services like care institutions is inadequate. Lone-parent families and families with numerous small children or of migrant background face a growing risk of poverty.

These economic developments and structural changes are accompanied by changes in the self-conception of women and men, putting emphasis on self-realisation and autonomy of the individual regardless of sex. Not only do these changes induce instability in gender roles and an erosion of the bourgeois model of the division of labour in families but they also affect the intergenerational relations between children and adults.

It is in this context that public discourse is increasingly aware of children as social actors. Since the signing of the UN (United Nations) Declaration on the Rights of the Child the understanding of children as subjects in their own right is spreading. The understanding of children as *economic actors*, as members of society who contribute also in economic terms to society's well-being, is still very much an unheard issue in Germany.

Child work

Despite statistical data showing ever since the late 1980s that the majority of school-aged children and youth in Germany has or has had experience with paid labour the issue of child work in Germany is discussed in terms of aberration and abnormality (Liebel 2004). Full-time school children are not allowed to work before or in between school hours, on weekends, after 6 pm, not more than two hours a day nor exceeding five days consecutively. Their legal work involvement is strictly regulated and limited to 'light and child-adequate engagement' in activities that are common for children and generally accepted by society. The concept used in this case however is not that of 'work' but rather that of 'leisure and learning activity', thereby implying that the activities by children are non-economic. 'Work' is generally ascociated with income-generating activities by adults, outside the home. Thus it is not surprising that research conducted to depict the situation of child work in Germany is generally limited to paid jobs (for an overview and critique see Liebel 2004; Wihstutz 2004). The studies draw a statistical picture but give little insight into the motivations and meanings of the work to children. Field work focusing on the everyday life of children and their time structuring during the afternoons draws a more complex picture of contemporary children in Germany (Furtner-Kallmünzer et al. 2002). Concerning the issue of domestic work, almost all children are involved in household activities (LBS-Initiative Junge Familie 2004).

Children in the division of family labour

In discussions relating to housework and care, children are seen as objects or as recipients of the pedagogy, care and housework of women. Up to the present, feminist discussion of housework and care does not see children as active participants in the division of family labour in the household. At best child work is seen in terms of the socialisation of young girls into their future role. Their contributing to the functioning of family and household organisation is not considered in terms of work. This results in age and gender discrimination as it is above all daughters who take on the housework and caring tasks for parents, where those parents earn their money out of home or are unable to fully engage in the family for other reasons (Corsaro 1997; Liebel 2004; Solberg 1997).

Research literature on the topic of family up to now has generally not considered the generational division of labour within the family. According to the latest report of the ILO (International Labour Organization) on child work (IPEC 2004), only those tasks that are performed in an outside-household context are to be considered as housework, and therefore understood within the context of work. Day-to-day work by children within the family is reduced to cooperation ('helping hands') and conceptualised as a learning experience (IPEC 2004, p.VII).

In the dominant image of childhood – as also represented by the ILO – a specific idea of the relationship between adults and children makes its presence felt: adults look after children. It is since the era of Enlightenment that 'childhood' has become a special time in the life-course with special institutions and places for children. In terms of functionality children are to learn and to acquire skills in order in future to be able to increase society's wealth. The generational order envisages that children are placed in a hierarchically weaker position and are limited in as to how they can participate and have access to society's resources. This 'seniority principle', as Elson (1982) terms it, ascribes parents with a responsibility towards children, and connected with this the role, indeed the necessity, of deciding over the children, their needs and how to care about it. Such a one-sided inscription of children's status as recipients hardly has conception of the ways in which children provide care and take on responsibility. Consequently, while 'children' in public discourse, minors are denied the capability of making a productive contribution to society.

The study: significance of work to children

Viewing children as experts on their own experiences the data collection to the study 'children and work' was elaborated by engaging in guide-lined conversations with children about their daily or weekly activities, their own feelings, perceptions and judgements on work. While talking with the children about their respective activities a broad concept of 'work' emerged, showing rich and complex perceptions. The investigation was guided by a concept of 'work' that was based on the following criteria: others profit from the activity, it is carried out regularly and may possibly be paid. Put in other terms, the commitment by children to take on specific tasks in their families meant no external person had to be employed and paid. Furthermore by taking on responsibility within the household, boys and girls support their parents to generate income (for further details on the research project see Hungerland, Chapter 17 in this volume).

The data are taken from 40 semi-structured interviews with open-ended questions with children between the ages of 9 and 15 in Berlin. The interviews lasted between 60 and 90 minutes and were recorded digitally. Each child was interviewed once.

Results

Almost all the children perform unpaid housework in their families. The motivations and the significance the work has for the children varies depending on the cultural and socio-economic situation of the family as well as their gender. Typical tasks that children are asked to do can be differentiated into self-care, routine family tasks and non-routine family activities (Brannen 1995). Self-care implies being responsible for oneself in the sense of self-maintenance like taking care of your own body and tidying away your own belongings. Routine family tasks include laying/clearing the table, washing up/filling the dishwasher, hoovering/dusting, washing clothes, ironing, making meals for others and household shopping. Non-routine family tasks refer to gardening, looking after siblings and cleaning windows/the car.

In the hierarchical structure of the family, mothers generally give directions to their children as to which tasks they have to carry out.

James, 12-year-old boy:[2]

[coming home from school] I stretch out half an hour and watch television and only when mum reminds me I take out the garbage.

Interviewer: She calls you?

James: She either calls from work or she tells me in the morning before leaving for work. And sometimes, I just don't notice…don't know if I do it deliberately but it is definitely the case that I never notice the dishwasher to be full and that I need to empty it because it needs to be done. In any case, it annoys my dad that I forget.

Jenny, 14-year-old girl:

Interviewer: You said you and your brother have split up the work to be done at home, or is there someone who tells you who is to do what and when this is to be done?

Jenny: My mum, voluntarily we won't do anything.

Interviewer: What does that mean? Could you describe how this works out?

Jenny: We always try to creep away secretly from the table but then she calls us back or she tells us other things to do and if we leave she asks us to take the garbage with us, yes.

Contributing to family life

Alongside typical household activities boys and girls perform other kinds of work that are neither explicitly demanded nor expected by their parents or other adults, but are rather selected and undertaken by the children themselves. In contrast to those which they do when prompted, children feel themselves to be responsible for the tasks they have chosen themselves.

When engaging in conversations with working boys and girls they reflect upon their work against the background of their specific familial situation. Depending on the cultural, social and economic background of the respective families and inner-family relations, the notion related to children's work is rather that of a contribution to family life than of work. The children give voice explicitly to the fact that they seek to help and give support through their commitment. They underline the importance of their work for their mothers, siblings and friends among others. It is above all children from single-parent or large families, as well as children in families from migrant backgrounds, who relate the meaning of their activities in terms of a contribution to the (familial) community.

The reward for their contribution is on the one hand pride in their own capabilities, on the other recognition and respect from adults. Through their work they sporadically transcend, in their self-perception, the 'play-space of childhood'.

GIRLS

In the interviews they often explain their cooperation in the family in terms of the desire to support their mother. They consider their mother to be the person in the household who is principally responsible and who is looking after children, while at the same time they perceive her as an individual with her own interests and needs.

Joey, 15-year-old girl, helps her mum:

> She [the mum] also has to perform well at school that's why I help her…it is a long time since she has been to school, that's why she had a few problems at first. I also help her with the laundry, taking it out of the machine, putting it on the line. Usually once a day I do the dishes. My mum does it twice a day 'cause we are so many. And then whenever I see things scattered around on the floor, I'll pick them up. And my little siblings are playing all the time and spread their belongings in the living room. And I have to clean up because nobody else would. My other brothers would just ignore the chaos, they won't be bothered. So it is me tidying and cleaning away because often people come by and all happens in this limited space. So I prefer to tidy up quickly…

By taking on tasks and responsibilities within the household, the daughter backs her mother to earn money outside the home, or potentially to develop her own training, while maintaining the structures of family life. The girl emphasises that she does not only take on tasks during her mother's absence, but also when she is back home. She frequently relieves her mum of activities or carries these out together with her. In her narration the girl pictures herself as an important contributor to the specific community of the family. She is explaining her motives for taking on responsibility within the household and for younger siblings by citing schooling needs of her mother.

Girls who take on responsibility for others outside the (nuclear) family unit explain their engagement through the pleasure which they experience in doing something good for others. They enjoy being together with people, undertaking joint activities and sharing time.

Jenny, 14-year-old girl (helping out at a horse farm):

> I belong to a group of friends and a friend of mine works there. If we want to horse-ride together she says, 'look, I still have to do some things.' Then we say, 'Okay, we'll help you. What can we do, what do you have to do still?' Then we finish it off together and she has gained time to spend with us, we can ride the horses or otherwise also clean the stables, feed the horses. We go out to the plains, do the hay and in return I am allowed to spend the night at the horse farm…

Interviewer: How did you get the idea?

Jenny: Hmm, it just happened. We didn't talk about it or something. It was just that I always spend my time there and I enjoy helping and it's not labour in that sense to me. It is just natural to help and to care, you don't just walk away and let others do the work.

They offer support above all to neighbours, friends and acquaintances of their parents. Their relationships are friendly and mutually beneficial, so that monetary reward is rather incidental or even indeed complex due to the emotional ties.

Juliane, 14-year-old (takes care of a small child at times, together with her twin brother):

Well, she [the mother of the girl child] is also a friend of ours and then she gives us 6 euros or so, sometimes she doesn't but then that is okay because we are friends with her. She would pay us sometimes but we haven't really talked about how expensive we are, and when she [the little girl] stays the night at our place and we take care of her, the little son of my mum's boyfriend usually stays in, too.

In the narration of these girls the idea of caring is closely linked to a sense of community. In their perception, community is generated through cooperation. They point out that they do not experience responsibility only for themselves but for others and the group as such. The basis of their orientations and actions is a feeling of solidarity which is based on reciprocity, mutual recognition and respect.

BOYS
In their narrative they perceive their mother as the one who is principally responsible for the household. They do not explain their cooperation with household and care work in terms of wanting to alleviate their mother's burden. Instead they indicate that their involvement in domestic work or with siblings is necessary since their parents or their mother is out of home earning money. They put emphasis on their household and care commitment to be of subsidiary nature, making clear that once mum is back home she is back in charge, too. These boys portray themselves as responsible substitutes, meeting their parents' expectations. They do not place their familial engagement in question, but rather describe it as self-evident.

Mike, 12-year-old boy (taking care of his younger siblings):

Well, my mum works and my dad helps out a little and when I am alone, my older brothers gone, I take care of my little sister and pick up my younger siblings from kindergarten...my older brothers did the same but now they are out-grown, they did this too when they were younger, it is on me as the middle one of all the children, it is okay for me because it means showing respect but sometimes I don't feel like it, sometimes it bothers me but that is normal.

Interviewer: Do you think it is right that you take on tasks in the family?

Yes, with us Africans it is tradition that you help doing the shopping and the household chores. It means showing respect to your parents. If they say 'hurry up, tidy up', then okay, I just do it, quickly cleaning, vacuum cleaning and then it is all done.

Other boys talk about their activities as carers outside the nuclear family unit, working as babysitters or taking care of animals. A boy shares the job of looking after a child with his sister. Similar to her he also grasps his work as an act of friendship. While his sister states that babysitting is a preparation for the future because she pictures herself working with children later on and becoming a mother herself, the boy develops an image of himself as a future inventor and computing strategist. Another boy has gained access to horses by working on an estate and, as he himself says, discovered his love of horses. Alongside the intensive caring relationship with the animals, the job is enjoyable for him above all because he can utilise his capabilities and receives recognition. In the interview he sees his professional future not in areas of care but as a stuntman or as a member of a police special unit.

Discussion

Differences in motivation

The theory of 'doing-gender' outlines how activities contribute to the social construction of gender. Tasks are not simply completed. Who is responsible for which areas and tasks is a question of status, hierarchy and dominance. In the end, through the daily carrying out of activities, wide-ranging and symbolically significant judgements about 'gender' are taken, i.e. how we are and should be 'women' and 'men' (Rerrich 2002).

In their narrative, the boys and girls involved in household duties and care work do not only describe what they do but they also give us an impression of their self-conception as children and as girls or boys. In the interview they create a picture of themselves and of how they want to be perceived. In interviews, processes and events are reconstructed according to memory and present interests and emotions. Thus, differences in motivations as depicted here between houseworking and care-taking boys and girls may indeed respond to differences in reason. Yet these differences may also respond to a specific way of 'talking' about oneself and the respective work in the interview situation. The children show themselves to be aware of the 'gendered' connotation of work and the public discourse on child work/child labour.

Respect and power

Girls and boys who take on responsibility in the household or look after their siblings describe themselves as competent, independent and capable of action. Contained within care work is always an aspect of power and hierarchy: with regard to their (younger) siblings girls and boys shoulder responsibility and achieve to a certain degree a particular position or a higher status in the hierarchy of siblings. In the eyes of the child in charge, the children to be looked after are dependent and reliant on them; they are, indeed, seen as 'children'.

James, 12-year-old boy:

When she [the younger sister] was still smaller she would love to play 'servant'. Yes, it used to surprise me, well to be honest, I also took advantage of that, I told her to fetch this or that for me or to serve toast with something on it. And she liked it but as she became older she got fed up with it. And well, while she was still smaller it was my responsibility in any case to take care for all the things she wanted to do…

The children perceive themselves as being (almost) on an equal footing with their parents. Responsibility is associated with competence and trust. Their parents or other adults from their community not only trust boys and girls to have the capabilities, but also signal to them that they rely on them.

Mike, 12-year-old boy:

They [the parents] don't dare to tell me to be careful concerning my younger siblings, I am 12 years old and they do not have to worry any more…

Solberg (1997) stresses the idea of the social construction of age, in her argument focusing on the age of children. She points out that the notion of what it means to be a child is very much family specific and a result of a continuous ongoing (implicit) negotiating process between parents and children. The concepts of a 'grown' and 'mature' child, or of a 'small' and 'dependent' child are subject to change over time and through the process of negotiation.

By taking on work and responsibility at home, preferably while their parents are away, children may experience how to 'grow', in the sense of gaining autonomy over time use and the chance to apply their skills.[3]

Micro-sociology observes that the engagement of children in the family is significantly influenced by the relationship which exists between children and their parents. Recent studies from North America show that children's cooperation in the household is also dependent on the quality of the relationship between members of the family, or between parents and children (Cheal 2003). If relationships between family members tend to be egalitarian, they have a positive effect on their reciprocal help and their willingness to take each other's concerns on board (Zeiher 2004).

Yet children also shoulder responsibility and are community-oriented in hierarchical child–parent relationships. According to Brannen (1995) this is due to the values and norms that are experienced within the family. If the identity of the family is based on the formation of a community, then children are perceived from the beginning as its members. They grow up with the thought that they belong, and can, and indeed must, contribute to the well-being of that community.

In the interviews the children show an awareness of the significance of their contribution to family life. Boys and girls portray themselves as members of a community, understood in the sense that each member of the specific community is able to contribute. The basis of children's responsible activities is their sense of solidarity and belonging to the family and community, which trusts in their capabilities and recognises their performance. Respect of one's own needs is considered to be a prerequisite for providing care and attention to others (Rommelspacher 1992). This counts for both children and adults.

Our findings indicate that children take much more part in the division of labour in families than is considered in public discourse. Shouldering responsibility within the family setting and in specific other groups they sporadically leave the 'traditional space of childhood' and thus gain to a certain extent more chances to participate in their family or group.

Children who, as described here, carry out caring duties and housework, within or outside their families, move in a field of tension between desire and obligation, capability and being overstretched. They feel responsible not only for themselves but for others and other things, too. Rather than entering a discussion about the 'good' or 'bad' aspects of children working, it might be more promising to approach the topic with a perspective based on the term of 'fairness' and 'sharing' between the members of the community, such as can be described a family.

Concluding remarks

The private household is the area in which the majority of children work. In the self-perception of children they contribute through their (unpaid) domestic work and care to a good, communal or family life. It is through their work that these boys and girls experience themselves as part of these specific communities, with their specific qualities recognised and regarded with respect. The organisation of family in its turn is challenged by structural and economic changes in German society. Children's engagement in domestic work and care becomes an important contribution to the organisation of family life.

The significance boys and girls attach to their domestic and care work respectively is influenced by their own personal interests and needs, which are affected by the cultural and socio-economic origin of the children and the relationships lived in the families. Boys and girls refer differently to their family commitment which may be due to differences in motivation. It may also be explained by gender-related different modes of talking about these specific work areas and profiling interests.

To understand the significance of work and especially domestic work to and for children, it may be useful to draw back on concepts of interdependency and reciprocity. Children working within the family and community context may be seen as participating and as embedded in a complex relationship between agency and structure, choice and constraint, autonomy and belonging.

Developing a concept of labour that recognises domestic work performed by children as a socially and economically significant contribution may be a first step to admitting children a stronger participatory role in society than has previously been considered worth the case.

Acknowledgements

My special thanks are due to Anne Solberg for her critique.

Notes

1. This paper is based on aspects of the doctoral thesis of the author on child work in Germany, dealing with the significance of child work from the child's perspective. It is part of a DFG (German Research Association) funded research project at the Technical University Berlin 'Children and Work'.

2. The children were asked to choose their own alias.

3. Solberg developed the concept of 'homestayers' (1997) in order to describe children as the new generation of housewives, as they are the ones who during the day spend their time after school at home, while their parents work elsewhere.

Chapter 8

'Helping at Home': The Concept of Childhood and Work Among the *Nahuas* of Tlaxcala, Mexico

Martha Areli Ramírez Sánchez

Introduction

The *Nahuas* of San Pedro Tlalcuapan, in the Central Mexico area, understand childhood as the period when all the unmarried children contribute with several different activities, paid and unpaid, to the development of the domestic group. During this time they are called *chamacos, miates* or *escuincles*. This concept of childhood, and the participation expected from the children, translate into a system of exchanges, of a reciprocal, indeterminate, continuous and long-term nature, which constitutes the *process of nurturing* for this community. Thus, the children are to provide help and work to their parents, who will, in turn, reciprocate with food, education, expenses for the child's wedding and inheritance.

The logic behind this phenomenon is one of reciprocity and exchange, which is always present in all actions of the *Nahuas*, but especially during the childhood stage when it can be more clearly appreciated. I will therefore define this period as *reciprocal nurturing*. In other words parents 'invest' in their offspring, receiving the children's work and help in exchange. On the other hand, the parents are 'indebted' to their children as the latter give them their work; they are therefore compelled to fulfil their role of parents. This logic of reciprocity lies within a wider cultural complex that includes the *Nahua* concept of person and the reproduction dynamics of the peasant family.

Consequently it can be suggested that in the *Nahua* concept of childhood the child is considered as a complete social actor since the moment of birth. This concept can be contrasted with those prevalent in western societies where childhood is defined and conceptualised by qualities such as fragility, dependency, tenderness, etc. These qualities are, however, attributed by the adult world.

The population and the place

The members of the *Nahua* ethnic group are considered descendants of the Aztecs. Historically, the Aztecs were the dominant group in economic, political and cultural terms until the Spanish conquest in 1492. Nowadays, they are still the largest ethnic group. There are lingual and cultural variants within the *Nahua* group. However, they all have the same origin. They are spread around 9 to 11 states of the Mexican Republic. Previous ethnography carried out in this and other communities in the *Nahua* region points to the existence of similar nurturing patterns. Then it would not be far-fetched to suggest that the thesis of this work may be applicable to other regions of the country.

The community where this study took place is called San Pedro Tlalcuapan situated on the foot of the volcano Matlalcueyet in the state of Tlaxcala. It belongs to Central Mexico in the Mesoamerican cultural area. It is two hours away from Mexico City by bus. Nowadays its main economic activities are migration to the United States and subsistence farming. The population is 2678 according to the census of the year 2002 registered by the local medical centre. This is not an official figure but seems to be the most reliable given the characteristics of the region. The number of inhabitants is variable due to the constant migration and to the fact that members of the family living in the United States are counted as living in the town by relatives. That is, if the person is sending money to their family, supporting their family, they count as if they were living at home.

The methodology and its inferences

This work has been conducted with an anthropological approach and can be qualified as an ethnographic exercise that intends to recover the local vision of the peoples studied, the *Nahuatl* for this particular case. The *emic* place vision has an important contribution to the discussion as it reduces the gap between the life in the community and researcher's *translations* or *interpretations* allowing us to particularise universal concepts.

The field work took place over a period of three years, with both short and long stays. The observation of a detailed record of the daily routines of 24 children, boys and girls from two to 17 years old, was kept. I would accompany each individual child for a week writing down their routines and talking to them. Those activities were registered as well as their translation in economic terms, in other words, how much money the child's activities contributed; this is because in indigenous-peasant societies a great amount of work is required for families to function.

Every activity performed by a member of the family means either an expense or a saving. If it was not performed by a family member someone would be paid to do it. Examples of such activities are: carrying drinking water, sowing the fields, harvesting, looking after domestic animals, building, cleaning, cooking, washing clothes, looking after sick people, younger siblings and newborn babies, milling corn or chilli, which are staple foods, killing animals for meat and participating in religious and secular festivities. In this sense, all activities performed by members of the family have an economic value. Data on several of these tasks were collected. Children participate in all of those activities. Some are specifically for boys or girls. This allows a further appreciation and understanding of work going beyond gender and age group division which organises it.

Participant observation and the fact that I was with the children while they were performing the tasks let us know what they were thinking at the very moment of the action. It allows clear explanation of what is done and for whom. From this perspective we can appreciate that not only is the child capable of doing the job but they know who they are doing it for and that they will receive a number of goods in exchange. Given this context, a quantitative tool was used to measure whether the hypothesis proposed during field work could be used as generalisations. For this purpose I designed and applied a 36-question questionnaire for 120 unmarried children: male and female. All of them were students: 50 per cent in the last three years of elementary school. The other 50 per cent were students of the three years of secondary school. This research intended to explore four main topics:

1. hours devoted to domestic chores, leisure activities, agricultural work and chores performed in neighbours' or close relatives' homes

2. incomes and expenses connected to their activities

3. paid and unpaid activities

4. of all the activities researched which ones were considered work and which not.

In order to take the time dimension into account as well, it was decided to include a diachronic component in the study. Thirty-six interviews with adults were conducted so as to evaluate the constants and changes in the situation of the children in Tlalcuapan. The people interviewed were 14 males born between 1930 and 1940 and 22 females born between 1942 and 1950. The interview was guided but allowed enough flexibility for them to talk about other topics. The questions asked were around general data with an emphasis on three main areas:

1. their childhood and how it compares to grandchildren's lives

2. they were asked to talk about their parents' childhood

3. paid and unpaid activities they performed during their childhood and who for.

The discourse of childhood

The approaches to the study of childhood have been based in exclusively affective considerations and *common places*. An important reference to study the topic from a different perspective is the work of Ariès (1987, p.540) who proposed that the origin of the concept of childhood and the feelings around it is the product of a social construct.

This concept was created toward the end of the Middle Ages and it has been reproduced by the families in industrialised societies. By a different account, Tobias Hecht (1998, p.92) argues that childhood should be defined through the context of the study of the home where the children live. He suggests that the sense

given to childhood is constructed in a *'relative'* manner and that is the result of practices not definitions.

Meanwhile, Marilyn Strathern (1988) points out that one of the particularities
of modern western societies is that childhood is considered as 'the childhood
extended by means of continuous dependency' (p.218); this way the adult–
dependency equation is established. Expanding on the concept, she says: 'the
children, in contrast are considered not able to act independently [...] they are
object to the adults' subjectivity' (p.219). Taking those concepts into account I
believe that documents such as *The Rights of the Child* and *The World of the Child*
issued by UNICEF generate an 'image' of infancy and childhood that was created
in the context of western culture under particular historical conditions. This construct is the basis for discourses, publications, etc., which report the situation of the
children of Latin America, Asia and the Middle East and give an insight into their
problems. However, they do not consider different historical moments or the
economic models in which children's activities take place.

Based on those official documents, a number of practices, ideas and public
policies have been developed, which portray a particular kind of childhood where,
as explained by Tobias Hecht, the parents should be the fundamental providers for
the children; 'the children...are the final consumer, and are [considered] inadequate to satisfy through production activities their own needs of being clothed and
fed' (1998, p.81).

Nonetheless, I think that applying unequivocal concepts about the world
cultural diversity is difficult and does not permit discussing the topic of childhood
in a more meaningful way. This case study intends to share the life experience of a
community and to present data to increase our understanding of the situation of
the millions of children that work around the world. Knowing about cases with the
characteristics found in the children of San Pedro Tlalcuapan could contribute
to it.

It is precisely in this community that the concept of 'childhood' considered as
universal and natural is not applicable. In San Pedro childhood is not seen as a stage
of fragility and defencelessness but quite the contrary. It is considered a period of
contribution to the family's economy, a key moment as the *Nahuatl* person is being
formed. A number of relationships between parents and children, bidirectional and
inter-dependent, are established within the family. They are characteristic of the
reciprocal nurturing where work plays a key role in that period of life rather than
being a problem that undermines and harms children.

Being a child in San Pedro Tlalcuapan

It is common in the community to hear the unmarried children being called *hijos de
familia* (family's son/daughter). In their eyes a single son or daughter should
perform a number of activities that correspond to their social status; if they are not
married, they are not men, not adults. Marriage is the definitive step between childhood and adulthood. Girls become women when getting married and a young man
becomes known as *cabeza de familia* or man upon marriage. During this period of
life before marriage children's work is available for their parents and close relatives.

It is the time of *giving*; the moment when those contributions will be rewarded lies ahead. In a strict social sense the childhood stage is a lengthy period. When the bodies of male and female children start to show evident changes they are called *mi joven* in the case of men and *mi señorita* in the case of women. However, the meaning is not the same as in the west.

Data collected during field work suggest the existence of a local concept of childhood that has not changed in the last 90 years similar to the one experienced by elderly people in the town and their parents. The same activities and responsibilities persist toward parents and their families, in spite of the fact that the standard of living in the community has significantly increased, due to the remittances sent by migrant relatives living in Oxnar and Costa Mesa, California, USA.

Despite clear biological development children continue performing their tasks with gradual increase in number and variations in function by age and gender. The activities change but their sense is the same. Data registered indicate that 100 per cent of male and females between three and 17 years old perform domestic chores, agricultural work and utilisation of land in the surrounding mountains. The number of hours per day devoted to work varies between 13 and 17; 95 per cent attend school; 98 per cent have relatives in the USA and receive money from them; 100 per cent expressed satisfaction with activities they perform; 100 per cent of children interviewed and observed tell the difference and classify the activities they perform in two categories: help and work; this discrimination is present both in discourse and through their actions.

Work – help: unmarried children's types of participation in the cycle of development

The ethnologic research of Catherine Good (2005) with the *Nahuas* of Guerrero, Mexico, shows a concept and meaning of work when they spent the time, force and effort in a collective action: they use the expression *'trabajando juntos como uno'* (working together as if one person). Work is something that is shared, that unites people and is dignifying.

Through this proposition we can understand what we mean when talking about *work* in a *Nahua* community. However, within that wide definition of work we can appreciate a meaningful variant and this can be clearly seen in the case of the children in Tlalcuapan. The internal logic of the family shows that the benefit of the actions performed during childhood will be reaped in coming years through very concrete actions: if the son or daughter is still living with their parents until the moment of getting married the parents will pay for the wedding party.

While working with these children one can appreciate the fact that they deeply differentiate the actions they perform, their sense, how they perceive their own work and what they think about themselves. They can differentiate *'work'* and *'help'*. The use of local categories with specific meanings is a characteristic of this place. My intention is to recover those concepts in order to explain the phenomenon observed; having explained that, I proceed on to the description. Based on three concrete situations experienced during field work – the first at the moment of applying the questionnaire at the schools; the second when interviewing adult and elderly men and women; and the third whilst observing the community in their everyday life – I arranged the activities performed into categories, following how they frequently differentiate them. These categories are as follows.

- *Help*: this can be understood as any unpaid physical activity performed for the benefit of a relative or person either close to the kin group or residential group. Basically, children of all ages 'help' close relatives and family friends. More specifically, older single sons 'help' more in activities where the product is directly used by the domestic group and activities requiring more physical effort are performed by male children. On the other hand, girls perform more activities for other families where no great physical strength is required but are rather time-consuming. Examples of these are: looking after younger children in other households or keeping the company of an elderly person, including that when they die, their children and grandchildren will take care of their soul by fulfilling all the ritual festivities associated with the dead.

- *Work*: any activity performed in exchange of an economic reward either in the formal or informal sector of the economy. It is subject to timetables, contracts and supervised by a boss. Paid work is not exclusive for the older male sons; some nine or ten-year-old children can be contracted for paid work. The wages obtained are added to the family income pool. This category of work is performed by both males and females. What varies is the amount of money children can keep for themselves. For example, money kept by male children is spent on parties, clothes and savings whereas the girls spend it on clothes and hair accessories.

Work and help are not opposite actions since they come together in some instances; namely when the family is 'helped' with money obtained in a paid job. In this case, two levels of action, 'help' and 'work', are combined to cover the family expenses and pay for the basic needs of the domestic group. Work and help permit reproduction of the domestic group as well as the growth of the family. Some families wait until their older children have grown up and work and help in a more significant way before having more children.

The function of work as an economic category is commonly recognised. However, activities conceptualised as 'help' generate goods and services for the community as well. In that sense it is important to explain them in some detail in order to understand functionality.

Levels of help

Within the domestic group are tasks such as looking after the younger siblings, cooking food, washing clothes, looking after the sick and the elderly – also participating in the preparation of wedding parties, baptisms, birthday parties, specially the girls' fifteenth birthday, family parties and funerals. Thus help functions as an exchange whereby members of the family interact. In other words, they act as sister, son, parent, etc. The definition of a good child includes being a child that helps.

Outside the domestic group is the type of help offered or received from an individual belonging to another domestic group. Its characteristic function is that performing it creates or reinforces bonds of trust with other families. This kind of exchange takes place among close relatives and neighbours. Usually the vehicle to provide this kind of help is unmarried children who are always available to help. Younger children, *escuincles, miates, miatitos* are the ones that do the *favores* (favours) on behalf of the father, mother or family.

Definition of these actions follows the fact that both help and work are elements constantly found in the domestic groups studied. In their own words, quoted contextually, 'I am helping my family or this is for my family's good'. The same activity under a different category would be 'I am working for my family'.

Adults say that help includes moral support and solidarity for a person that fulfils his or her own obligations. Work is subject to timetables and the supervision of a superior. In this sense parents work whereas children do not.

'Help' and 'work' contribute to the family's income pool in a place where the economy is based on seasonal agriculture, national and international migration and no welfare system exists. It is an indigenous peasant environment. Help substitutes all the range of welfare services available for citizens in other countries. For the *Nahuas* from the state of Puebla 'the money that a man gives to his mother is a symbol for his dependency towards her as the main source of domestic services' (Mulhare 2003, p.274).

Childhood in a system of reciprocity and exchange

Everyone 'helps' members of their family especially those with whom they share households. In a deeper sense nurturing includes the transmission of values. An example of this is again taken from the *Nahuas* of Puebla:

> The purpose of instilling 'icnoliz' [word for respect in Nahuatl] is mainly to maintain good relationships between siblings. Fraternity is paramount in a domestic group where siblings must work together with their parents in order to fill the family barn and the common income, icnoliz functions as a guide for pre-ferred behaviour in the Nahua family. (Taggart 2003, p.8)

From an ideological point of view work and respect go hand in hand but to reward the outcome of work is to give respect as well. Children between the ages of 12 and 17 are most productive; however, what they contribute is not repaid immediately. Parents will use the surplus to build a house, buy more land or have more children. When a son or daughter decides to marry, parents will pay for a big party. That is the moment to give back part of what was received. At this time the child will get back the work provided to the family and will also get part of the inheritance in the form of land to build a house on. They will become adult then. Parents begin to provide a different kind of help: advice, moral support within the community and when the grandchildren are born. The cycle of exchange and reciprocity is thus continued. This fresh debt will make the new adults take care of the parents when they reach old age as well as taking care of their souls when they die. In this sense exchanges define the relationships in the family and the community.

The children with their work especially circulate around the community transferring their work and building more social relationships between families. I never found a case of individuals seeking to terminate such relationships, quite the opposite. Someone with no relationships with other persons and families does not get community recognition. A person who does not participate in the exchange and who does not share is not considered a good person. Work and help are ways of forming relationships and a means of transmitting fundamental values aimed at the making of *Nahua* persons. This is what I call reciprocal nurturing that gives the children a social role comparable to that of an adult in the western world.

Spaces of conflict

The first impression one gets from this system is almost ideal: that is to say, it shows great solidarity. Nevertheless, this family logic whereby children are growing up is changing and generating spaces of conflict. In this regard the elderly people in the community say they have always worked and argue that children nowadays 'are not what they used to be, they get sick easily, they are more delicate'. A possible explanation for those transformations is the accelerated change faced by the community, the influences from the migrants when they come back and the extent of the national education programme which lacks specific provision for areas with indigenous bilingual populations.

An example of this is currently taking place in the classrooms of elementary schools where teachers transmit practices and discourses about childhood as well as topics included in the new nationally prescribed textbooks. The introduction of new models results in tensions within the family. Children are taught what a child should and should not do regarding topics such as hygiene, values, etc. When children come home they have to work in the surrounding mountains, look after domestic animals, sow, help and so on. It is at home that tensions become evident. Poorer families face new conflicts arising from economic demands of education such as purchase of school uniforms, use of resources or the decision on who will study. This newly arrived concept of what a child should be confronts traditional cultural patterns with ideal models. This proves that those models are not universal or natural, given that they *have to be* taught and learned in these communities.

It is not my intention to say that schooling is a problem given that Tlalcuapan has had an elementary school since around 1920. What have changed are content of education and goals of schooling. Labour migration has also introduced new patterns: it is expected that education helps people to get a job and speak English so that they can migrate later. However, generally speaking most parents do not regard education as having a value *per se*.

Younger couples express wishes that their children will not be 'dirty' like themselves which in this context means being indigenous and peasants. At the same time they wish children to be hard-working, good people with no vices. However, they do not manage to conciliate the patterns learned through formal education with the long-standing local tradition of raising children which fails both at dialogue and practical level. The new concept of childhood that has arrived in Tlalcuapan contradicts values, the concept of person and networks in the community.

Final considerations

In Tlalcuapan it is unmarried children in the family who drive development of the domestic group. Family life in an indigenous peasant environment is not built by individual effort. They achieve goals through exchanging work with relatives and from outside the family. It is difficult to think that children would respond to another logic that is different from that of work. These children think of their future and their own value as being capable of working. They are aware that they are building relationships. Mulhare (2003) documented the case of a girl who left her parents to live with neighbours, arguing that they did not value her work. After she moved out her parents visited and bought her a pair of trousers. Her response was that they were not going to buy her with a pair of trousers.

All this leads to the understanding that not all activities performed by unmarried children can be categorised as exploitation. They are part of a kinship system (Robichaux 1996) that functions under specific cultural norms. Therefore, we do not see poverty as the main reason behind the children's work. The experience of shared work, always considered as a highly valued activity, has been documented (e.g. Good 2005; Mulhare 2003; Taggart 2003) in different areas of Mexico. Thus, the study of childhood allows us to understand the internal logic of the peasant family.

Lack of knowledge of local cultural traditions has limited outcomes of programmes seeking to transform the reality of working children. It is also important to discover local patterns of education coexisting with the processes of globalisation and accelerated change. A further challenge would be to recognise that modernisation projects aiming to develop poor countries and eliminate child labour are displacing important cultural traditions.

Part 3

Work and Competence

Chapter 9

Children's Work as Preparation for Adulthood: A British Perspective

Jim McKechnie and Sandy Hobbs

Over the last decade researchers in Britain have demonstrated that it is common for children to work. The typical pattern is for children to combine part-time employment with full-time education (Hobbs and McKechnie 1997; McKechnie and Hobbs 2001).

The focus of research has shifted over the last decade. Initially researchers focused on establishing the nature and extent of child employment. This took place against a backdrop of discussions regarding the effectiveness of legislation. In the mid to late 1990s the emphasis switched to debates regarding the relationship between part-time work and education. In this context concern was expressed about the negative effect of work on students' engagement with, and performance in, school. In the early part of the twenty-first century the emphasis has changed once again. In the last few years there has been a growing interest in the contribution that students' part-time employment could make to education.

While the focus of research questions may have changed over time there has been a consistency in societal attitudes to part-time work in Britain. The legislation introduced to cover the employment of children, the Children and Young Persons Act 1933 which is still in force, accepted the idea that combining work and school was acceptable as long as it was 'controlled'. Implicit in this was the view that such employment was a form of control over children's antisocial behaviour and that such work experience had a positive socialising effect.

In the intervening years, even though evidence mounted to suggest that such employment was not benign, the positive view of work dominated. Steve Cunningham's work provides a persuasive argument highlighting the role of permanent state officials in maintaining and perpetuating this view of children's work (Cunningham 1999). In the latter part of the twentieth century two key educational reports, the Crowther Report and the Newsom Report, added to this perception by highlighting the positive effects of such part-time employment.

The intriguing aspect of all this is that there was no evidence upon which to base such perceptions or attitudes towards work. The research evidence that did exist up to the 1990s had tended to draw attention to problems associated with part-time employment, for example the negative impact on education. The re-emergence of the study of child employment in Britain in the 1990s has not resulted in a research base that allows us to address the issue of the contribution of work.

However, the general view is that such work has potential to make a positive contribution. When the topic of children's employment is raised in general conversation it does not take long for a number of views, or clichés, to emerge. For example, such work experience 'teaches children the value of money', 'gives them a taste of the real world of work', 'makes them realise what it's like to work', 'makes them more responsible'. While these assumptions are easily identified, the evidence to support, or challenge, them is lacking.

This chapter reflects our initial attempts to consider how researchers might explore these claims and evaluate them. We focused on one specific assumption, that work in some way exposes children to 'the real world of work' allowing them the opportunity to learn about work in a way that prepares them for adulthood.

An obvious problem is how do you start to evaluate such a view? What is meant by the 'real world of work'? In these preliminary investigations we adopted a simple approach to operationally defining this issue. If children's work does prepare them for the 'real world of work' then we should be able to identify similarities between their job experiences and the experiences that we associate with adult employment.

It is worth noting that while we draw on research findings from three studies the primary aim was not to investigate this issue. In effect we collected additional data which we thought would allow us to evaluate the assumption we were concerned with.

There are three studies that we will draw on in this paper and each one had a slightly different focus; however, we will suggest that when we take the findings together they provide some insights into the idea that children's work prepares them for adult employment.

Study I

The primary aim of this study had been to explore the relationship between educational performance and senior school students' part-time employment (McKechnie, Hobbs and Hill 2002). In Scotland senior school students are referred to as S5 and S6 students; S5 students are on average 16 years of age while S6 are typically 17 years of age.

The project:

- was designed around a questionnaire-based survey
- surveyed all students in a given area: N = 1860 (S5 – 1183: S6 – 677).

To explore the extent to which school students' part-time work may or may not mirror adult employment we explored the issue of training. Students were asked to provide information on whether they had, or had not, received training in their current jobs and in their former jobs. This latter group is important for two reasons:

- they provide information on those students who had worked in the past but were presently 'unemployed'
- for those students currently working it provides information on their previous work experience.

First let us consider the extent to which training is or is not a part of the work experience of this group of employees.

Table 9.1 indicates that for current workers in both year groups training is a common part of the employment experience, though it is more common among the employed older students. This contrasts with the pattern for former jobs. Among the older students approximately half of the students report no training in former jobs, while this rises to 61 per cent for the younger students in S5.

Table 9.1 Training

School year	Work status	Training %	No training %	N
S5	Current workers	63	37	538
	Former workers	39	61	466
S6	Current workers	81	19	451
	Former workers	51	49	376

There are two possible explanations for this. First it is possible that students may have forgotten any training in past jobs. Second, it may be the case that the type of jobs that students held when younger were less likely to involve training.

There is some support for this latter position when we look at the link between training and job type (see Table 9.2).

Some job types are more likely to have involved some training experience, for example hotel and catering, waiting and shopwork. Previous research has shown that these types of jobs are more common as school students age (McKechnie, Hobbs and Lindsay 1998). The types of jobs that children are involved in when younger are the very jobs that are not associated with training, for example delivery, babysitting, door-to-door sales. This might lead us to the view that, when it comes to training as an adult-like aspect of work, the jobs that children are involved in when younger are less adult-like in this respect. Before we move on to consider this hypothesis let us look briefly at the type of training that students received.

Students had been asked to provide details on the type of training they had received. For both S5 and S6 groups the most common form of training was

Table 9.2 Current job type and training

Job type	S5 training %	No training %	S6 training %	No training %
Delivery	14	86	20	80
Hawking	18	82	–	100
Shopwork	79	21	88	12
Babysitting	9	91	8	92
Waiting	78	22	72	28
Hotel/catering	67	33	85	15
Other	54	46	75	25

'job-specific training', for example how to work a till, provide silver service. Among S5 less than 10 per cent received any training in fire and safety, food hygiene or health and safety. For S6 this figure was just under 20 per cent.

However, our main concern at present is the consideration of our hypothesis that younger child employees are less likely to receive training, and by implication their work is possibly less adult-like.

Study II

In this study we were concerned with comparing the work experience of 15-year-olds (in school year S3) with that of 16-year-old students (in school year S5). Once again, while it was not the main aim of the study, we included some material on the extent to which employment mirrored 'adult-like' experiences of work (McKechnie, Hobbs and Anderson 2004).

This study was a questionnaire-based study, comparing the experiences of S3 with that of S5 students, N = 520 and 274, respectively.

This study focused on two aspects of the 'adult-like nature of work'. First we considered the issue of training, to test our hypothesis that part-time work at younger ages may be less likely to involve training. Second we asked students to inform us about the nature of their work experience, in particular the extent to which they worked alongside co-workers, dealt with customers, handled money and finally the procedure by which they were paid.

Training

A comparison of the 15- and 16-year-olds' experience of training supported the idea that younger employees were less likely to receive training than their older peers. This difference was consistent for current workers and former workers (see Table 9.3).

Table 9.3 Training 14–15-year-olds vs. 16–17-year-olds: current workers

Age group	Training %	No training %	N
14–15	52	48	121
16–17	78	22	93

As in the previous study we found that there was a trend indicating that training was associated with job type. Furthermore, while a number of S3 students reported some training, those jobs held by younger students were significantly less likely to be associated with training experiences. Previous research has indicated that gender is associated with job type. In this study the data trends indicated that females might be more likely to receive training compared to males. However, we could find no evidence that gender was significantly linked to training.

Work experience

In this study we had also considered other aspects of children's work experience. To varying degrees they reflect the complexity of the tasks that employees may or may not do and the adult-like nature of the experience.

WORKING ALONGSIDE OTHER CO-WORKERS

On a four-point scale students indicated the frequency of working alongside others. The analysis showed that for current workers older students were significantly more likely to work with co-workers all of the time. In contrast the 14–15-year-olds were more likely to indicate that they hardly ever or never worked with co-workers ($\chi^2 = 41.7$, df = 3, p < 0.001).

DEALING WITH CUSTOMERS

Once again the responses indicate that among current workers 16–17-year-olds were more likely to deal with customers on a regular basis as part of their work. Among younger students a large percentage had some dealing with customers but this age group were more likely to say that their work rarely involved dealing with customers ($\chi^2 = 26.7$, df = 3, p < 0.001).

HANDLING MONEY

We also examined the extent to which students did or did not handle money as a regular part of their work. In this case there was no significant difference between 14–15 and 16–17-year-olds ($\chi^2 = 6.9$, df = 3, p > 0.05).

METHOD OF PAYMENT

Among adults it is common to be paid through a bank account. In exploring the method of payment it was apparent that 16–17-year-olds were significantly more likely to be paid via a bank account. A small percentage of younger students, less than 10 per cent, were paid in this manner. It was far more common for them to receive payment as cash in hand ($\chi^2 = 68.2$, df $= 1$, p < 0.001).

For the 14–15-year-olds there were no significant gender differences associated with any of the above aspects of work. For 16–17-year-old workers the only gender difference to emerge was that females were more likely to work alongside co-workers than their male counterparts.

Where does Study II leave us? Based on this material it is possible to argue that younger students are more likely to work in jobs that are unlikely to involve training, working with others, dealing with customers or receiving payment in the standard adult form, i.e. through bank accounts. Against this background we could be heading for a conclusion which suggests that, on the basis of our original operational definition, younger students are involved in work that is less likely to be adult-like or prepare them for adult work.

Study III

In the third study, 14–15-year-olds were interviewed about their jobs. In total 70 students were interviewed; 52 out of the 70 had worked at some time. The interviewees had been drawn from a larger study comparing the employment of children based in rural and urban contexts (McKechnie, Stack and Hobbs 2001; Stack 2004).

The interviews covered a range of topics including how they had secured employment and the future benefits of their work. In the context of this paper we will focus on two specific aspects of the interviews, namely the issue of skill attainment and contribution to future employment.

We have already suggested that based on Study I and II one might argue that younger students' employment is less likely to contribute to preparation for adult work. This view was reinforced when we asked our interviewees about the attainment of skills based on their work.

Skills

A small minority of the students who worked were involved in activities that drew upon previously acquired skills; three were paid to play music, one was a gymnastics teacher and another taught computing.

However, the fact that most of the jobs did not involve any training was clear to the respondents. This was reflected in the apologetic tone adopted, shown in the use of 'just' in many of the responses:

Just cleaning and stuff.

Just working at the counter.

I just help out washing dishes.

The pattern of responses suggested that our earlier conclusion may have some justification, namely that younger children's work may contribute less to adult work preparation. Other aspects of the interview responses challenged such a conclusion.

Future impact

In another part of the interview we wanted to explore students' views about the contribution that their work experience may, or may not, make to their future. It's interesting to look closely at the responses to this type of question. Fifteen students responded by saying 'no' or 'don't know'. However, nine of these children then went on to mention some benefit.

This pattern of response occurred in a number of places throughout the interviews and suggests that some of the issues that we were exploring were 'novel' to the interviewees, i.e. they had not given much thought to these aspects of their work before. We will return to this issue in the conclusion to this chapter.

When asked about the contribution to the future the largest single category of responses, 18 in total, referred to the ability to deal with people. Some examples of the responses illustrate this:

Get on well with people… I can sell anything.

How to work with others.

Working with people…customers as well as staff.

There were 22 answers that fell into categories which probably overlap: time management, being organised and reliable, and being confident and patient:

Organising my time.

Discipline.

…now I'm really confident because I've had to work serving people…Yes, it's given me good interpersonal skills.

The evidence from the interviews with these younger workers suggests that while they do not perceive their jobs as opportunities for developing work-related skills they do view their work as contributing to other skills, so-called 'soft skills'. These 'soft' skills include interpersonal skills, communication, confidence, etc. In Britain there has been recognition that such abilities are crucial for successful transition into the adult labour market and are as important as more 'concrete' job-specific skills. In this context then younger children's work could be thought of as contributing to preparation for adulthood.

Conclusions

We started this chapter with the intention of evaluating whether children's work can be viewed as a preparation for adulthood. The approach we adopted set out to consider the extent to which children's work experience mirrored aspects of work that we associate with adult employment.

The results support the view that this work can be thought of as providing a preparation for adulthood. However, the extent of this preparation is mediated by age, type of job and gender.

Study I and II could lead one to assume that it is less likely that younger children's work has any long-term contribution to make. This conclusion is challenged by the findings from Study III. By shifting the focus away from concrete experiences – for example training, working with co-workers, etc. – it becomes apparent that these younger workers perceive the contribution of work in terms of the attainment of 'soft' skills.

Clearly there is a need for researchers to explore these issues in more detail. Some have already started to do so; for example, Leonard (2002) has focused on newspaper delivery and identified the opportunities for learning in this 'routine' task.

We indicated in our introduction that in Britain the emphasis has switched in the area of child employment to highlight the 'potential for learning'. If we are to travel down this road then it is paramount that we do so using an effective evidence base. We need to move away from the 'assumptions approach' that has driven policy and legislation in this area for a number of decades in Britain. In making this move we think the present chapter highlights a number of methodological issues that need to be considered. These are:

- Need for clear definitions of concepts. First, general assumptions about the impact of work, for example prepares children for the adult world of work, need to be clearly operationalised. Second, concepts such as 'training' and 'learning' in the work context need to be carefully defined. In the present studies we have used the term 'training' in a general sense that reflects our adult conceptions of this term.

- Pluralist approach to methodology. We need to acknowledge that different sources of information provide different types of information and have the potential to offer different types of insight into the same phenomenon.

- Recognition that children may not have 'thought' about aspects of their work. In Study III it was apparent that many of the interviewees were addressing issues about work for the first time. From a research perspective this raises a number of issues.

- Need for developing a range of techniques including the need for 'triangulation' of sources, for example job descriptions, perceptions of work and observations of work.

In Britain the last 15 years has seen the issue of children's work gaining the attention of some academics, policy-makers and non-governmental organisations. However, the decades of neglect that preceded this present level of interest has left us with a limited *understanding* of children's work.

Chapter 10

Working Children in Fez, Morocco: Relationship Between Knowledge and Strategies for Social and Professional Integration

Bernard Schlemmer

This chapter presents the first findings of a field survey carried out in Morocco.[1] It seeks to address an obvious yet understated paradox:

- every study on 'child labour' highlights its dangers for the child[2]
- the answer, they say, lies in primary education for all
- yet every survey of the Moroccan education system reveals it to be failing to pass on to all children – even at primary level – the basic knowledge they will need for adult life.

Faced with that clear contradiction, it is necessary to establish the facts with respect to:

- the major handicap it might be for a child to go to work before compulsory school age
- and how much better a future he or she might have as a result of going to school.

Explaining the paradox

'Child labour' studies

These studies, most of them commissioned by international organisations or NGOs (non-governmental organisations), all correspond to the same paradigm: child labour *per se* is an evil that must be eradicated. They are therefore, *ipso facto*, purpose-oriented: analysing child labour in order better to eradicate it.

They follow a standard line of inquiry:

- which children are working
- what kinds of work they do
- how working affects their education, health and their physical and mental growth
- why they are working so young and what can be done to improve the situation.

Such questions lead to more or less predictable answers in studies that tend to resemble one another, irrespective of date or location:

- working children come from underprivileged parts of the population
- girls mainly work in the domestic sphere, and boys in agriculture and the 'informal sector' (or grass-roots economy)
- their education and health, of course, suffer as a result
- poverty is the main reason why they are working so young, in addition to the 'traditional mindset' and the shortcomings of the existing education system
- efforts must therefore be made to assist the poorest families, to open local populations up to progress, to improve the quality and supply of education and, in the meantime, to bring in up-to-date legislation to combat the 'worst forms' of child labour.

The solutions proposed, by the way, always address issues concerning the rights of the child rather than labour rights.

Education system surveys

These can involve academic research where the thinking, at least, is not geared to producing a predetermined set of results. But the researchers are not the same as those working on child labour, and their analysis takes no account of the actual circumstances of working children. The social sciences conducting educational research tend to adopt the views of the institution they are studying: that school and labour are incompatible.

School-age children, they argue, must go to school full-time if they are to stand any chance of success in adult life. They are aware that some might have to work to pay their tuition fees, of course, but regard them in the same light as other 'problem cases': physically, mentally or, indeed, socially handicapped children.

Published research on the education dilemma in Morocco, then, focuses almost exclusively on supply-side shortcomings. Backed by irrefutable quantitative data, it ascribes the fact that children are not being educated to infrastructure problems and inadequate means. Apart from notes about traditional teaching methods prevailing in rural areas, and about boys being treated differently from girls, there is practically not a word on the demand: *it obviously exceeds the supply so why talk about it?* But our research shows that many children stay away from school not because access is barred by economic or material difficulties, but because school-taught knowledge is not considered a prerequisite of social success.

Ascertaining the facts behind the paradox

Seventy-five per cent of the sample population interviewed – young adult males[3] in the traditional working-class district of Fez Medina – had started work before the age of 15.

Finer analysis of that population divided into two subgroups – those born before 1974 and those born after – shows that while the overall proportion working before compulsory school age has remained more or less consistent, there are differences linked to the starting age:

- at one extreme, it has risen with the increase in access to education (33.5 per cent of boys born before 1974 had worked since they were six or seven, and had never been to school, compared to 22.5 per cent of those born since)

- at the other, however, the increasing difficulty in gaining access to higher education (with figures down from 6.2 per cent of those born before 1974, to 2.3 per cent of those born since) has resulted in higher numbers dropping out of school to start work.

On the whole, children are enrolling in school more naturally at the compulsory age, and fewer are staying away. But can one really talk about school being institutionalised when, at the same time, increasing numbers of working-class children are dropping out at an increasingly early age?

Conventional criteria for breaking down the sample population:

- the social background and educational capital of household heads (about which enough has been said)

- rural–urban differences, which are slowly attenuating

- gender differences, which are also attenuating but at an even slower pace: twice as many girls remain deprived of schooling as boys.

Is school or labour the route to social and professional integration?

There is no room here for a detailed account of every method I have had to devise to measure the various routes to social and professional integration. Let us just take the following index, which I managed to develop through questioning socially and professionally integrated young men on the one that they themselves and each of their brothers had taken:

- 'low-level' integration, for routes leading to a low social standing linked to underpaid, unstable, and relatively unskilled lines of work

- 'normal' integration, for routes leading to a social and professional standing shared by the majority of one's entourage

- 'successful' integration, for routes leading to a degree of upward social mobility linked to a more highly respected status than that of one's father
- 'outstanding' integration, for routes leading to what is perceived to be genuine upward mobility.

Routes to integration by levels of educational attainment

Table 10.1 shows clearly that it does make sense to earn a diploma; that the baccalaureate in particular is a barrier against total failure; and that chances of success improve with enrolment in secondary education.

But it also shows that while dropping out before the end of secondary school may increase the risk of low-level integration, it does not rule out other possible outcomes: drop-outs can achieve some degree of success, if not genuine upward mobility.

Table 10.1 Social and professional integration by level of educational attainment: total sample population

	Unemployed graduates %	'Low-level' integration %	'Normal' integration %	'Successful' integration %	'Outstanding' integration %	Total %
Baccalaureate holders	37.0	-	5.0	26.0	32.0	100
Secondary schooling	-	21.5	57.0	21.5	-	100
Little or no schooling	-	38.0	48.5	14.0	-	100
Total	3.0	37.5	42.0	15.5	2.5	100

Next we distinguish between individuals that never went to school at all; those that started primary but then dropped out; and those that stayed through to the end of primary and even started – but did not finish – secondary (see Table 10.2).

While attending school is obviously useful, the benefits become clear only to those staying the course at least until the end of primary school. More importantly, the figures in Table 10.2 back up the unorthodox view suggested earlier: that some boys who have never been to school still manage to achieve not just a 'normal' level of social and professional integration, but even some genuine successes.

Most of those that had dropped out claim the decision to abandon their studies had been theirs, possibly because they want to avoid implicating their parents. The latter, for their part, say they were hostile to their son's decision and had tried to change his mind. This may reflect what, in psychoanalytical terms, could be called

Table 10.2 Social and professional integration by level of educational attainment: little or no schooling

	'Low-level' integration %	'Normal' integration %	'Successful' integration %	'Outstanding' integration %	Total %
Completed primary and/or some secondary	38.0	38.0	24.0	-	100
Dropped out of primary	33.0	60.0	7.0	-	100
Never went to school	44.5	37.0	18.5	-	100
Total	38.7	48.5	13.7	-	100

a 'double link': two mutually exclusive sets of parental instructions with, on the one hand, implicit guidance not to follow such expensive studies and, on the other, an explicit command to stay on in the classroom (undermined by little more than symbolic sanctions). In actual fact, parents give up making their children go to school, even though it is compulsory, with astonishing ease. It would appear not to matter that much to them if they left; see Box 10.1.

Box 10.1 Who decides to stop schooling

1. **Boys born between 1960 and 1974**
   | | |
   The family, for reasons other than financial 48.8%
   The family, for financial reasons 11.0%
   The boy 37.8%
   The school 2.4%
2. **Boys born in 1975 and after**
   The family, for reasons other than financial 30.8%
   The family, for financial reasons 12.4%
   The boy 51.4%
   The school 5.4%

Source: personal research (B. Schlemmer 2000–2003)

Notwithstanding the economic crisis that has racked the region since the 1980s, i.e. since our second cohort reached compulsory school age, the proportion citing financial reasons for leaving school has hardly grown at all. And in spite of a slight rise in the number of boys expelled or refused entry by the school, the figures there remain highly marginal. Meanwhile, it is unfounded to interpret the substantial increase in very young boys deciding to leave school as evidence that more of them have stopped wanting to go: it has more to do with parental opposition to such a move having declined to the point of 'laissez-aller'. So the difference actually lies in the fact that parents feel increasingly less of a need to do anything about ensuring their sons' education. Their relations with the schools system today could best be described as distant.

Furthermore, the age at which the children are deciding to leave has fallen dramatically. In the past, 67.7 per cent were over the age of 12. Today, 59.9 per cent are under 12, and 43.1 per cent between 9 and 11.

The interviews have shown that parents give up trying to assert their point of view so easily – or even do not really have one, regarding their duty as having been done once the child is enrolled – because the idea of school as the only route to social and professional integration is alien to them. School-taught knowledge is not considered crucial in Fez, a city where the craft industries are an open option for out-of-school children, and where master craftsmen are suspicious of any child intellectually too well equipped not to grow into a fearsome competitor; indeed, it is even felt to be a handicap or at best a waste of time (see Schlemmer and Gérard 2004).

Our survey does not reflect the situation of all working children in Morocco as a whole, just boys in the city of Fez. It is important to bear this in mind since in order to make sense of its findings one needs to be aware of how knowledge is perceived in that city's craft industries – which dominate the local economy. When we carry out the same survey in Casablanca, where such industries are far less influential, we will probably come up with a different set of results.

In the meantime, analysing the case of the boys with little or no schooling but who, with a solid traditional apprenticeship, have found it relatively easy to achieve a good level of social and professional integration has not exactly been a completely fruitless exercise.

P.S. The editors of this book have just written to me, telling me – with leniency – that my paper is very interesting but suffers from a lack of conclusion. But how to conclude? The fact that school is not a guarantee for a successful social integration on the labour market is not precisely an astonishing discovery, even if more significant is the fact that child labour could be as reliable a way toward this integration as school is, at least when academic studies are not carried on up to, let us say, university or so. Have we to conclude that schooling is useless? Obviously no! But school, it must be said, is failing to fulfil its role as a medium for social integration. 'We want an education system whose methodology and content are adapted to our reality' stated the Movement of Working Children and Youth (Kundapur Declaration). How can we answer such a rightful claim without dismantling the principle of 'the same school for all'? How can tighter links be forged between training and work without playing into the hands of employers, or giving up on general learning and the preparation of personalities for adulthood in the broadest sense of the term? Can a school education feasibly be made compatible with productive paid labour? Disadvantaged children at school tend to take in only what they feel might be of use to their parents. And the latter recognise the value of school, but believe – with, sadly, some justification – that it is not meant for their children. So we have a dilemma that needs resolving. Work, even when performed in unacceptable conditions – and should, as such, be rendered off-limits to minors – is instantly valorising to the children themselves (despite their generally being denied worker status at every level), their parents (who regard a child's earnings as secondary income, falling some way short of an adult's), employers (who profess to see them in terms of the burden of responsibility rather than as a lucrative source of profit) and fellow workers (who treat them as incompetents). They are highly conscious of the fact that they are being useful, that they are doing their bit to keep the family going; boys take legitimate pride in performing their duties 'like a man'. But at what point does such thinking serve merely to maintain the status quo and underpin exploitation? When should work cease to be considered positive? All that I am able to conclude is to ask for a serious reflection on these questions, from social scientists throughout the world. It should be obvious. But it is better to underline it, since the pressure is so high to consider that a working child is necessarily a victim of child labour, and the strain so great to obtain hastily statistical results on the 'education for all' agenda.

Notes

1. Within the framework of the Franco-Moroccan *Programme de recherche sur l'insertion et les savoirs au Maroc* (PRISM).

2. The term 'child labour' is used throughout this chapter in keeping with the International Labour Organization definition (cf. International Programme for the Elimination of Child Labour – IPEC), which does not mean to say that we agree with it.

3. In regard to gaining information on the female population, the survey ran into what proved to be enormous difficulties.

Chapter 11

Working and Growing Up in America: Myths and Realities[1]

Jeylan T. Mortimer

Almost all adolescents in the United States do paid work for considerable periods of time while attending high school. Unlike working youth in Germany, and other countries with the apprentice system, their jobs typically have no formal connection to their schooling. Students seek these jobs so they can have their own spending money, save money for college, and engage in sometimes expensive adolescent lifestyles. Some are helping to support their families. Most American parents encourage their children to work because they think that employment has benefits for them that are not usually obtained in school. Most important, they believe that working will teach their children to be self-reliant and to obtain general knowledge about the workplace (how to act at work, what to wear, the need to be on time, etc.), pertinent skills (especially 'people skills' fostering smooth interpersonal relations), and positive work orientations (a positive work ethic and recognizing the importance of being able to take responsibility when others depend on you) that will enable them to participate effectively in this sphere in the future.

Notwithstanding these potential benefits, teenage employment is not without its critics. In contrast to parents and teenagers, some developmental psychologists express grave doubts about the value of paid work experience for children (Steinberg and Cauffman 1995). They argue that children are allotted simple, repetitive work by their employers, which provides little learning opportunity and no chances for advancement. Some teenage work is stressful, presenting difficulties for children who have not yet developed adequate coping skills. Moreover, the critics allege that the kinds of jobs that are available to youth – in fast-food restaurants, grocery stores, gas stations, and retail outlets – cultivate negative attitudes toward working in general and poor work habits. But their strongest fear is that paid employment will distract children from their schoolwork, interfere with their capacity to do homework, and diminish their academic achievement. They also worry that teenagers who work may come to think of themselves as adults, reject adult control over their behavior, and take on problematic activities, such as substance use, which adults sometimes engage in during their leisure time. Their resentment of child-like treatment could foster defiance and various forms of deviant behavior.

Many educators share psychologists' concerns about the conflicts between school and work. They also worry that students who work cannot fully participate in the vast array of extracurricular activities organized by the school to foster student growth and exploration of non-academic interests and activity domains (e.g. sports, music, dramatics, fine arts, etc.).

This controversy has fostered widespread public attention and debate (see National Research Council 1998) and a growing empirical literature, mostly focused on whether hours of work have deleterious consequences for high-school student achievement, as indicated by grade point average, time spent on homework, and high-school drop-out. Whereas long hours of work are found to be associated with lower grade point average, less time spent doing homework, and other achievement indicators, the question remains as to whether working, and especially more intensive work, accounts for these problems. A plausible alternative explanation for these associations is that youth who already have little interest and capacity for schoolwork, or whose families have limited resources and do not encourage higher education, choose to work longer hours so as to prepare themselves for future full-time labor force participation.

Though youth work is the focus of many studies (see Mortimer 2003 for a review), they tend to be rather limited in scope. Rarely is the quality of work available to young people considered, as investigators focus on the most easily quantifiable dimension of adolescent work experience, the number of hours worked per week (or year). Furthermore, research is usually restricted to the consideration of outcomes during, or shortly after, high school. Little attention has been directed to the longer-term benefits or costs of teenage employment.

The Youth Development Study (YDS)

For almost two decades, University of Minnesota researchers have been following a cohort of teenagers as they complete high school, enter postsecondary schooling, and become established in the full-time labor force. A panel of 1010 randomly chosen ninth graders registered in the St. Paul (Minnesota) School District agreed to participate in the study; 1000 of these completed first-wave questionnaires. Whereas the character of the youth labor force differs greatly across the various regions of the United States, St. Paul is quite similar to the nation as a whole on a variety of demographic and work-related characteristics. The population of St. Paul was approximately 272,000 at the time of the study, located in the 'Twin Cities' (including Minneapolis) metropolitan area that had over 2.5 million residents in 1990. Socio-economic indicators for the city of St. Paul and for the nation as a whole, as documented by the 1990 US Census, are quite comparable (e.g. per capita income, percent below the poverty line). However, the citizenry of St. Paul is somewhat more highly educated than that of the nation at large, and St. Paul had relatively good employment opportunities for adults and for youth (Mortimer 2003). In 1990 the rate of unemployment was 4.7 percent in St. Paul, and 5.5 percent in the national labor force; rates of labor force participation were 63 percent and 60 percent, respectively.

Of course, youth will have fewer work opportunities in the more economically depressed inner cities of the country (see Newman 1999 on working teenagers in New York City), and experience different kinds of work in rural areas (see Elder and Conger 2000 on teenagers who work on farms and in small rural communities). Still, the circumstances of youth who work in St. Paul are most likely similar to those in many other mid-sized American cities.

The panel was surveyed annually throughout high school – from the ninth (1988) to the twelfth (1991), with superb retention (93 percent) during this period. The initial panel was 74 percent White, 10 percent African American, 5 percent Hispanic, and 4 percent Asian (the remainder did not place themselves in any of these categories or considered themselves mixed race). Median household income was in the range of $30,000–39,999; 62 percent of the families had incomes at or below this level. Among the parents, 27 percent of fathers and 19 percent of mothers were college graduates: 59 percent of fathers and 61 percent of mothers had not attained more than a high-school education. Twenty-three percent of the panel lived in single-parent families.

Yearly questionnaires, administered in classrooms, tapped experiences in work, occupationally relevant attitudes and values, and plans for the future. Respondents' parents were also surveyed by mail to obtain accurate socio-economic background information and parental attitudes toward youth work. After the respondents left high school, they continued to be surveyed annually by mail. The questionnaires addressed work experiences and orientations, and obtained monthly records of educational attendance and both part- and full-time work. Through the most recent 2004 survey administration, when most respondents were aged 30 and 31, fully 76 percent of the panel have been retained. We have supplemented the annual surveys with qualitative interviews of selected respondents to better understand the transition from adolescence to early adulthood, and the role of early work experience in this process.

The large YDS data archive has enabled us to address many of the controversies about teenage work – about the character of teenage employment, whether working is beneficial or harmful for adolescents, and whether it has longer-term consequences with respect to a variety of outcomes in early adulthood, including mental health, higher educational attainment, the acquisition of full-time work, and income. The findings of this research have been summarized in *Working and Growing Up in America* (Mortimer 2003) and a large number of additional publications and reports. Given space limitations, we focus here on just a few prevalent myths, and the corresponding realities, of teenage work in the US context.

Myth 1. The poor quality of teenage jobs enables little learning opportunity and has no positive impact on work values and orientations. We find that as they progress through high school, young people take on jobs of greater complexity and supervisory responsibility, and that they receive more employer-provided training (Mortimer 2003). Further, most young people perceive their jobs rather favorably, reporting opportunities for learning several employment-relevant skills, such as being able to take on responsibility, learn about the importance of being on time, and how to deal with customers, supervisors, and co-workers. For example, when asked in the eleventh grade whether their jobs gave them 'a chance to learn a lot of new things,' 43 percent replied that this was 'somewhat true' or 'very true,' and another 42 percent said it was 'a little true.' Moreover, our longitudinal research finds that as perceived learning opportunity at work increases, both intrinsic and extrinsic work values are fostered (Mortimer et al. 1996). As youth learn about the workplace, they become more aware of the diverse kinds of rewards that employment has to offer, and come to value the inherent rewards of work (e.g. opportunities to be helpful to others and useful to the society, opportunities to express one's abilities and interests at work, and other intrinsic benefits), as well as those that can be obtained from a job (e.g. income, security, advancement opportunity, and other extrinsic benefits).

Myth 2. Teenage work interferes with high-school achievement. This second myth is predicated on the assumption that working and educational activities constitute 'zero-sum' games. Specifically, hours spent working commensurately diminishes time spent in school-related activities. We find no evidence, however, that adolescents who work more or less intensively have significantly different grade point averages or spend significantly different amounts of time doing homework, after adjusting for prior differences (measured upon entry to high school) in social background, attitudes toward schoolwork, and achievement (Mortimer and Johnson 1998). Most students combine their schooling and work roles effectively, often negotiating with employers to limit their hours of work when academic needs dictate (Mortimer 2003). Indeed, other research suggests that the 'zero-sum' premise is fundamentally flawed: as teenagers work more hours they tend to withdraw from their less productive activities, such as watching television (Schoenhals, Tienda and Schneider 1998). Other studies that take into account processes of selection to work likewise find no significant differences in high-school academic achievement depending on hours of work (Schoenhals et al. 1998; Warren, Lepore and Mare 2000).

Myth 3. Teenage work is stressful and diminishes mental health. Consistent with much research on adults, we find that adolescents who report more stressors at work, including time pressure, exposure to noxious work conditions (heat and cold), work overload, uncertainty about their job tasks, and responsibility for outcomes that are perceived as outside their control, report more depressive affect during high school (Mortimer, Harley and Staff 2002). Still, we find few persistent additive effects of teenage work on depressed mood after teenagers leave high school. (A similar pattern has been noted with respect to alcohol use, see McMorris and Uggen 2000; intensively working students drink more alcohol while they are in high school, but have similar patterns of alcohol use to their less intensively working peers when observed in the years immediately after high school.) Interestingly, however, we find evidence that job stressors in adolescence enhance resilience with respect to the same work stressors four years after leaving high school. That is, for youth who experienced relatively few work stressors in adolescent jobs, self-esteem and self-efficacy declined steadily, and depressed mood increased, as early adult job stressors rose. In contrast, those who experienced more job stressors in adolescence were significantly less responsive to work stressors at this time (Mortimer and Staff 2004). We conclude that most job stressors that teenagers experience on their jobs are not overwhelming; though momentarily stressful, these 'eustressors' (Shanahan and Mortimer 1996) enhance future coping capacity.

Myth 4. Teenage work is deleterious for early adult socio-economic attainment. Our most recent research focuses on the question of long-term impact. By working during high school, do teenagers lessen their chances for socio-economic attainment? According to the logic of the critics, by disrupting school achievement, adolescents who work limit the likelihood that they will attend and graduate from college. Given the importance of higher education for subsequent occupational and income attainment, their life chances will be eroded accordingly. In addressing this question, we have found it useful to distinguish between different types of adolescent work careers, differentiated on the basis of their duration and intensity. Four types are revealed: 'steady work,' at high duration and low intensity, involving employment during almost all months of observation during high school but moderated, on average, to 20 or fewer hours per week; 'most invested,' at high duration and high intensity, involving rather continuous employment of over 20 hours per week on average; 'occasional,' involving moderate employment during about half the period of observation; and 'sporadic,' involving near continuous high intensity employment. A fifth pattern, involving no work in high school, is rare (characterizing only 7 percent of YDS respondents).

Our analyses (using hierarchical linear modeling techniques) show that steady workers have a clear advantage in obtaining the highly coveted four-year BA/BS degree (Bachelor of Arts/Bachelor of Science). Of all five types, the steady workers were the most likely to do so. Importantly, their advantage could not be accounted for by numerous bases of selection to these patterns of work. During the years following high school, the steady workers 'trade off' immediate income and employment gains as they pursue postsecondary degrees (Mortimer 2003; Mortimer, Staff and Oesterle 2003).

Our most recent analyses (Staff and Mortimer 2005) show that steady work is particularly beneficial for youth who enter high school with little educational promise, those who have little interest in school, relatively poor achievement, and lower educational aspirations. Such young people more frequently pursue the more intensive, 'most invested' or 'sporadic' work patterns during high school, which are followed by more rapid withdrawal from formal education and the acquisition of full-time employment. But when they do work steadily, they acquire a capacity to combine schooling and working in moderation; this combination serves them well if they subsequently attend college. In the American context, college students are usually expected to pay, at least partially, for their educations, and the poorer socio-economic backgrounds of 'low promise' youth make it especially likely that they would have to bear part of the cost. 'High promise' youth likewise benefit from steady work (as opposed to more intensive, and especially, sporadic employment) during high school. But they have relatively high rates of BA receipt if they follow other trajectories as well: occasional work, and no work at all. Their greater resources, both psychological and material, enable them to achieve higher educational degrees without having to combine school and early work.

Conclusion

Findings from the YDS indicate that four of the myths and fears surrounding teenage employment are largely unfounded. Our findings, taken together, point to the conclusion that adolescents are rational actors who strategically position themselves, in light of their predispositions and resources, for entry to the full-time adult labor force. They follow two general strategies. The first, and most beneficial, involves investment in education, combined with moderate but steady work. This enables youth to reap the benefits of employment (learning about work, developing work values, and obtaining generic workplace knowledge and skills) without lessening their capacity to do their schoolwork, prepare for college, participate in extracurricular activities, and engage in all the various activities characteristic of the highly regarded 'well-rounded' adolescent lifestyle (Shanahan and Flaherty 2001). We find no evidence that moderate work, combined with schooling, diminishes socio-economic attainment; to the contrary, our analyses indicate educational attainment and wage gains for those who combine school and work both during and following high school.

The second strategy youth pursue is to invest in more intensive work in adolescence, which enables them to take on more adult-like work while still in high school, thereby gaining work-relevant knowledge and skills, learning and advancement opportunity, but also more stress. This second trajectory precedes more rapid movement into the full-time labor force. Those who have already encountered adult-like work stressors in teenage jobs develop a greater capacity to deal with work stressors when they are encountered in the early adult occupational career.

Particularly for youth who do not have the advantage of having well-educated, high-income parents, work, and especially steady work during high school, poses distinct advantages for subsequent educational attainment, which augurs well for further occupational and income gains. But all adolescents can benefit from moderate work experience, given the near exclusive focus in the American high school on preparation for college. Employers, and even employers of college graduates, look for evidence of work experience when selecting among otherwise similarly qualified applicants, unlike Germany, Japan and other countries where pathways of transition from school to work are more clearly institutionalized (Kerckhoff 2003; Mortimer and Krueger 2000). American young people, upon leaving school, must find jobs on their own. Their fashioning of distinct work trajectories, during high school, consistent with their interests and resources, appears to serve them well in this distinct school-to-work transition regime.

Note

1. The Youth Development Study is supported by grants titled, 'Work Experience and Mental Health: A Panel Study of Youth' from the National Institute of Child Health and Human Development (HD44138) and the National Institute of Mental Health (MH42843).

Chapter 12

Between Prohibition and Praise: Some Hidden Aspects of Children's Work in Affluent Societies

Manfred Liebel

In the relatively affluent societies of the northern hemisphere, work carried out by children has also become a controversial topic for discussion. Against the background of the state prohibition of child labour, a multivalent and contradictory discourse has developed which shows signs of double standards. The following contribution traces hidden aspects of the topic, focusing above all on the work of children in show-business and in the school context.

'Allow children to work,' demanded the German weekly newspaper *Die Zeit* (No 44, 25 October 2001) on its title page, and went on to explain: 'Transform kindergardens into laboratories and studios. An appeal against ennui and monotony.' 'Standing at Pump 4 for a good cause' was the title used by another German newspaper (*Die Tageszeitung*, 19 June 2002), reporting on the day that 'for the first time a "social day" took place in Berlin. Instead of sweating in the classroom, 400 schoolchildren went to work, harvesting strawberries, working at petrol stations or in party political offices. They gave their earnings to aid projects in the Balkans.' 'Young. Courageous. Entrepreneurs. – Schoolchildren as entrepreneurs –'. Under this slogan the German Children and Youth Foundation staged a conference on 19 October 2004 at which children were to learn from US experts how they could establish their own firms while still at school.

These examples show that work by children in affluent societies is clearly no longer as anathema as one might have expected given the complaints that were made for many years by teachers and child carers that 'child labour' was taking control of children again and turning school once more into a neglected part-time occupation. In the following chapter, with reference to the work of children in show-business and school, I want to ask to what extent 'double standards' are operative here, and how the experience of work is represented from the perspective of working children and what it means for the children themselves.

Children in the media – elitist child labour?

The vigorous expansion in the media and advertising market has brought about many very attractive new working opportunities for children. They range from participation in public performances within a show-business and media context to the designing of their own websites. The variety and extent of these activities can barely be comprehended, but I shall now go on to consider the work of children within the media.

Many of these jobs are attractive, because they offer relatively high chances for earning money, but also because they are accompanied by public attention and correspond to narcissistic desires. Working on radio, in television or even in film is seen as a privileged activity by children. The expectations of lucrative payment are in this regard particularly attractive, as is a popularity which is accompanied by high regard and an improvement in the social standing (of the child and its parents) among one's contemporaries. Another factor which cannot be disregarded is the parents' pride in their offspring.

While in European countries the media and show-business have only become a broad field of work for children in the past two decades, there is a longer history of this kind of work in the USA. Towards the end of the nineteenth century a mania had already broken out for child stars to appear in theatre plays: such dramas became box-office successes. Old plays were updated, adding roles for children. Prominent opponents of child labour suddenly turned into ardent supporters of children appearing on the stage. The US sociologist Viviana Zelizer (1994) observes that, paradoxically, at this time children were being used on stage to portray and propagate the new child image of the 'priceless child'. During the economic depression of the 1920s, the charmingly innocent film child, whose spirit softened the hearts of the rich, became both an emotional sounding-board and a projection surface. The child gave people hope once again for a new and better future and therefore served as a therapeutic device for feelings of impotence within society.

These double standards, deriving from the myth of childhood innocence, make themselves present above all nowadays in the children's beauty pageants and especially in relationship to girls. Every year around one million girls under 16 take part in these competitions. It is a billion-dollar business, which is held together through sponsorship, advertising, designers, photographers, hair-stylists, modelling schools with other branches of the economy, not least the cosmetic industry. The children's beauty pageants, in which even babies take part, are seen as an ideal hunting-ground for modelling agencies and other 'talent-seekers'.

Participation in beauty pageants is, as a rule, not yet connected with the children having their own income; they are rather seen by children and above all their parents as a kind of springboard for a 'marketable career'. Many parents are deeply convinced they are only doing the best for their children, even that they are giving them a great gift for the future. Through promoting their child, the parents seem to be driven by the latent desire to unlock resources that would otherwise have remained closed off to them. These are aspects of life and resources to which they cannot gain access through their own efforts because of their age, but in which they can participate – through their children.

In European countries parents are often also the driving force seeking to steer their children into a career in the media. Television channels, catalogue retailers and agencies are literally besieged by parents. For every contract a large number of children apply, often at the behest of their parents. The level of pressure can often be great, since, after the time-consuming interviews, castings, make-up and hair-dressing courses, model courses in order to learn the typical model catwalk, one must also bear in mind the uncertainty of whether the child will get the job. During the casting the children are subject to an evaluation which is generally not made public. It can be even more stressful to wait for a decision about a role, and this can use up more energy than the role itself.

Being named as a star can bring recognition, success and fame to the child who has been selected, be it through relationships, independent effort, talent or chance. The potential child star is given a glimpse of importance which, although akin to a promise for the future, will with all probability not turn into reality. The formula, familiar from the world of celebrities and communicated through the media, 'famous = beautiful = successful = rich' is triggered by the celebrity process which can create the desire for a continuation of such a lifestyle. In such a case, the experience that the 'career' ends at the latest with the onset of puberty can be a painful one.

As important as the question as to the impositions, risks and seductions may be, it is just as necessary to ask how the children themselves judge their work in the media and what they do, or try to do, about it on their own initiative. In our investigation carried out in Berlin (see Hungerland *et al.* 2006) those children working in the media were well aware that their jobs are temporary and that their celebrity can have both positive and negative aspects. Some complained that their kind of work isolated them from other children. One prominent problem they articulated was that they had little input on set and merely had to carry out instructions. Moreover, they criticised the fact that the money they had earned was not available to them, as it is paid into a secure account to which only the parents had access.

The Swiss psychologist Gabrielle Bieber-Delfosse (2002) talks of 'elitist child work' with reference to work in the media. In so doing, she encourages one to think about 'divisions' in the fields of work of children. At the same time, the media work of children is not, as Bieber-Delfosse assumes, elitist merely because it is accompanied with prestige, fame, relatively high earnings and the promise of a 'career', but also because it creates in children the impression that they belong to the 'chosen ones'. Beyond that we have to be aware that work in the media is often open to those children whose parents possess more 'social capital' than others (and perhaps also more economic and cultural capital) and who assist their children in finding job opportunities through active intervention and the making of contacts. Such work would therefore be elitist in the sense that it is available to children with upwardly mobile and ambitious parents, and available to children who for their part understand how to bring themselves into play on the media labour market through ambition, determination, self-presentation and eloquence.

Furthermore an aspect of its elitist character might be the fact that media work is not considered within the dominant social consciousness to come under the aegis of morally repugnant child labour, but is rather seen as a kind of lucky break and as a springboard for a better future. It is not considered worthy of condemnation, but as worthy of being aspired to. And the fact that it can take on forms which leave little space for the subjectivity of the child and can often open the door to abuse and exploitation when carried out on the impetus of the parents tends to be overlooked. In this sense, work in the media is to be understood as a mirror image of those mechanisms which keep the capitalist economy functioning and which judge human beings either as winners or losers.

Such a selective legitimation of media work by children leads implicitly to an additional devaluation of and discrimination against other areas where children engage in work; fields of work which are not formed according to the same ideological structure. Here we are talking about areas in which child work means help and support of others, and therefore has a social impetus; or areas in which children simply look for opportunities to earn a little money in order to emancipate themselves from the authority and the normative standards of the adults around them.

School – a new field of children's work?

To be counted among the hidden aspects of work by children are also those activities which up to now have been seen as belonging to the education sphere and regarded solely under pedagogical or, at best, educational–economic aspects. Above all, school has become a field in which children engage in economically significant activities.

This led in the 1990s to the assumption that, with regard to obligatory school attendance and the school performance of children, one was dealing with a – or even *the* – 'modern' form of child labour ('school work'). This assumption was based on the fact that school takes up an ever greater part of the life and the daily routine of children, subjecting them to a regime of externally determined performance criteria. The Danish sociologist Jens Qvortrup compares 'school work' with 'children's manual work' and emphasises that the latter has 'gradually lost importance qualitatively. It has changed from being the predominant activity of children to being a residual one, a relic of bygone times, while school work has developed from a rudimentary form to the predominant one' (Qvortrup 2000, p.28; see also Qvortrup 2001). The Austrian sociologist and economist Helmut Wintersberger demands a revision of the 'historical' view of children's work, so that it include at least 'the work of children for school'. Like Qvortrup, he sees school as 'a new form of children's work' (Wintersberger 2000, p.177; see also Wintersberger 2005).

It is however distracting to categorise children's school attendance as 'child work', since this refers simply to the time demands that are made on children and to formal analogies between school work and industrial labour. It is not clear where, apart from the appropriation of economically relevant competencies ('human capital'), the specific quality of 'work' in the school situation would be found (for a more detailed critique, see Liebel 2004, pp.131–4). As a result, such an understanding of school work thwarts any insight into the new processes of communication, which have been observed in recent years, between school and the world of work. Following the argument that school ought to convey something of the experience of economic life, but also often due to the fact that schools lack their own resources (since they are no longer provided with enough of them by the state), state schools themselves also become sites of economic trade and pupils – whether they want to or not – become 'economic agents'.

We have to distinguish here between two fundamentally different forms of economic activity in school life. On the one hand, for example through 'partnerships' with commercial enterprises, who, as sponsors, give the school 'a helping hand' and in this way gain direct access to the pupils or the teaching situation, the space of the school becomes a field where particular economic interests can get involved. On the other hand, new models of the connection between work and learning are developed, in which, in the realm of the school itself, economic activities, for example in the form of production schools, are introduced. These are not to be seen as symbolic or work-analogous activities, but rather the pupils are empowered or enabled to produce their own economic achievements themselves.

While the praxis of sponsoring and intervention by commercial enterprises in European schools only began in the 1990s, such praxis is long since established in the USA and Canada. In a study on the battle of the global players for market power the Canadian writer Naomi Klein (2001) presents a large number of examples. For example she reports that market research enterprises, such as Channel One, recruit teachers as 'partners' and together with them develop models of teaching situations in which the pupils are to draft a new advertising campaign for Snapple or develop a new design for drink dispensing machines for Pepsi Cola. In New York and Los Angeles, high-school pupils constructed 32 cartoon commercials for Starburst fruit sweets and in Colorado Springs pupils designed adverts for Burger King that were displayed in their school buses. 'Finished assignments are passed on to the companies and the best entries win prizes and may even be adopted by the companies – all subsidized by the taxpayer-founded school system' (Klein 2001, p.94).

Klein also found a school in Vancouver, Canada, where pupils worked for several months for the restaurant chain White Spot to develop the concept and packaging for an instant pizza, which is now on their kids' menu. The following year, the pupils developed a complete plan for birthday parties in the restaurants of this chain. The pupils' presentation included 'sample commercials, menu items, party games invented by the students and cake ideas' (Klein 2001, pp.94–5). Aspects such as general safety, possible food allergies and low costs, as well as sufficient flexibility, were taken into account. According to one nine-year-old boy, the project meant 'a lot of work' for him (Klein 2001, p.95).

Once more, with reference to the USA, she reports on market researchers experimenting to send children and adolescents home with disposable cameras and have them take pictures of their friends and families; in one task set by the sports equipment firm Nike, they were to return with documentary material on 'the place they most liked to be at'. Such exercises are legitimised by the market researchers as 'educative' and 'ability-enhancing', and are even approved by some educationalists. Thus the headmistress of a primary school in Massachusetts explained the purpose of a taste test involving a brand of breakfast flakes as follows: 'It's a learning experience. They had to read, they had to look, they had to compare' (Klein 2001, p.94).

One more example from Naomi Klein's account, which the author terms 'perhaps the most sinister of these experiments': in the USA, Coca-Cola organised a competition at various schools in the course of which a strategy was to be developed for the distribution of free Cola coupons to pupils. The school that developed the best advertising strategy was to win $500. One school in Georgia that took the competition particularly seriously proclaimed a Coca-Cola day on which all the pupils came to school in Coca-Cola T-shirts and assembled for a photograph in a formation representing the name 'Coke'. They were instructed by leading employees of the firm and learned everything about the black bubbly fluid. Then, however, something went wrong. One pupil ventured to come to school in a Pepsi T-shirt. For this sin he was promptly excluded from class. The headmistress justified this exclusion with the words:

> It really would have been acceptable…if it had just been in-house, but we had the regional president here and people flew in from Atlanta to do us the honor of being resource speakers. These students knew we had guests. (Klein 2001, p.95)

The tasks taken on by the pupils or imposed on them have considerable economic significance, although they are considered rather as 'leisure pursuits' in the traditional sense or even legitimised as part of the school's task of education. At any rate, their economic yield for the firm that commissions them is considerably higher than the 'reward' – if any – given to the children and adolescents. From at least two of the examples, however, it also becomes clear that the children are certainly aware that their activities are work, and a type of work from which others profit rather than they themselves, and which is thus not accepted without protest.

At the same time, the aforementioned examples from Naomi Klein are not identified as children's work. That comparable activities are also not taken into consideration in the discourses about children's work allows us to see how fixed remains this separation, which may be traditional but is now redundant, of the spheres of work and leisure, or of work and education. It allows us to see clearly that, in these spheres, in terms of 'elitist child work' – double standards are at work.

Since the mid-1990s, in Germany 'a clear trend towards an economy-oriented school' (Vollmer 2005, p.41) can be observed, as part of which children become economic agents within the school (to the following see Liebel 2006a and 2006b). In part, a new subject 'Economics', or new combination-subjects are introduced, in part so-called school pupils' firms are established or work placements are extended and also freshly conceived. This new trend is accompanied by the propagation and establishment of cooperation between schools and businesses, which are frequently designated as 'pedagogical partnerships' and are intended to lead to an 'economics-oriented education landscape'. These efforts are primarily directed towards achieving an 'emotional rapprochement or a reconciliation' with the economy, and in particular industry (Vollmer 2005, p.42), i.e. a reduction in prejudice within the schools towards any possible influence by business.

In the financially deprived German schools the offers of help from business are ever more frequently welcomed. A representative study of school cooperations by the German Youth Institute (*Deutsche Jugendinstitut*) demonstrated that the development of contacts to sponsors was the schools' highest priority with 69 per cent (Behr-Heintze and Lipski 2005, p.15). It is estimated that there are already more than 1000 cooperation agreements between schools and businesses in Germany.

In most German federal states, the state regulations have been rewritten to such an extent that the products and marketing strategies of individual firms can be included within the teaching plan. In this manner, products can be tested in the learning environment, products manufactured by the pupils themselves can be compared with the professional product or 'production-line analyses' can be produced. One example: from a lesson centred around Pampers (produced by *Procter and Gamble*) an 'experimental competition on nappies' for Years 6 to 10 was developed. With teaching materials from the 'Business and School' Institute, 36 chemical producers were able to have their products become the subject of chemistry teaching. Products and materials are often placed in a new and creative context. Materials and remnants are turned into art; cardboard is used for the production of furniture and as material for a fashion collection.

In many schools, the topic 'Advertising and Marketing' has in the meantime become a 'significant topic for cooperation' (Vollmer 2005, p.97). As a result, for example, pupils carry out market analysis on specific products, conceive innovative products such as legal costs insurance for young people or new attractive textile patterns for a firm, or they develop new marketing concepts under contract for a firm. To give one example: at an open day at one grammar school, pupils carried out a questionnaire on the paper tissue SNIFF® which provided insight into which motifs 'came across well' in particular age groups and therefore identified a particularly good group of consumers. At the same time, the pupils discovered that the product is not perceived primarily as an item for use but as a 'special object'. Such contract work can most definitely be productive for the firm involved.

Such activity can be profitable or indeed vital, above all for firms who direct their products at young people and need to identify foods and trends in a timely fashion. One example: within the framework of a 'pedagogical partnership' with the firm *bofrost* at a grammar school, pupils from the tenth year created models for 'innovative designer cakes'. The product manager and the marketing manager from *bofrost* cast their expert eye over the results and discussed the various cake motifs with the pupils. The marketing manager gave particular praise to a 'mobile-phone cake' with the words: 'Digital communication is an important part of young people's lifestyle'. The results were submitted as an entry in the European Commission's 'Food for youngsters' competition.

Alongside the 'pedagogical partnerships' and school pupils' firms in Germany as well as other European countries (above all Denmark), there are a series of schools and other pedagogical institutions in which work and education are consciously linked with one another and in which the work carried out by children transcends simulation and symbolic activity. The starting point for such institutions is the thought that assuming social and productive tasks furthers independence and interest in learning in the children. The children ought to gain through acting in socially 'non-playful' situations the experience that can achieve something important for themselves and their environment and can be a fully valid member of society. Some of these institutions place themselves expressly in the tradition of educational reform embodied in production schools and on occasion name themselves in this tradition.

Economic activity and work do not always mean the same thing in every context. While in production schools particular attention is paid to the labour process itself and the social relevance (or also the ecological aspects) of the products manufactured or the services provided, in the 'pedagogical partnerships' and pupils' firms it is generally business aspects, i.e. a 'business idea' and profit-gaining 'entrepreneurial activity', that are at the centre of the interest. At the same time, both models can in their everyday practice touch on ethical and business aspects whereby one may well ask the question as to which aspects (should) have priority.

One of the striking aspects of the production schools that exist nowadays in Germany is that they are not part of the state school system and are only tolerated as a kind of private school. They are limited to children and young people who are unable or unwilling to fit into the state school system, or who have failed and are considered, in official terms, to be 'resistant to learning' and 'unsuitable for school'. Current state school policy makes use of the services of these schools on those occasions when the dominant school pedagogy has reached its limits and can make no further suggestions. This policy implicitly demonstrates that, akin to commercial enterprise, it has no interest in the educative effect of work experience in so far as it does not serve 'career planning' or the cultivation of entrepreneurial thought.

In contrast to this, school pupils' firms and similar forms of 'entrepreneurial' activity by pupils enjoy much encouragement and financial support. They have their place within the state school system and are sponsored, with state endorsement, by financially powerful foundations who are not seldom closely associated with banks and entrepreneurial organisations. Whereas the production schools are, at best, tolerated, so that already disadvantaged children and young people do not end up completely marginalised, the school pupils' firms are accorded a higher value in the 'transition from a welfare-based society to a society based on individual provision and responsibility' (Edelstein 2001, p.15). These institutions too are able to communicate some experience of the world of work, in a way which is similar to those of production schools, but where they do this, they are operating at the margins or beyond the bounds of what is seen as the 'appropriate form' of 'economic competence' in affluent capitalist societies.

Conclusion

Through the examples of working in the media and in school we have seen that work by children is no longer generally rejected and condemned, but is evaluated in ambivalent and contradictory ways. In doing so, we have seen that the label 'child labour' is reserved for such 'traditional' activities which serve first and foremost as a way of earning money, whether on the basis of material need, or for reasons of (supposed) consumer lust. Such activities are considered to be 'child labour' in so far as, according to a bourgeois understanding, they damage children and correspondingly are to be seen as unacceptable or hostile to children's interests. Yet the question as to what is appropriate for children or what damages children is dealt with selectively. In so far as they fit into the pattern of an upwardly mobile lifestyle ('career planning'), whether on the part of the parents or the children, the activities of children are not condemned as 'child labour', although they do in fact endanger the children involved, but, instead, are understood to be 'normal' or are even ennobled through other prestigious terms ('artist', 'film-star'). The same is true, even if it is less openly admitted, for the use of the creativity of children for economic purposes ('trend-setter', 'entrepreneur'), in particular when it happens within the context of pedagogical institutions.

Viviana Zelizer (1994, p.75; see also Zelizer 2005) has understood the controversies of past decades about the pro and contra of children's work as a debate about the 'legitimate and illegitimate economic roles for children'. The growing ambivalences and contradictions in dealing with the work of children now show that the pro and contra have reached a new level and doubts are increasing about the clear distinction of these roles, as well as the desire to redistribute these roles. Since at the latest the 1980s it is not simply purely an either/or but one needs to distinguish areas and forms of 'non-acceptable' and 'acceptable' work.

In place of a straightforward 'no' to child labour, a 'no' to 'necessary work' has arisen which is nowadays usually equated with 'exploitative child labour'. This 'necessary' or 'exploitative' child labour is located almost exclusively in the poor southern hemisphere of the globe (see ILO 2002; for a critique see Liebel 2001a). In so far as the northern hemisphere is referred to, it is associated with 'child poverty' and solely seen as its consequence or it is localised with reference to migrant children and stigmatised as a consequence of a 'lack of love' for one's own children.

In contrast to this, partial areas of the work of children are now legitimised and affirmed, because they are supposedly 'no (longer) necessary'. They are ennobled as a kind of 'productive hobby', which is assumed to be the result of a whim and is up to the children. A closer analysis of what might be considered the given social conditions is not carried out. At the end, it appears that only that work by children finds recognition which comes into existence under privileged circumstances or is usual in so-called better circles. Almost unnoticed, this form of legitimised children's work becomes an elitist form of children's work (not only in the field of the media).

This kind of selective legitimisation of children's work demonstrates that the recognition it is shown becomes ideology and this in a double sense. On the one hand, the recognition ostensibly accords with the desire of children no longer to be satisfied with the passive role ascriptions of an excluded and segregated childhood, without truly enabling self-determined access to the world of work. On the other hand, it ensures in a haphazardly selective way the production of the motivational preparedness in children to fulfil predefined tasks and duties without resistance. This form of selective recognition is on the one hand down to the fact that in 'post-industrial' societies many activities by children, thus far not seen as work, become economically significant; on the other hand it serves to maintain the subjected status of 'modern' childhood and to keep its subjective potential for agency at its disposal.

Part 4

Participation of Working Children

Chapter 13

Children's Work as 'Participation': Thoughts on Ethnographic Data in Lima and the Algarve

Antonella Invernizzi

During the last decade we have seen increasing documentation relating children's work to experience of autonomy that potentially promotes inclusion with working children's participation promoted in many different arenas. It is in that context that this text aims to explore the question: 'How can children's work be understood as a form of participation?' although it sets out to do so within a very narrow framework that focuses on working children's everyday lives. The analysis is based on two qualitative studies carried out in Lima (Peru) and the Algarve (Portugal)[1] that mainly focused on children's work in family settings. The primary hypothesis of this research is that children's work can be concurrently examined in terms of survival, socialisation, participation and exploitation. Furthermore, it is borne in mind that these are all somewhat interdependent dimensions of children's experience and therefore there is need for an overall view in order precisely to understand the content of any of them.

After some comments on how 'children's participation' is intended within this analysis the text will outline some key decisions children appear to make in their work or are able to take because they work. As an illustration, the decision to quit school in order to work will be examined in greater detail. In order to understand its rationale, elements relating to dimensions of 'survival' and 'socialisation' will also be examined. The conclusion returns to comment on the notion of children's participation.

Children's participation as a means to increased self-determination

Article 12 of the UNCRC (United Nations Convention on the Rights of the Child) is the usual reference for defining children's participation, stating that the child has the right to express his or her views in any proceeding affecting his or her life. Those views should be given due weight in accordance with the age and maturity of the child. There are good arguments for believing that is a view of participation that is too narrow although it is an adequate basis for the object of this text. When referring solely to Article 12, the issue of working children's participation actually appears to be extremely broad.

On the one hand it encompasses many different and contrasting definitions and objectives, depending on the approach adopted. It might be considered a feature of an educational process for adult citizenship, a means of increasing effectiveness of projects and programmes, an aspect of mediation aiming to increase children's self-confidence and self-esteem, a contribution toward democracy thus toward a new form of children's citizenship or as a means by which to empower children and increase their self-determination. Very often a single text cites more than one of these aims as potentially positive outcomes of children's participation. Thus they become arguments justifying the need to promote children's participation processes. However, one also has to bear in mind that some objectives might clash with others. As we shall see later, children might for instance want greater self-determination in their current situation and reject educational processes that implicitly postpone it until a later stage in their lives.

On the other hand, children's participation embraces activities in diverse domains. Some participatory situations address decision-making in relation to changes at personal and family level. Others set out to influence changes in community or organisations. Others aim to promote children's participation in local, national or international policy-making and political realms. One can theoretically place them between two poles of a continuum. At one end we would find participatory processes as actions and practices that identify, recognise positively and use children's decisions, their competence and their autonomy as they exist in everyday life. At the other end we would find practices bearing notions of children's rights or citizenship as a starting point and where adult-created structures attempt to give children a voice. Many participatory processes, however, are situated somewhere between the two poles. Working children around the world have been involved in a wide diversity of participatory processes that range from more structured ones in international policy-making to the most 'spontaneous' ones in their everyday lives. Despite limited impact on shaping international policies on child labour, working children's participation has certainly been influential in creating knowledge that proves their competence as social actors as well as providing foundation for the potentially meaningful and positive character of their work.

The examination below actually focuses on a very limited aspect of children's participation: i.e. individual decisions which appear to give children increased self-determination or, at least, self-preservation. These are decisions made in 'natural' settings and thus have no connection with any adult-specific and formal attempt to promote their rights.

Decisions children take because they work

Because research in Portugal and Peru focused mainly on children's work in family settings or any instance related to family life, participatory situations examined here are limited. There is indeed a degree of interest in looking at family organisation of work since the International Labour Organization (ILO 2002) recognises that this form of child work predominates worldwide. However, examination excludes, for instance, those decisions made by working children living on their own or living where they work.

Participation is a rather abstract concept and not part of the informants' vocabulary in either Lima or the Algarve. When analysing ethnographic data, it is nonetheless possible to identify a significant number of decisions children take because they work or in their work. Situations are very varied and whereas some children appear to have the most minimal possibility of choice others appear to take diverse and very influential decisions. Young people decide to work or not to, in what to work, take decisions on how to use income, leisure time, clothes and other purchases. Some decide how to manage and organise their work. There are more 'controversial' decisions whereby young people sometimes decide to support family economically instead of going to school or learn to work rather than go to school. In Peru some children were able to decide where to live, with whom and thus move out of the family home.

The latter three are 'controversial' because they are generally seen as being against the child's 'best interest'. It may be argued that they cannot be treated as 'decisions' because they are parental decisions rather than children's or because the child is 'just reacting' to an adverse situation instead of deciding. In the Peruvian study (Invernizzi 2001) a principle was developed in the analysis that challenged that assumption. It was argued that:

> Each time: 1) a child decides something; 2) that goes against parental views of his or her best interest; 3) and/or conflicts with familial 'best' organisation for economic survival; 4) but is nonetheless authorised or, at least, gains reluctant consent of adult or parent; 5) then the overall event shows the child is somehow entitled to make that decision.

We might thus include the above processes in the category 'participation'. An example drawn from research in Lima is the child's decision to create his or her own business in the street instead of helping the mother at her sales pitch. Some children maintain a distinction between 'help' and 'work'. 'Help' is generally an unpaid task whereby the child conforms to organisation and direction of an adult or another young person. 'Work' in this context is an independent business whereby the child autonomously organises tasks and manages income. In some cases allowing a child to start an independent business is economically less viable than collective organisation within the mother's business. However, some mothers clearly accept a young person's independence, the reason simply being that he or she 'wants it'. That entitlement to independent activity appears to relate to cultural views of childhood, wherein economic independence of a child through his or her work is positively viewed at an early age.

In the Algarve some situations also correspond to that scenario. For instance, many parents in rural areas consider young people's employment is often too hazardous and involves high levels of economic exploitation. However, they sometimes have to compromise by accepting the adolescent's firm decision to work. A few of them say they ultimately contacted the employer and checked working conditions which meant that in due course they agreed with the child's decision.

That situation proves that children make key decisions. However, the fact that they conflict with adult views is not a main characteristic of children's decisions but more so a rather inflexible means of proving they are independent and not under adult influence. Proving children's ability to be independent has actually long been a key feature of accepted experiences of participation and fear of manipulation is probably the main reason. It is actually a position that has been challenged, showing that participation is often a matter of a shared decision with adults (e.g. Alderson 1998) based on inter-dependent relationships rather than absolute independence of the child. From this perspective one has to acknowledge that many children make important decisions with adults and this equally has to be recognised as a form of participation.

On this basis another set of ideas may be understood in terms of participation. For example, we can consider the gist of a group discussion held in a Portuguese class where the majority of pupils had repeated experience of failure and/or school desertion. The debate became slightly heated when pupils were asked to discuss the idea that work jeopardises education. One girl agreed with the idea: 'If we people want to get a good job, we need to know languages...there is no future in construction'. A firm reply came from two boys: 'If farmers do not work, what shall those who speak English eat?', 'What will doctors eat if we all go to university?', 'Who will build their houses?' etc. The discussion then focused on professional opportunity in relation to professional training: being qualified does not mean having a job. Some young people expressed a view that if children do not want to study they must be allowed to work and even at lower ages. Indeed, some children do leave school and some of those clearly in order to work.

One might argue that those young people do not have the knowledge and competence required properly to examine employment opportunities related to access to professional training and the labour market. One might also suggest that they are perhaps simply reporting parents' views put forth to justify the fact they have been withdrawn from school in order to work on the family farm. In this case, the decision to leave school in order to work would not be considered a form of 'participation'. However, such assumptions can also be challenged and, by looking at the context where young people live, the rationale for their decision might become evident.

Survival, socialisation and identity construction: the context of children's decisions

The context in which children make key decisions about work comprises many different elements of diverse nature and work may present certain advantages and disadvantages that relate to a specific context.

Standard of living and economic contexts certainly require considerable attention. Peruvian reality includes very harsh economic conditions for much of the population and children's work often remains essential to cover basic needs. Although Portugal also shows high rates of poverty compared to other European countries they are not comparable with Peru. Generally speaking, family dependency on children's work is less significant in Portugal. Children's contributions remain, however, essential for the survival of some families from the most economically disadvantaged groups, particularly those who live from agriculture and animal husbandry or those affected by adverse circumstances such as accidents, illness or unemployment. Leaving school in order to support the family economically is part of the reality for a small number of children met during research and is a decision defended as legitimate by many others. For them, this is not the best solution but often the only one: not recognising these difficult economic conditions appears to be very stigmatising.

Children's work is nonetheless not simply driven by economic constraint. Complicated and sophisticated processes involving children in family activities are related to social and cultural aspects as well as economic ones. For example working children in Lima often explained work as a way to 'help their mother' or 'help their siblings'. Such forms of mutual support within the family essentially include intricate practices whereby, for instance, a child takes responsibility for the cost of a sibling attending school or what a family regards as a shared project to improve accommodation quality. The contribution of each member of the family is calculated and gradually money required is saved. It would be easy to dismiss such projects as mere reaction to poverty but they require considerable competence. In fact, some mothers in Lima say 'working for the stomach' to describe work that provides very little income. However, the expression does not only describe economic qualities but is characteristic of daily efforts that do not leave space for any other project and, thus, is source of a feeling of impotence. An identical activity can be 'working for the stomach' in one case but conversely be part of a plan leading to improvement in family living standards in another. Children's contributions might be outstanding in such detailed projects that allow some families to overcome or keep out of the worst forms of poverty and thus ensure education and more viable economic conditions. The decision to leave school at a particular time might exactly be in order to carry out such plans and allow a way forward for new projects. Furthermore, the same decision might appear to undermine a child's education in a personal perception of a child's rights but it might be that it promotes the right to survive (or to education) of other siblings.

Such situations indicate how far inter-dependence in family relationships (Morrow 1994) is a key element in understanding working children's experience as well as their decisions. Inter-dependence relates to the contribution to family survival as much as sharing decisions. Cultural and social dimensions give specific content to these forms of inter-dependence wherein work may be positively valued in some cases. Paradoxically, the hypothesis here is that those images of childhood that are more favourable toward children's work (and generally seen as main causes of child labour) are also those often promoting more protected working conditions for inexperienced children and higher degrees of autonomy and participation for experienced young workers.

There is, however, a second set of considerations elucidating the context of children's work, rationale for decisions and specifically the context in which some of them abandon school to work. Here they are categorised under the label of 'socialisation and identity construction'. In the Peruvian study, observation of routines and informants' views often identified positive outcomes of children's work as a learning process. Clearly, one cannot dismiss harsh living conditions and their impact on what children are expected to learn. In extreme poverty the more the child is independent the more he or she is likely to survive if adult support is no longer available at a certain point in time. Parents' death and illness are part of the equation. However, poverty and insecure living conditions should not obscure the fact that children's work may be positively valued for general educational poten-tial. Learning relates to ways in which children and adults might not only depart from 'work for the stomach' but more generally have an impact on their environment and their own life.

Literature on children's work in European countries accentuates facets of socialisation, i.e. working experiences and source of reference for future jobs (for instance: Morrow 1994). Similarly, in southern Portugal young people often mention them but adults mostly emphasise those dimensions of work.

Ethnographic data actually suggest at least four questions on 'socialisation through work'. What are the reasons given for work being an appropriate experi-ence for children or, conversely, a negative one and to what kind of work does it refer? What about the acquisition of skills and competence and construction of the child's identity? What can we learn about the relationship between work and school? Which activities are considered appropriate for learning and preparing the young person's future?

Although the third question is certainly most relevant for understanding school abandonment, it might be useful to briefly describe a few findings relating to the others. Let us begin with the first question. In many adult and child infor-mants' view, work can be a suitable experience for a child depending on specific work or tasks and on other considerations. A challenging finding in this respect is that it may be appropriate to ensure a child a kind of 'protected' environment. In a number of families in both Lima and the Algarve adults said they needed to organise activities that allow them to keep children under supervision. Mothers working in the streets of Lima said that leaving children at home alone all day long while they worked was a risky alternative as some children would not attend school or eat properly. In Portugal as well, the question of supervision was seen as essential by several parents. They said that they needed to organise activities with children, especially where leisure activities were scarce. For young people in rural areas work was a pursuit for avoiding boredom especially during summer holidays. According to that logic young people helped in restaurants, shops or other family businesses, spending most days with relatives. Some parents with jobs took children with them. This mainly refers to part-time work alongside school but the question becomes even more relevant when, as we shall see later, the child no longer attends compulsory school. Clearly, the idea that work may be a source of protection and supervision is relatively challenging in a context where we normally merely assume children must be protected from work. Findings far from indicate that children do not suffer abuse and exploitation in these contexts. Rather than denying any of these dimensions, what need to be examined instead are the precise mechanisms that respectively create ample protection, supervision, and training, as well as exploitation and/or abuse.

The second question more specifically concerns what children learn through work. It is actually a broad question including social, economic, cultural, emotional and even aesthetic traits. Some learning is strictly related to specific activities. Street-working children in Lima learned for instance about places to buy cheap sweets and to cope with heavy traffic. Similarly, a Portuguese child responsible for several goats learned precise skills for tending them daily. Other skills and competence might have more general relevance; for instance ways of interacting with middle-class clients in Lima was valued a useful skill for work requiring that contact. In rural areas some Portuguese adolescents expressed interest in working in shops in order to see: 'how it is when one works with money'. Such interests are very dependent on situation but also children's preferences. Some informants stressed the idea that choice is not about specific work that would be good itself rather more than the fact a child likes it and may be able to discover interests and talents that might be meaningful for generation of income later in life. Another, more general thought about learning through work is about control of the environment. Control over use and management of money was frequently mentioned by both Peruvian and Portuguese informants.

Self-esteem and confidence are other key aspects described as important positive outcomes of work experience when, precisely, it allows greater control over the environment and taking on projects. In southern Portugal, for instance, Diana (15 years old) said that through employment during the summer she gained confidence in her abilities and determination in personal projects. Not all children share this view but some consider positive outcomes thus. Positive facets of work in terms of learning and identity actually contribute to explain why some children decide to work and what kind of work they choose. Diana's employment during summer holidays was illegal, not only because of age but also because it was during the night. The illegal nature does not, however, diminish the importance of advantages and rationality in her choice.

The key question helping to understand school abandonment is certainly about the relationship between work and school. The assumption of an automatic correlation between children's work and poor school performance or non-attendance has been seen as simplistic and attention should be paid to problems within the school system (for instance: Boyden et al. 1998). In Latin America where enrolment rates are actually relatively very high, questions arise about, for instance, outcomes of years of education for the most economically deprived children. They most frequently face failure and repetition and, paradoxically, school attendance does not necessarily make them literate and numerate as one would expect (Boyden *et al.* 1998).

The Portuguese portrayal of education is also problematic. Professional qualifications remain a relatively difficult objective: one in two young adults (aged 18–24 years) is an early school-leaver, i.e. did not complete secondary school or obtain professional qualification. The Portuguese situation is far from the European Union (EU) level, where 'only' one in five is an early school-leaver (Franco and Jouhette 2002). Furthermore, one Portuguese young adult in four did not complete nine years of compulsory school (Ministerio da Educação 2003). Among questions that need to be addressed in both Peru and Portugal is access to school, the efficiency of the school system, educational content, distance from children's own culture and the working world.

In relatively problematic educational contexts one might better understand why even in Europe some adults and young people say full-time work is a proper experience for young people to learn and adequately prepare their future. Such statements especially focus on young people with repeated failure or delayed in studying for different reasons. Generally, adults in Portugal said that education is the main means of giving children a decent future and make genuine efforts to guarantee attendance and professional training. However, some similarly say that 'not all children have a head for school' or 'can achieve at school'. What they observe in their communities is that if school, professional training or academic studies brought in better incomes and more stability, work experience at a low age might guarantee avoiding the worst forms of poverty.

Work remains more generally positively valued as a part-time activity beside school. Contact with the working world appears to offer complementary knowledge and skills, allowing contact with different occupations a young person might take up in the future. The noteworthy assertions here are about what a child likes, their talents and inclinations. It may be tending goats or sheep, driving a tractor or selling in a market and good that the child shows interest and pleasure. A further suggestion made by informants, however, is that part-time work alongside school may also provide alternative skills and aptitude if educational projects fail or the economic situation becomes problematic. Flexible ideas about socialisation are seen as more sensible than idealised paths.

Approaching work as part of young people's socialisation has also some implications in the way informants define abuse and exploitation. If work is 'good' because the young person can learn, some young people also consider that work that does not allow them to learn is a 'bad' thing and in some cases defined as abuse. Young people's perspectives may be essential in ascertaining indicators of abuse and thus promote preventative and protective actions in partnership with them.

After exploring informants' views and experiences one may be surprised that dominant discourses on child labour often seem to ignore the complex reality they face. In Portugal, any work (including light or part-time work) is forbidden before age 16 or completion of compulsory school and dominant discourses on poor educational achievement often blame pupils' work. That approach certainly chiefly contributes to denying rationality to young people's practices. Instead, one has to consider some of the above arguments regarding their socialisation and survival under very difficult circumstances. When struggling to keep a family business going, helping ill or disabled parents, or very negative school experiences, some of them might consider spending up to 12 or 13 years in compulsory education (instead of nine years) as not necessarily 'in their best interest'. This is more likely if later in life they are unable to afford professional training, complete it or find a job in the profession learned, situations relatively common in their communities.

Conclusion

Accepting children's decisions such as leaving school in order to work as legitimate examples of children's involvement in decision-making may seem a rather inappropriate method of viewing children's participation. The purpose of this text is not to argue that these children are taking 'right' or the 'wrong' decisions but to argue that the rationale of such decisions is often denied instead of being rigorously examined. Unverified assumptions about the child's best interest are often bases for denial which does not allow for a more holistic view on their situation and thus on a wider range of actions and policies that could promote their interests and well-being. More importantly, the argument offered here is that the 'natural' decision-making processes outlined above do not differ, in their nature, from other processes we normally consider as genuine children's participation but are nonetheless differently and negatively labelled.

However, in order to adequately consider the above decisions as 'children's participation', there are different arguments that require attention. First, and even if considering one specific issue, one cannot identify any single 'right' decision that may be applied to all working children. For instance, the majority of children in southern Portugal and many in Peru wanted to go to school and ideally complete professional training. However, this does not invalidate the decision a few of them in particularly difficult situations made. In other words, children's opinions need to be measured against their normal lives and experiences which are very different indeed.

Second, the dominant framework of children's participation that generally promotes autonomous decision-making processes whereby adults are only facilitators or supporters appears to be unable to deal with many children's experiences in normal life contexts. Inclusion of adults around them is also required.

Third, assumed lack of participation should be challenged. If it is rightly argued that children's participatory rights have to be promoted this implicitly leads to the frequent belief that children do not participate of their own accord. Very little attention is paid to how they naturally make valuable and influential decisions about their lives. Such practices have been a resource for a number of working children programmes since they existed.

Fourth, if we accept that children make valuable and rational decisions we also have to admit that the dominant framework in which working children's experiences are replaced is precisely the one that invalidates the significance of their action and competence. Generally, school abandonment would be understood in terms of lack of protection, parental abuse or even lack of discipline when it comes to school attendance rules. Similarly, even less controversial decisions (such as working part-time alongside school) might be entirely invalidated by national and international legislation.

Finally, and consequently, one might conclude that to promote children's participation adult agendas might sometimes need to be adapted to conform to children's views rather than attempting to make their participation fit within an adult agenda. It might be too optimistic, for instance, to believe that children's participation will systematically increase effectiveness in the elimination of child labour if children (and adults in their communities) have no say on what is good or bad work, what advantages of work have to be compensated in other ways and, finally, what work needs to be eliminated.

Note

1. See Invernizzi 2001 and 2003 for the Lima study and 2005 and 2006 for the Algarve study. The research project 'Children's Exploitation, Socialisation and Participation in Economy. A Comparative Analysis of Child Labour in Peru and Portugal' has been funded by the Swiss National Science Foundation and carried out at the Centre for Family Research, University of Cambridge, between 2001 and 2004. Fieldwork in Peru (1994–1997) was mainly concerned with ethnographic methods: observant participation in the streets of Lima, interviews with children and parents, street social workers and young adults who have been working during their childhood. A specific feature has been a small scale action-research project where some families have been allocated a credit for improvement of their street trade. During field work in southern Portugal (2002–2003) ethnographic methods have also been the principal methods although findings presented in the text are also based on the outcome of questionnaires passed in three schools, interviews and group discussions in the same schools, and group discussions in leisure centres. A specific strategy of this piece of research has consisted of inviting four adolescents living in rural areas to take pictures of their working activities and provide a testimony that has been published in a local newspaper.

Chapter 14

Child Employment in Northern Ireland: Myths and Realities

Madeleine Leonard

Despite a plethora of studies which demonstrate that paid work is a common feature of children's lives during their school years, many societies continue to ignore or trivialise the work that children do. If Northern Ireland is taken as an example, attempts to organise a conference around the theme of 'Children's Work in Developed and Developing Societies' in 1996 had to be cancelled because of the disbelief that children worked in Northern Irish society. The participants who were specially invited because of their supposed expertise and policy responsibilities for children and childhood in Northern Ireland felt that such a conference was futile on three grounds: first, not many children work in Northern Ireland; second, the small numbers that do are involved in child-specific and child-friendly work such as newspaper delivery work; and, third, existing legislation on child employment more than adequately protects children at work and promotes their interests. All three propositions are false.

In response to general apathy about this issue and because of knowledge of research on children's employment in other countries, Save the Children commissioned a piece of research on child employment in Belfast in 1999 and it is this study which forms the empirical framework for this chapter (Leonard 1999b). When the report was published, the conference was successfully rescheduled but many participants had difficulty in considering that there could be any similarities between the paid employment experiences of children in developed and developing countries. Of course major differences exist and many contributions to this volume amply demonstrate vast disparities between the working experiences of children in different corners of the globe in terms of level of choice, motivations, remuneration, working conditions and so on. Yet despite these differences, some similarities are also apparent. Child employment wherever it manifests itself reveals ongoing disparities between the rights and needs of children compared to adults. Wherever they live, children generally experience less power than adults and, wherever they live, children experience greater difficulties in voicing their concerns and coaxing adults to listen to what they say.

Highlighting children's paid work in developed countries is not just about rendering visible an invisible aspect of children's lives; it involves questioning many key concepts of contemporary western childhood which position children as economically dependent during their school years. It also brings to the fore and renders more complicated taken-for-granted relationships between children and adults in their guise as parents/guardians, teachers, employers and the legitimacy of the role of the state in sometimes providing a legal framework within which these relationships are played out.

The research in Belfast focused on the perceptions and experiences of 545, 14–15-year-old children drawn from 12 schools deliberately selected to take account of possible gender and class factors. A combination of methods was utilised including questionnaires, focus group discussions and tape-recorded interviews with working children. One in five children under the compulsory school leaving age of 16 were employed at the time the research was carried out. This increased to 63 per cent if previous employment experience and babysitting were taken into account. Gender had little impact on participation but there was a tendency for girls and boys to be over-represented in some occupations reflecting a gendered child labour market in some ways similar to the ongoing gendered nature of the adult labour market. Class also had little impact on participation although there was a greater tendency for working-class children to have jobs than suggested in other accounts (Hobbs and McKechnie 1997; Middleton and Shropshire 1998; O'Donnell and White 1998).

The research revealed that children were employed in a myriad of occupations commonly considered as adult rather than child work. As reflected in other studies, children worked in cafés, restaurants, pubs, shops, hotels, factories and building sites (Hobbs, Lindsay and McKechnie 1996; O'Donnell and White 1998; Pond and Searle 1991). One of the most common forms of child employment in Northern Ireland is newspaper delivery work. This has also emerged as a key type of work in a number of UK studies (Hobbs, Lavalette and McKechnie 1992; Hobbs and McKechnie 1997; Lavalette 1996; O'Donnell and White 1998). The prevalence of this type of work among children has enabled adults to subsequently treat newspaper delivery work as a type of work specially created for children to take account of their 'inferior' abilities compared to adults. This view is often extended to cover child employment in general. The creation of special child-type jobs such as newspaper delivery work enables adults to continue to maintain a separation between adults and children in relation to the labour market. Many adults in developed societies continue to believe that the labour market separates the adult world from the child's world. Adults work and children attend school. This fails to recognise that school itself could be considered as a form of work (Qvortrup 1999); that many adult jobs have been specially created in response to modern and generally incorrect notions of childhood (Oldman 1994); and that the introduction of compulsory schooling has merely enabled children to restructure their work to fit around the school day (White 1996).

However, the prevalence of special categories of child employment enables adults to maintain and uphold various myths of contemporary childhood. One of these concerns the competency of children. As Qvortrup (1994, p.4) acknowledges, 'the adult world does not recognise children's praxis because competency is defined merely in relation to adults' praxis'. This is in line with the ongoing tendency to see children in the process of becoming and not yet complete. In the same vein, children are considered not as different to adults but as lesser than adults. As Waksler (1986, p.74) puts it, 'in everyday life we adults take for granted that children as a category know less than adults [and] have less experience'. Hence children are not and cannot be proper workers. But they can be encouraged to take up money-making hobbies such as newspaper delivery work. Such work is thus not considered as real work. It is relegated to the margins of the economy and becomes conceptualised as a harmless, unskilled pastime which can enable some children to earn some pocket money.

Seeing children's earnings as pocket money rather than wages enables the continuance of another myth and that is that children are irrelevant to the household economy. They are economic burdens. They are economically useless albeit emotionally priceless (Zelizer 1985). Of course, many children do earn low wages and do not work sufficient hours to become economically independent but within the structural constraints imposed on them by their positioning as children in developed societies, some make important contributions to the household economy while others practise greater levels of autonomy and agency in spending earnings rather than pocket money. Another myth upheld by the existence of special types of child work is that the work that children do is generally unskilled. Some researchers also hold this view. Mizen, Bolton and Pole (1999) for example argue that children rarely gain any skills from their employment. However, much depends on how skills are defined. A detailed examination of newspaper delivery work revealed that children were involved in ensuring papers were delivered in time to correct addresses, dealing with adult customers, collecting money and balancing books (Leonard 2002). In these ways, the job reflected strong parallels with many types of skilled adult jobs. However, children themselves tapped into influential adult definitions and tended to dismiss their work as unimportant, as trivial, as marginal and as unskilled. This reminds us that while children are social actors in their own right and are able to illuminate the everyday practices and meanings which constitute their social worlds, such meanings and practices are created and recreated within the context of not just children's own experienced worlds but also within wider social and cultural structures and through relationships with the adults who construct and mediate these (Christensen and James 2000).

Child employment presents an example of the myriad of ways in which adults and children live their daily lives in shared spaces. Child employment enables children to interact with adults in ways that transcend other relationships that they experience with adults where generational concepts of maturity and competence are more constraining. Child employment reminds us that children relate to adults in different ways in different contexts (Mayall 1994). The research in Belfast indicated that children reassessed their relationships with three sets of adults: parents, teachers and employers (Leonard 2003). Many children did not inform teachers that they worked outside school hours partly because of their perception that teachers would disapprove and partly because they wanted to maintain autonomy over their non-school lives. With reference to their relationships with parents, many children felt that having a job enabled them to challenge the institutional status of their position within the home. Within the family children are often perceived as vulnerable and in need of protection. Discourses of protection often render invisible the power of adults over children who are in their care. As one of the primary 'everyday spaces' (Holloway and Valentine 2000) of childhood, the home emerges as a venue where adults are positioned as providers and children are positioned as passive consumers (Woodhead 1997). Work blurred existing boundaries between adulthood and childhood where work was commonly considered the preserve of adults. Work enabled children to negotiate a level of autonomy from the structural and material constraints of family life. Many children suggested that parents viewed them as more responsible and competent because of their ability to work and earn an income. While many parents expressed concern that work would negatively interfere with education, many children in conjunction with their parents made rational decisions regarding balancing commitments between work and school. Hence many children demonstrated competency in weighing up the pros and cons associated with working while attending school and tried to achieve a satisfactory equilibrium between the two.

While several children were aware of their tendency to be exploited by adult employers particularly in relation to wage levels, nonetheless some children highly valued the trust placed in them by employers to carry out work tasks competently and reliably. For some children, work provided opportunities for them to assert their autonomy and to be treated as serious, valid contributors to the employment relationship. Some children felt that they were able to negotiate less hierarchical relationships with employers compared to other adults. By working alongside adults doing similar work to adults, children were able to negotiate more individualised conceptions of themselves as co-workers rather than children. These opportunities to be 'adult-like' were rated positively by the majority of children although many felt that the degree to which they are economically exploited needs addressing. Nonetheless, throughout the research, children demonstrated the often complex ways in which they negotiated and renegotiated their relationships with adults. Often this resulted in them challenging, diluting and transforming traditional appropriate roles.

Consequences for child labour legislation

The prevalence of jobs such as newspaper delivery work among children enables the state to maintain its justification for the scant treatment of children in its legislative framework. By viewing newspaper delivery work as an ideal occupation for children, the state moves to naming other types of occupations or workplaces as particularly suitable for children and the legislation becomes shackled to a limited list of dos and don'ts in relation to what types of jobs children can legally undertake and during what hours. Occupations classified as suitable for adults are classified as unsuitable for children. This separation of children from aspects of the adult world of work draws on dominant images of children as immature, incompetent and irrational. It undermines notions of children as responsible social actors adept at managing their own space and time. Instead it constructs children as vulnerable, innocent and unable to negotiate the public world of employment. According to Nasman (1994) when children are made visible in legislation as a special category of persons, they are in effect identified as different from others and because of their minor status are often placed in an underdog position.

In relation to child employment laws, rights-based features of work such as employment conditions or remuneration remain absent from the legislation. Children in Northern Ireland are not covered by minimum pay legislation and in all cases were paid less than those covered by the legislation. In this sense children are not being treated as proper citizens. Indeed one of the key differences between how the state treats adult and child workers is that the former are considered within rights-based discourses while the latter continue to be influenced by protectionist discourses. There is a lack of acknowledgement that protecting child workers might best be achieved by promoting their rights in the labour market. As Landsdown (1994) argues, children continue to be perceived as having needs rather than rights. I interviewed the only employment officer for Belfast responsible for ensuring the limited legislation that exists is enforced. He proudly told me that during his 14 years in the job, he had never had to deal with one single case where the legislation was being flouted. This is hardly surprising given that over 90 per cent of the working children who took part in the research were unaware that any legislation existed. Moreover, there is no incentive to use outdated, ineffective legislation that limits children's employment opportunities and does little to promote their interests.

One of the most interesting features of children's own accounts of their work in Belfast was their perception that they had a right to work (Leonard 2004). There were many aspects of their working lives that were open to exploitation in relation to employment conditions and remuneration yet children had little recourse to any organisations or institutions that could be utilised to promote their interests. Trade unions in Northern Ireland continue to position children under the age of 16 as school pupils rather than workers. The legislation continues to position children as weak and dependent and thus continues to be structured around protecting them rather than providing frameworks for empowering them and promoting their interests. Yet when children's own perspectives and experiences are brought into the equation, they illustrate their ability to discuss the pros and cons of their own working situations.

The research in Belfast demonstrated that children want to be and are adept at managing their own life-worlds (Alanen 1988). They are often more competent than what they are presumed to be by adults. They are capable of making measured judgements and acting rationally when they are given the opportunity to do so. Ignoring children's own experiences of work and their own perceptions of work often results in misguided policies that do little to protect children or promote their interests. In developed societies, policies relating to working children continue to underestimate their abilities and fail to acknowledge that children are experts of their own working lives. If children were consulted and their views taken into account, then policy initiatives concerning working children would look very different. Indeed, when children's own perspectives are taken into account, they move beyond the limits of protection to suggesting frameworks whereby they would be empowered in the labour market. Policy responses continue to fail to recognise that it is children's lack of status that promotes their vulnerability and children's lack of power deepens their vulnerability (Landsdown 1994; Van Bueren 1998).

Working children's own experiences and perceptions of their work should be a crucial source of information for policy-makers and all those involved in collecting knowledge about the nature and extent of child employment. While there now exists a wide-ranging body of research into children's paid and unpaid work, there remains a need to develop research programmes that would further illuminate children's working lives. Such programmes could usefully explore not just how children's experiences differ in relation to age, gender, class, race and ethnicity but how their knowledge and understanding of different work practices draw on, feed into, produce, reproduce and challenge the local, regional, national and international frameworks within which they live their daily lives.

Chapter 15

Vocabularies, Motives and Meanings – School-Age Workers in Britain: Towards a Synthesis?

Christopher Pole

Introduction

From the campaigning work of voluntary sector organisations (MacLennan, Fitz and Sullivan 1985; O'Donnell and White 1998; Pond and Searle 1991;) and the trades union movement (GMB 1995; TUC 1997), through to school surveys by academic researchers (Balding 1997; Finn 1984; Hobbs and McKechnie 1997; Mizen 1992), research has consistently revealed that between one third and one half of British school age children are in paid employment at any one time; and that before they leave school between two thirds and three quarters will have held down some form of paid employment. Projected on to the British school population as a whole, it is estimated that somewhere between 1.1 and 1.7 million school-age children are currently working.

While it remains that jobs traditionally regarded as the preserve of children in modern capitalist societies, newspaper deliveries and babysitting, provide the single biggest sources of employment, it is now also beyond doubt that the employment of most school-age children involves a broad range of jobs. The vast majority of children are employed illegally, either transgressing the limitations on hours, occupying prohibited jobs or, in most cases, failing to obtain a local education authority permit to work. Children as young as nine or ten have been found working, but participation rates increase with age and although boys start earlier than girls, there are few significant gender differences in overall rates of working. Although the participation in paid employment by children in Britain today is well documented, its purpose is far less clear. Much of the existing research has been concerned to establish the extent and location of childhood employment rather than to examine its meaning to those who perform it and its significance to their lives.

The concern of this chapter is with the nature of children's work and their reasons for engaging in it. It seeks to offer an analytical framework which recognises the significance of work not merely in (traditional) work experience or socialisation terms but also in respect of the more immediate relevance of work to childhood and children's lives. In this sense, it is about the relevance of work to children as independent social actors, capable of making their own decisions and shaping their own lives and also about the structures and conditions under which childhood labour is conducted. In acknowledging the view that childhood is not fixed but socially constructed and that children are social actors, capable of engaging with, responding to and influencing their own social lives in meaningful ways (James et al. 1998; James and Prout 1990/1997) the chapter focuses on what children actually are (i.e. paid workers) and upon their motivations for seeking out and participating in paid work. However, the approach here and in other output from this study (Mizen et al. 1999; Mizen, Pole and Bolton 2001) is also to recognise that agency is also moderated by the structures within which it is exercised. In this sense, while we are interested in the meaning of work to children's social lives and in this particular case in their motivations for engaging in it, we are also interested in the material conditions of that work and of those that propel children to it.

The research

The research[1] was designed to capture the subjective experience of children's employment, to listen to children talk about and reflect upon their work, without losing sight of the importance of the structural context within which it is conducted. In order to provide systematic detail on a wide range of issues relating to children's work, not least questions of motive and rationale, the study was designed to work closely with a group of 70 working children, each of whom agreed to participate in the project for a period of 12 months. Throughout the field work, a number of complementary and linked qualitative research methods were deployed which involved gathering data through semi-structured interviews at the beginning and end of the 12 months; discussions in small groups of between three and five students; bi-monthly thematic work diaries; individual discussions of diary entries; and children's own photographic accounts of their work using disposable cameras, together with an additional written account. This chapter draws on interviews and diary discussions.[2]

In asking the children to participate, one objective was to generate a sample of children working in jobs broadly illustrative of the types of employment that children in Britain are currently known to do (Hibbett and Beatson 1995). A further objective was to ensure that the children came from diverse socio-economic backgrounds. To this end, the children were drawn from six comprehensive schools located in contrasting geographical areas of England and Wales and drawing their students from contrasting socio-economic catchment areas.

The sample was also comprised of equal numbers of boys and girls, children from different minority ethnic groups; it covered the school years 8 to 10 and, when the research began, included students aged between 11 and 16 years of age.

Children's work

Questions of motivation for working are especially important when we consider the types of jobs that children do. While existing survey research has gone some way toward identifying the categories of children's employment, it provides little indication of its character; of the types of workplaces, tasks, quality and work relations that govern children's experiences of work. In short, we have very little idea of what children actually do when at work. At first interview, children in our study were asked to describe their jobs. Table 15.1 gives a general picture of these jobs and is useful in demonstrating the scope of their employment.

Table 15.1 Main type of employment at first interview

Type of employment	Frequency
Babysitting/child care	4
Newspaper deliveries	2
Other delivery – milk, leaflets, take-away food, etc.	4
Shop/retail	14
Food serving/preparation	15
Waiting tables/glass collecting	15
Farming/animals	4
Outwork	1
Construction/landscaping	2
Hairdressing	4
Entertainment/art – performing, art, etc.	4
Cleaning – agency, commercial, domestic, etc.	7
	Total 70

However, a principal concern of the study was to obtain a clear appreciation not merely of the type of jobs that the children did, but also of the nature and meaning of that work through children's own accounts of it. It is this attempt to capture the lived experience of childhood work that facilitates the analytical approach of this chapter. Nevertheless, the simple tabular representation of the types of work that the children did is useful, illustrating general trends. For example, it suggests that opportunities for skilled work, or at least a job involving some element of skill, were rare. For most, employment meant unskilled repetitive work at what might be described as the edge of the formal labour market. In most cases, this work was little different to that performed by adults and, as we have argued elsewhere (Mizen *et al.* 1999, 2001), this alone casts doubt on what some commentators have characterised as a specific children's labour market. In highlighting the kinds of jobs that children do, our work demonstrates that in many cases children and adults compete in the same labour market for low-paid, low-skilled and poor-status jobs.

As Table 15.1 shows, most opportunities for work came from the service sector, particularly in catering, retail and distribution and personal services. However, few large service sector organisations employ school-age children. For example, most public house chains and hotels, big supermarkets and grocery retailers, franchised restaurants and fast-food outlets operate a minimum age criterion as part of their formal recruitment polices. For children, therefore, service sector employment usually means small employers, particularly the smaller catering establishments that have proliferated alongside the large fast-food and chain restaurants. These restaurants, cafés, sandwich shops, fish and chip shops, mobile burger bars and hot dog stands, coffee and tea shops that make up this independent sector are frequently family run and in order to maximise profit levels which are often fairly modest, the use of part-time and casual labour is common. For these types of organisations children can offer a willing source of cheap and flexible labour, which is available at short notice and requires little by way of formal training, tolerates irregular hours and whose expectations of work are low. Much of this work is dirty, hot and arduous. As kitchen 'hands' in restaurants, hotels and cafés, the children worked fetching equipment and utensils, carrying provisions, disposing or recycling waste, working their way through sinks of washing up, loading and unloading heavy dishwasher baskets, preparing piles of vegetables or trying to keep some semblance of cleanliness in the turmoil of meal-time activity in a busy, often cramped, commercial kitchen:

> I just like do the cleaning up and do a bit of washing up so they can keep on top of it 'cos the girls that work there like, one's my mum, and they don't really have time to clean up when they are serving during the day [...] (Ronan, 15, factory canteen worker, Midlands city).

Outside of kitchens, the children had also found employment in public houses and social clubs. Although rarely employed as bar staff, they were frequently responsible for collecting and washing glasses, replenishing stocks of bottled beers, soft drinks and bar snacks or pushing their way through crowded, smoky, bars to empty ashtrays. Others worked in take-away restaurants and pizza parlours, relaying orders to the kitchen, answering the telephone and handling payments; or washing up, cleaning floors and walls, clearing tables, serving food and working cash registers in restaurants and cafés.

This pattern of low-quality work was repeated in retail and distribution, the other major source of employment for the children. Although several of the 70 children had found work with bigger retailers such as department stores or local supermarket chains, where conditions were sometimes better, the experience often remained tedious:

> I go down, get designated a checkout and sit down and for four hours put things through the till. The only vigorous part of it is learning all the different numbers for the weighing machine [...] (Ian, 15, supermarket checkout, East Anglia town).

In the main, retail employment also meant smaller employers. Some of the children were employed as shelf stackers in corner shops, supermarkets and off-licences, while others worked as checkout operatives.

> That's when I go in [Saturday], we have got a load of milk, I have to put that all in the fridge, then I go on to do the bread, then I do all the sweets, then I put all the tinned stuff out, and the drinks, and then I help on the till (Sarah, 14, convenience store, East Anglia town).

The 'better' retail jobs were to be had in florists, electrical, clothes and shoe shops. Others, exclusively girls, worked as assistants in hairdressing salons, washing hair, sweeping up and making drinks for customers and other staff.

Perhaps more traditionally, children also worked undertaking home deliveries for newsagents, and take-away food restaurants; they posted leaflets door to door and called to collect money for family businesses. For some of the boys, opportunities for employment were to be found delivering milk to doorsteps well before the school day had even started:

> Well I get up at, start at 5.00, finish at 8.00 that's on a school week and in the holidays I start at 5.00 and work until 10–11.00 [am]. (Luke, 14, milk deliveries, Midlands city)

Finally, others had worked in various capacities as cleaners. For two of the boys this involved periodic employment for a large agency supplying contract cleaners to national sporting and cultural events. For some of the girls, cleaning jobs reflected the seasonal requirements of the local labour market when they found jobs during the tourist season as 'housekeepers' in holiday parks, cleaning caravans and chalets. Others provided cleaning services to offices and shops throughout the year or cleaned the homes of neighbours and family friends:

> I clean for one of my mum's friends, she needs a cleaner so I do that [...] Well just like I have to Hoover everywhere and that, load the dishwasher, and just clean up... (Sarah, 14, domestic cleaner, East Anglia town).

Why do children *choose* to work?

Given the low quality of these jobs, then questions of motivation become central. Put simply, why do children choose to enter employment when the vast majority of the opportunities for work offer no more than routine and low-quality experiences of work?

In some respects, this may appear to be an unnecessary question to pose. The obvious common-sense answer, supported by many of the studies of child labour cited earlier, is simply that children work for money. However, evidence from our research, and that of other studies conducted in the UK and elsewhere, suggests that, as is often the case, the simplistic answer is not the only or the complete answer. Moreover the simple question 'Why do children choose to work?' assumes a number of things which require unpacking if we are to get closer to an understanding of the significance of child labour to children's contemporary and future lives.

In the first instance, the question assumes that children have a choice of whether to work or not. While there is no evidence from our study that children have been coerced into working in any overt sense, by parents or anyone else, there is evidence which suggests that where money is tight at home, then the child may feel a moral obligation to contribute to the household economy. In this, our research supports some of the findings of Leonard (1999a, 1999b) whose work revealed a greater propensity for childhood labour in disadvantaged areas. Similarly, Hobbs *et al.* (1992), Middleton and Shropshire (1998) and Lavalette (1996), with slight differences of emphasis, found that children from poorer backgrounds tended not only to work longer hours than their peers in more affluent circumstances, but also worked for less money. Collectively, these studies may be seen as posing something of a challenge to the assumption that, at least in the UK, children's participation in work is a matter for the children themselves, and is a matter of free choice. While this may, in broad terms, be the case, the concept of choice, in some circumstances, is mediated by a social responsibility that the child feels towards his/her family and its specific economic circumstances. Evidence from our research emphasises the role of children as active participants in economic and social family life.

In addition, we might also add pressures felt by many young people in respect of the need to fit in with dominant youth culture. In order to do this and thereby achieve what might be seen as a form of social inclusion, or at least a means of avoiding social exclusion, children need access to the trappings that define or accompany that dominant youth culture. This may include access to certain leisure pursuits in the form of entrance and participation fees or specialist equipment for sports or cultural activities. Moreover, our research suggests that taking part in everyday teenage life demands a certain level of consumption. Not ignoring the social class, gender and cultural differences that may be relevant here, in general our data revealed a need for access to the 'right' kinds of clothes, accessories and make-up, music, magazines, food, drinks and places to 'be', which often brought with it not inconsiderable transport costs. Indeed, recent research into children, identity and fashion (Boden *et al.* 2004) reveals the significance of label culture particularly among boys, fuelled by the present boom in sports fashion, from a very young age. The point to emphasise here is that pressures to participate as unexceptional young people in ordinary or everyday youth/childhood pursuits means that children need access to money. For some, this was not a problem, being supplied almost without question by their parents. For others, however, the only way of financing such a lifestyle was via the income from their own labours. While it may be argued that the accoutrements of lifestyle represent wants rather than needs and are, therefore, of a lesser order in the context of children and young people's lives, there are others (White 1996) who argue that wants represent participation and inclusion and should not be dismissed as the mere ephemera of marketing and conspicuous consumption. Similarly, the longing for (cultural) artefacts or aspiring to particular kinds of status, what might be conceptualised as desire, also seems important to the construction of young identities, as it both shapes and is shaped by the social construction of childhood or youth. For many children and young people, taking a job is the only means of financing a participative, socially included life. To ignore that, for many children, the needs of ordinary childhood present themselves as pressures to work would, in our view, be not only to fail to understand some of the ways in which childhood and youth is constituted and constructed in the early twenty-first century, but also to ignore the financial situation within which many children live their lives.

Vocabularies of motives

Having raised a number of important questions about the extent to which children engage in work on the basis of free choice it is perhaps appropriate at this stage to modify our original question 'Why do children *choose* to work?' to 'Why do children work?'. Taking as read that access to money may be the principal reason for many children, this does not, nevertheless, tell the whole story. For example in her study of Danish child workers Frederiksen (1999) asked children to write a piece about why they worked but to 'leave out having an income'. The children revealed a number of reasons other than those relating to the pay they would receive. Similarly, Mansurov (2001) and Ingenhorst (2001) also highlight a range of reasons for child labour in Russia and Germany respectively as does our own work (Mizen *et al.* 2001).

Rather than simply list and elaborate on these various reasons which are best read in their original locations, the intention now is to attempt to extend our understanding of why children work by adopting an analytical approach based upon Mills' (1940) conceptualisation of motives, which has more recently been adopted by Hockey (1996) in his account of the motives expressed by academics for their participation in PhD supervision. The topic may seem a long way from that of child labour, but the analytical approach is one which focuses on an examination of the social contexts in which people account for their conduct by giving close consideration to the language they use to describe and provide reasons for their activities. They are, therefore, providing vocabularies of motive for their actions. In identifying such vocabularies from their own experiences, be it of PhD supervision, child labour or other activities in which the individual is centrally involved, the approach can provide insight not only to the meaning of the activity but also of the material and structural conditions within which the activity is conducted. For example, Hockey (1996) identifies two vocabularies of motives to aid his understanding of doctoral supervision. In the first, the motives outlined by his interviewees are specific to the institutional context and structural constraints of higher education. They are perhaps the kinds of things one might expect to hear from PhD supervisors as they describe the demands of their role. In the second, Hockey suggests a set of what he terms alternative, mythical motives which supervisors could give as reasons for supervising. These are more personal, relating to the individual circumstances of the supervisor and his/her relationship with the supervisee and to the place of doctoral supervision within the wider work and life experiences of the academic concerned.

Adapting both Hockey's (1996) and Mills' (1940) approach it is possible to articulate at least two vocabularies of motives for children's participation in work. The two vocabularies relate to different perspectives within childhood studies. One, which might be seen to accord with traditional perspectives on childhood, can be called the developmental vocabulary. Such a vocabulary may be located within socialisation perspectives on childhood which have traditionally character-ised this stage in the life-course, as a means of preparation for adulthood in general and, more specifically, child labour as a means of facilitating entry to an adult or 'real' labour market. The second vocabulary we can call the operational vocabulary as it pertains to the lived experiences of participation in work as voiced by the child workers. This articulates more readily to what has become accepted as the new sociology of childhood (James *et al.* 1998), which sees childhood not merely as a state of becoming, but of being in its own right.

In the context of children and work, a developmental vocabulary of motive, though drawn from interviews with child workers themselves, incorporates those accounts of work which relate to the general socialisation thesis of childhood. This vocabulary might be seen to engage with a traditional and anticipated view of the role of work in children's lives. The vocabulary might include largely longer-term, positive developmental aspects of work participation such as the fol-lowing:

- It helps me learn things about working life.
- It gives me real experience that will help me get a job.
- It means I have something to put on my CV.
- It is a way of learning the value of money.
- It will show that I know what it's like to work.

In addition an operational vocabulary, drawn from the children in our study and also based on their words during interviews, would include the following:

- It gives me a taste of independence.
- It takes a bit of stress off the family.
- It means I can buy and do things.
- It's a way of socialising with my friends.
- It makes me somebody.

Here the vocabulary is more personalised and based on the role of work not merely as preparation for the future, but as an activity with significance for the here and now. It also shows relevance not just to the children themselves but also to their family, friends and to wider social participation.

The value of this vocabularies-oriented approach to understanding the signifi-cance of work to children's lives is that it allows us to consider the motivations for children's work within a frame of reference which goes beyond some of the binary divides of structure and agency, being and becoming, investment and gratification, etc., that often characterise debates within the sociology of childhood. Vocabularies of motive, taken from the expressions of the children, recognise the significance of their own experiences and understanding of work. At the same time, they locate that significance and those experiences within wider structural motives for work.

Socialisation and developmental perspectives have traditionally seen children's work as investment for the future. Moreover, much of the rhetoric which underpins the rationale for school-initiated work experience, in which the great majority of UK schoolchildren now take part, continues to be underpinned by this perspective. While there may be merit in such a position, it has often failed to recognise the more immediate and contemporary relevance of work to children's lives. However, from children's accounts of their work in our own and other studies cited in this chapter, it is clear that the role work plays in children's lives has significance both for its capacity to prepare them for future adult work roles and for its immediacy. Clearly, children take a great deal from their experience as young workers, which for many are central to the construction and consumption of childhood in and for its self. At the same time, they also recognise its potential to contribute to their futures.

In terms of understanding children's motivations for work, the vocabularies of meanings allow us to juxtapose the interior subjective perspective of the child-worker (operational) with that of the external world which is concerned not with what children are but with what they may become (developmental). At the same time, given that each of the vocabularies is based on the views of the children themselves, it is possible to hold both perspectives simultaneously.

Conclusion

This brief chapter has argued that the motivations for children's participation in work cannot be explained simply by reference to socialisation theories, which emphasise child labour as a form of investment, or by reference to the lived experience of work, alone. Children have clear reasons for engaging in work, which are shaped by the immediate demands of the complexities of their social lives. Equally, children recognise the possible longer-term significance of experience of the working world.

While the emphasis on children as independent social actors is important for an understanding of childhood as a stage of the life-course, it has also been the intention to demonstrate that, as with any social actors, children do not exercise free will or choice in a way which is devoid of context or structure (Qvortrup 1997). The data presented here demonstrate the existence and complexities of many different kinds of childhood which may be shaped by gender, social class, ethnicity, local economy, geography and perhaps many other variables. In seeking to understand childhood, therefore, we are not merely concerned with beings rather than becomings (James et al. 1998) but with the social context of being. This analysis of motivations for work is an attempt to recognise the significance of lived childhood experiences, but also to situate them within a social, cultural and political framework. The use of this vocabularies approach has allowed us not just to see children both as beings and becomings (Lee 2003; Prout 2004), but also to recognise that children themselves understand the consequences of their contemporary actions not simply for their relevance to their immediate lives but also for their futures.

Notes

1. The study upon which this paper is based was funded under the ESRC (Economic and Social Research Council) programme 'Children 5–16: Growing into the Twenty First Century' (Award No. L129251035). As well as the author, the research team included Dr Phil Mizen and Dr Angela Bolton, to whom thanks are expressed and acknowledgement is given that the chapter draws on work that was conducted collectively.

2. A fuller assessment of the project methodology can be found in Pole, Mizen and Bolton (1999).

Chapter 16

Child Work and Child Labour in Italy: The Point of View of the Children

Maria Teresa Tagliaventi

A controversial subject

Whenever we consider child work performed by minors of less than 15 years of age the discussion becomes complicated.

In fact the phenomenon is extremely complicated and composite in the south where it coexists with situations of extreme poverty and lack of resources as well as in societies with advanced economies where social and economic development appear to make joining the work force at an early age unlawful.

Not much attention was given to this problem in Italy until the 1990s, probably because child labour was an insignificant phenomenon and had almost disappeared following promulgation of a law in 1967 that prohibited any type of work until school leaving age had been attained (or until 14 years of age) and the introduction of sanctions to protect children's rights to health and education.

Since the end of the 1990s attention to the subject has progressively grown and, partially through studies and research projects, greater understanding of the problem has been promoted; however, the difficulty in exploring the phenomenon has also emerged quite markedly along with the general confusion about the subject and the incomplete results of research.

To demonstrate this it should suffice to analyse estimates made by scholars, research organisations, institutions and trade unions over recent years which differ from each other by hundreds of thousands with fluctuation of between 50,000 and 500,000 working minors. In some cases the paradox has even been reached in which the same institution or researcher, during different but not distant periods, obtains successive estimates that deviate greatly from each other for the same or similar age groups although starting from different methodological premises (Moretti 2004).

But then, in addition to relying on the black labour market and private dimension, child labour has other specific applications that make it particularly difficult to detect and analyse. Among those are the limited numbers of incidences of the most serious forms of child labour, which make it extremely difficult to perform extensive investigations. The multidimensional nature of the phenomenon, the territorial discontinuity of its distribution and because of the distribution, the phenomenon is mottled like a 'leopard skin' in Italy and exists in different contexts. There is also the life cycle of children's working experiences as children and adolescents that is irregular over a period of time (ISTAT 2002).

Concerning the specific applications mentioned, moreover, a conceptual difficulty must be added to this in defining what is work and what is not work in childhood and adolescence because in the 'container' of child work we usually include radically different situations ranging from child prostitution to criminal activities and from conditions of total destruction of the personality and dignity of the child involved to situations that are absolutely not damaging in the child's course of growth (Schibotto 1990; Tagliaventi 1999a).

Finally, it must be remembered that prejudices and the ideological purposes of various institutions and organisations that conduct research who 'see only what they want to see' and disseminate partial information or information that refers to specific contexts and pass it off as universal[1] sometimes come under the heading of data and contrasting visions of the phenomenon of child work.

Therefore it is difficult to deal with such a multifarious subject considering the multiplicity of facets in which child and pre-adolescent work takes physical form and which is not always comparable to adult employment.

The work of the children may be remunerated or not, productive or reproductive, family or extra-family, illicit or legitimate, etc. Additionally, various types of labour exist in connection with different sectors of activity such as jobs that differ with respect to the time employed (work performed intermittently or only in the summer or work performed daily), jobs performed by males and females, those that are varied because of the characteristics and context of the working environment and, in particular, because of the relational aspects connected to them (Tagliaventi 1999b).

Finally, it must be borne in mind that there are jobs that are not always recognised as such, and that, alongside older forms of exploitation of child labour, new forms are emerging that are more sophisticated and apparently less damaging to the physical health of the children and are therefore accepted without response by the collective conscience.

Although public opinion today is ready to be moved and protest because a boy in a cellar must sew shoes, no attention is dedicated to the one who is obliged to remain for many hours on a cinema or publicity set or obliged to participate in a show that takes place late in the evening for months or a child who undergoes strenuous and difficult sports training and is uprooted from his normal living environment in order to be built up scientifically like a professional athlete (Moro 1999).

Some characteristics of child work in Italy

Although there is still open debate on child work in Italy at present, it is possible to outline some recurrent characteristics that contribute to defining the phenomenon in our country through various research projects that have been carried out, especially those conducted in specific territorial contexts that are of a qualitative nature (Fontana 1995; Golini, Sgritta and Gigantino 2001; Mattioli 1996; Paone and Teselli 2000; Tagliaventi 1999b) as well as surveys conducted at national level using a representative sample of the population and commissioned by the Ministry of Labour and Social Policy from ISTAT (Italian National Statistical Institute) which was published in 2002 (a synthesis in Micali 2002). There are at least four common aspects that emerge from the various sources:

- the great variety of forms of work and manners of expression
- the distribution of child work throughout the nation (although there are several territorial specificities)
- the fact that the phenomenon is no longer exclusively connected to economic needs and poverty – although some forms of child work motivated by the need to increase a precarious family income remain
- the indirect conflict of the phenomenon with school or the greater presence of the working student with respect to the exclusive minor worker.

Concerning the differentiation between child labour and child work as described in the introduction there is no unity of thought on the subject among various research projects.

Generally, research projects commissioned by trade unions tend to stress the connection between child work and social exclusion, while those promoted by various universities propose a more articulated panorama that stresses, according to different contexts, conditions of exploitation or of non-damaging work that children may experience.

A point of agreement among researchers who have worked on the topic concerns child labour among foreign children, especially if they are clandestine or unaccompanied, because their activity often takes place in situations of compulsion and slave-like economic activity that are closer to forms of deviance than forms of work.

Child and adolescent labour among foreigners in Italy, nonetheless, is still a largely unexplored terrain and research available has often attempted, due also to the objective difficulty of performing this type of research, to reconstruct the characteristics of the phenomenon by starting with Italian adults who work with immigrant children rather than through direct collection of children's own accounts of their life experiences (Bertozzi 2004).

An important study on child labour, mentioned earlier, which helps us delve more deeply into the subject matter is the national ISTAT research that was commissioned in 1999 by the Ministry of Labour and Social Security in collaboration with ILO (International Labour Organization). The investigation dealt specifically with children and pre-adolescents involved in production for the market (paid labour) and several non-market-oriented types of production (unpaid labour) including production of goods for their own consumption according to ILO[2] indicators and drawn from different sources of information that included literature on the topic and interviews with selected witnesses, sample surveys of children and analysis of phenomena related to child labour.

The surveys taken among the children were carried out as part of an experimental research project at schools and in two research projects conducted among families. In particular, regarding the latter:

- more in-depth study of child work was included within multi-purpose examination of families and concentrated on childhood and adolescence (on a sample of 24,000 families that were considered representative of the Italian population)

- an *ad hoc* module was included with the research on the labour force on 'the first working experiences of young people'. This research, which is the largest project that ISTAT has conducted among families, called for a sample of 75,000 families for each quarterly cycle which was more than triple the number of families involved in the other investigation. The research was addressed to children between 15 and 18 years of age who were interviewed on work ultimately performed before they had reached 15 years of age. The interviewees who had not been 'caught red-handed' showed less reluctance in describing their now past experiences and, at the same time, since they were sufficiently 'grown up' had an appropriate concept of work.

ISTAT estimates according to this research state that some 144,823 minors under 15 years of age were working in 2000. Among these about 44,000 were working regularly. Most of them were seasonal jobs. In relative terms this means that three minors under 15 years of age work for every 100 children in their age group. The incidence increases with age with 0.5 per cent among children between seven and ten years of age, 3.7 per cent among children between 11 and 13 years and 11.6 per cent among children who are 14 years of age.

Among working minors 31,500 persons may be considered exploited. Exploitation means labour involving at least one of these characteristics: 'dangerous, takes place at night, fatiguing, performed instead of going to school, does not leave the child free time to play, be with friends or study'.

The most serious distribution of the phenomenon concerns, on average, one minor between 7 and 14 years of age for every five minors of the same age employed in any type of work. Contrary to minors who perform any type of work the incidence of exploited children in the sample population becomes rather important only for minors aged 14 where the figure reaches 2.7 per cent (ISTAT 2002).

The point of view of children on child work and labour

Not all research projects took into consideration the point of view of children on the objectives pursued. I shall refer only to two research projects that take children's points of view into consideration, and from which some useful information may be gleaned: the previously cited ISTAT research, and a qualitative research performed by the author (Tagliaventi 2002).

In the ISTAT research the judgement expressed by children about their work was rather positive: 35 per cent of the children stated that they preferred to work rather than to go to school and 72 per cent of them said they enjoyed their working experience 'a great deal' or 'enough'. The work performed does not seem to have limited in most cases the time the children had available to play, or to have damagingly limited school attendance (90 per cent of boys and 89 per cent of girls stated that their work left them time to do their homework).

Thus according to the children's opinion their first work experience is not seen as an obstacle to their growth and personality. Alongside this information, nevertheless, there are 1.2 per cent of girls and 8 per cent of boys who recall their working experience as being dangerous and 42 per cent remember that it was very fatiguing or fatiguing enough.

The research I carried out is qualitative with specific objectives that include examination of the motives and significance that children attribute to their activity while considering them social actors capable of producing knowledge about their reality.

The research was conducted in 1999 in several different places (Palermo, Trento and Rimini, cities in the south and north of Italy which are deemed representative of different climates and socio-cultural conditions). In-depth interviews of 70 pre-adolescent workers[3] (collecting life-stories) were completed with parallel views of 25 children involved in focus groups for the purpose of combining what had emerged empirically. The subjects, both male and female, had either in the past or at the moment of the interview maintained a continuous working activity.

The research brought to light how the children represented their experience and revealed the fact that they had joined the labour force at an early age in different ways, how this conditioned their socialisation and the construction of an identity but also, above all, how they are capable of taking action that the adult world generally does not recognise as being suitable for them and of attributing significance to these actions, albeit they are reconciled by the characteristics of their age group.

Again, in this research, the image that emerges of work is rather positive. The majority of the children are satisfied with work they perform although they are well aware of and capable of discerning negative aspects from positive.

In detail, if the children personally chose to work, positive aspects of their job are more significant than negative even if they carry out hard work. An important factor is the possibility they had to choose to work and the fact that they can always choose to change their mind if they do not like their job.

As for the positive aspects of their work, children claim that it gives them immediate and tangible satisfaction. The finished product is easily and quickly managed by boys and girls, gives them autonomy and the opportunity to stand out from the others. For those who work outside the domestic environment especially, their job allows them an early social contact with adults, and making them participate in a relational context different from the one formed by the family or friends. Boys and girls emphasise that their work is a way of having a social identity that is sometimes impossible to achieve in other environments.

Regarding identity, since working activities are carried out through social relationships, they respond to the need for identity. However, the process of building an identity develops through work, school, friends, family, recreational agencies and the community one belongs to.

Thus, in my opinion, work becomes a risk when it is the only opportunity a boy or girl has to build his or her own identity and not simply an opportunity among others. When work does not give them the chance to become part of a group or to leave it, to feel like a child, a son or daughter, a friend, a worker, a student, a player, etc., then there is a risk of defining it as child labour or prejudicial work. When, on the other hand, the children are free to move and to live in different environments, to be a bit of everything, then work can be defined as an important resource to build an identity, comparable to others.

Undoubtedly, albeit with all due care in dealing with a problem-fraught phenomenon such as child work, what children think of their work differs a great deal from what many adults think, who are responsible for their education, especially educators, teachers, pedagogues and the parents of minors who do not work and who generally demand that minors under 15 years of age be removed from actual working situations. But if adults do not consider or ask themselves why working activities are not only requested but also judged as quite positive experiences, they will not be able to look at early work in the right way or to provide alternatives to these satisfying activities. All of this obviously forces a reconsideration of conceptual paradigms of childhood and calls upon all agencies concerning the socialisation of children.

Notes

1. Recent investigations conducted by trade unions do not, unfortunately, escape this. An example is the utilisation of non-representative sample populations of minors, located territorially in precise areas of Italy, and the generalisation of research results that arrive at rather dubious estimates of the phenomenon.

2. The research considers children involved in domestic activities or work within their family as inactive. Children must also have performed at least one hour of work during the year previous to the survey. Therefore, all more or less light economic activities performed by children and all work deemed to have negative effects on their health, education and normal development are included in the concept of child labour. All illegal activities involving minors are not included that cannot be defined as work.

3. The pre-adolescents were between age 11 and 15 years.

Chapter 17

Work – A Way to Participative Autonomy for Children

Beatrice Hungerland

The discourse on working children in Germany

Bringing up the issue of working children in Germany usually evokes two kinds of reaction. The first supposes that children's work is an indicator of a growing poverty rate among families with children. The second assumes that an increasing number of school children's jobs proves the young people's disproportionate consumer-orientation or similar self-centred motives such as the fulfilment of narcissistic demands (this is said of children working in the media). They seem to give evidence of the baleful procession towards an individualistic society.

The only exception to such a negative view of children's work can be found when work is performed in an educational setting. This is true, for example, for pupil firms in schools as it is seen as providing the children and youths with skills they might use in future and therefore can be regarded as a kind of investment (for a detailed discussion on the subject see Liebel in this volume, Chapter 12). Nevertheless this ascribed value does not affect the negative public attitude towards children's work performed outside of institutional control. The public discourse only allows two attitudes towards working children: either as being endangered or as being dangerous. In both cases working children are regarded as victims and the only solution lies in their pedagogical treatment. Such a strategy of making children victims and objects is a general phenomenon in public discourses about children (cf. Bühler-Niederberger and Hungerland 2002), but it is certainly true for the issue of child work.

A new approach towards working children: the Berlin project on 'children and work'

What the children themselves think about their working activities, what they do, why they do it and what they gain from it has thus far been hidden from view. Our research project at the Technical University of Berlin, programmatically entitled 'What does work mean to children? An empirical study focusing on the aspects of social participation and the acquirement of skills'[1] was launched to ask the children themselves for their own subjective view of their work. The study was carried out between 2002 and 2004 and aimed to ensure that work by children is not perceived first and foremost as a social problem that has to be tackled, but rather that children are taken seriously as reflective, active subjects in all conceivable aspects of their lives. Children are regarded as social actors who are able and interested in playing an active role in society. Their work experiences are therefore seen in the light of offering or restricting opportunities for participation.

In order to open out the complex and relatively unexplored terrain covered by the meaning which children ascribe to their work, we used the research technique of 'Grounded Theory', developed by Barney Glaser and Anselm Strauss as the methodological basis for our investigation.[2]

What we now can state about the meaning of work for children in Germany is based upon 38 open, keyword-guided interviews we carried out with children in Berlin between the ages of 9 and 15. Access to the field of research was made possible by informing schools whereby we sought to ensure involvement by all types of school spread across both eastern and western districts of the city. Beyond this, we directly sought out children working in the media through casting agencies; in addition, we placed an advertisement in a children's newspaper distributed free to schools throughout the region, as well as approaching children while they were working.[3]

What is 'work'?: the need to conceptualise children's activities

Earlier research had only referred to paid work, because it tended to investigate the legal status or the causes and effects of 'child labour'. Concentrating on gainful employment ignores the fact that a great amount of work that is performed by children is not being paid.

From pre-test interviews with children about their work experiences, we had learned that children frequently do not perceive their work to be work as such, whether it be paid or not. Children themselves would reconstruct the idea of a work- and labour-free childhood by ignoring the productive aspects of their own activities. In order to be able to delineate our research object, we could not leave the definition up to the children themselves, but rather had to make a decision about what is to be considered to be work.

As we wanted to study children as social actors and gain an insight into the chances and limitations that different activities enabled them to confront, we had to include non-paid activities in our investigation. Emphasis was put on the fact that this work nevertheless had an economic relevance. We considered the domestic work of children to be a contribution to the family economy,[4] since it enables parents to put themselves at the disposal of the labour market.

We suggest that the direct, as well as indirect, contribution that children make to the family economy does have an effect on their position vis-à-vis the adults within the family. It is through their contribution to the family's capital in economic terms that the child gains a different kind of significance other than simply as the recipient of benefits. This process of being ascribed a significance, or indeed of ascribing it to oneself, could also extend beyond the framework of the family and lead to a new evaluation of children within society, from being 'useless' to being useful children again (see Zelizer 1985 and 2002). One of our research questions was therefore concerned with investigating whether children perceive such a re-evaluation coming from the adults, but also whether they themselves perceive it in this way.

The different types of work and their meaning for the children

The children interviewed carried out the following outdoor activities: delivering newspapers and advertising leaflets, babysitting, working in a factory, working in gardens, mowing lawns, cleaning out stables, looking after horses, giving extra tuition, selling at flea markets, doing voiceovers, participating in film-making, belonging to an opera choir, renting out bicycles, helping in gastronomic enterprises, helping in a bakery, carrying out magic tricks, filing books and busking.

Apart from that they told us about many kinds of domestic activities within the household: caring for siblings, taking small children to the doctor, cleaning the bathroom, cooking, shopping, washing up, filling and emptying the dishwasher, vacuum cleaning, whipping dust, sweeping, caring for pets (feeding, cleaning, walking dogs), emptying wastepaper baskets, doing the washing and ironing.

Of the children interviewed, 26 were undertaking paid work, divided equally according to gender. Altogether 22 girls and 16 boys participated in interviews. From their details it is clear that the number of children working without being paid is higher among the girls (9) than the boys (3). All children who regularly carry out paid work or already have experience in 'jobs' also carry out unpaid housework, although it has to be said that children from families in a higher-income bracket generally do less housework.

The meanings which work has for children must be discussed against the background of the hierarchical relationship between the generations. The status of this relationship between children and their parents is mirrored in the categories of work activities chosen. Work expected or initiated by parents must be ascribed another meaning for the children as opposed to work organised by the children themselves. This analytical distinction is a point of connection with those discourses that already exist around child work. It is also intended to show that the dichotomising perspective, which sees working children either as 'endangered' exploited victims or as 'dangerous' individualised consumers, has to be overcome if we are to gain new and differentiated insights into the meanings of work for children.

Unpaid work expected by parents: an unavoidable duty

Helping with the household and looking after younger siblings is expected by almost all parents and carried out by almost all children. Admittedly the number of activities and the amount of time taken up by them does vary. These tasks are in general organised, directed, delegated and supervised by the mothers. The gender division of work still seems to be unbroken with regard to the responsibilities of domestic and familial work.

By working in the household and in the garden, the children alleviate the burden on their parents and place time at their disposal. Such a transference of work responsibilities is legitimised by parents in their turn by pointing to the didactic benefits of such work (see Zeiher 2004). But tasks which are given by adults with pedagogical intentions frequently do not correspond to the desire expressed by children to carry out meaningful and useful, i.e. serious, activities and to be recognised for their capabilities. They find instead that their inferior status within the community is cemented. The children clearly perceive whether they are being given a 'genuine' responsibility or whether these are tasks which are handed down to them as members of the 'pedagogical moratorium childhood', for the purposes of learning.

Among themselves, children scarcely talk about these collaborative activities, as they are not something about which one could be particularly proud, nor something that it is worth complaining about.

Interviewer: And do you tell others about what you do around the house?

Michi (14): If someone asks me, then yes, but not unless they do.

Interviewer: Does anyone ask?

M: It tends to be rare, it's not really the major topic of conversation amongst my friends, the question of who does what at home.

This is down to the fact that this kind of work is not socially valued, something of which children are also very aware. On the other hand, this kind of work is to be understood as the expression of generational hierarchies within the family, which leave limited room for manoeuvre and remain unquestioned in the social relationship of adult to children:

Interviewer: And are there things that you disagree about in the family?

Xiayanxi (11): Yes, there are, if I don't tidy up my room, or if it's not properly tidied up.

Interviewer: And how do you work it out?

X: I go and tidy it up. [...] You do have to do your duties around the house from time to time, but the other duties, they are more fun.

Interviewer: Can you say why that's the case?

X: Because, well, if you're sweeping, you get so dirty, but you earn money doing the other things.

There seems to be an unspoken consensus or it is taken for granted that parents or adults can tell children what they have to do. The children have the feeling that they have little room for manoeuvre with regard to such tasks; they find them unavoidable and natural, or even unpleasant and boring.

Against the background of the generational hierarchy there are variations in the families depending on their identity as a family and the meaning of the tasks of its members for one another. The meaning varies according to how far the child is integrated or participates within the community. The dominance of the parents can be more or less visible, depending on how authoritarian or democratic the structure of the parent–child relationship is.[5]

Paid work expected or initiated by parents: gaining cultural, social and economic capital

Some parents support the paid work of their children, because they hope them to gain different forms of capital from it (in the Bourdieuan sense, 1983). Alongside the gaining of economic capital, which is not in the foreground in Germany (or whose primary status is at least not admitted), work can, or is supposed to, serve the acquisition of cultural and social capital.

The didactic experience of paid activities is frequently named clearly as the primary motivation which children presume their parents have in supporting their work:

Interviewer: What does your mother think of the fact you babysit?

Juliane[6] (14): I think she considers it good [...] that we take on responsibility as well, and I think she considers it good that one learns how to do that, since I want to have children myself later and one has to be able to do these things.

Through these kinds of work, children can, want and are supposed to test themselves in acquiring different skills. Children believe that adults approve when they develop self-confidence, and learn both responsibility and the value of self-earned money through working. For parents and children, the pedagogical aspects are of primary importance here, while the material gain made through such work is also seen as an educative factor. The money the children earn does not go into the household pot. Often some of it is saved in a bank account for their future but mostly they have at least some of it at their own disposal. Learning to deal with money one has earned oneself and learning that activities possess a value also belong to those competencies that children are expected to acquire.

In these tasks, both parents and children place value on the fact that they are fun and thus have the character of leisure activities. For the children themselves, the 'fun factor' is often rated more highly than the possibility of earning money.

Interviewer: Would you say that your acting is work?

Milena (11): I don't think so, okay, I earn money in doing it, but I wouldn't see that as work but rather as a hobby, no, not as work.

Such activities are primarily restricted to children from middle-class backgrounds, because they are generally made possible through the social contacts of the parents. In part, considerable time commitments are demanded of the parents (the mothers), in order to facilitate the work (castings for the children working in the media, background/networking in the case of babysitting). This work is paid best of all: it is made possible through the parents' social contacts and is dependent on the family already possessing sufficient social capital.

Only a few of the children interviewed by us indicated that they were obliged to contribute to the family income. Admittedly this may be down to our selection and the taboo nature of the topic. At the same time, in materially less well-off families, in particular single-parent households, the economic element cannot simply be ignored.

Younger children tend to work in consort with their parents, delivering newspapers together and helping them on flea market stalls. For them, therefore, earning money is not the primary motivation, but work is rather a common activity and also has the character of a leisure activity:

Kelly (12): It's good to do stuff together, then you can have a chat at the same time, or we take the dog with us, then you don't need to take it for a walk afterwards. The dog's always happy when we pack the newspapers into our rucksacks.

Paid work organised by children themselves: having money at one's own disposal

The majority of paid work that children told us about does not take place on the initiative of the parents, but instead is sought and organised by the children themselves. Since this is a voluntary activity, the children ensure that fun and income generation are combined. The possibilities of children finding an appropriate job are admittedly limited, as the youth protection regulations allow children under the age of 14 only a few activities which offer such potential. In doing so, children look for niches in the labour market that is for the most part closed to them, and make use of 'structural opportunities'.

Paid work offers children the possibility of having their own money at their disposal beyond or in addition to pocket money and gifts. The value of the work done becomes visible in their self-earned money. This admittedly only applies to child work to a limited extent: one should not underestimate the fact that the same work, when performed by adults, is clearly better-paid than when carried out by a child. In some cases, children carry out this work against the wishes of their parents. Both undertaking an activity that is not supervised by adults as well as having their own money at their disposal gives children a degree of autonomy that they scarcely find elsewhere.

Handy (11): And on Saturday for example, a friend and I wanted to go to the cinema, and so we did magic tricks, loads of them, until we both had 5 euros and then we went to the cinema. Well, I'm not really supposed to do that...

With the passage of time, the novelty of such work wears off. At the same time, the children remain closely connected to their activity, regardless of whether they are contractually bound or not. Becoming accustomed to the independent availability of one's own money is one of the reasons that children keep such jobs until they are old enough to find a better paid position.

> Leo (15): Now, well, in the meantime it is a little stressful, because it's every week, every Friday, always newspapers. There are also people who insult you, or say something else and are unfriendly but you always have to stay friendly. And at some point you've had enough. But because I get money for it and still find the job quite good from time to time, I keep doing it, until I get another proper job where perhaps I'll have more fun doing it, and maybe earn a bit more money.

Moreover, children feel a high level of obligation towards the job and the responsibility they have assumed which means that they cannot give it up even if it is much less fun that it was. This contradicts the assumption that in northern industrialised capitalist countries responsibility for others is less significant for most children who take on paid self-organised work (see Fuhs 2001).

A thoughtless consumerist attitude was not to be found among the children we interviewed. During the interviews, children only occasionally suggested that they bought clothes or designer items. These children emphasise the social value of such trademarks that is helpful in positioning oneself within one's peer group. The children do however also spend their self-earned money on presents for family, relatives or for friends. They therefore use their own money to strengthen emotional ties in a symbolic fashion.

> Interviewer: What sorts of things have you done with your money?

> Victoria (13): …first and foremost, I buy presents, because I've got lots of friends and relatives in the Ukraine, mostly relatives, loads of them! And then, every month, you know, it is someone's birthday, and they're always disappointed when there's no word from Germany and so, in the main, I've got to buy more presents.

We were able to observe that through their work children were keen to take on responsibility within their family. Although all children earning their own money stated that their income was at their own disposal, they see their activity as supporting better cooperation among the family members, when they are giving a part of their self-earned income into the household pot. This finds expression, for example, in the fact that some children do without extra pocket money from their parents. They think that the money they have earned themselves is sufficient and are content to be much less of a burden on their parents. Other children contributed money for purchasing computers, furniture, or financing travel, things that otherwise had financially burdened the family or even could not have been afforded.

A child's autonomous decision and a commitment towards community do not contradict each other. On the contrary, if they are able to make a contribution to the economic well-being of the family, the children clearly feel themselves to be valued.

Unpaid work organised by children themselves: autonomous and community oriented

Alongside those activities which children are given by adults and self-organised paid work, there are a series of self-selected and self-organised unpaid tasks which children take on both outside and within the family. The children explicitly mention the fact that their work should provide help and support.

> Joey (15): I just think it's good when people commit to others, as I wouldn't like it when... Well, I would also like it if somebody would voluntarily join in [...] For example I often help old people like my neighbour. I help her with shopping and all that. And sometimes she pays me, but mostly I don't take the money. I don't want it. When we go shopping, she buys me some sweets, for example, and that's enough for me. I like doing that.

The gratification gained through this work is twofold. On the one hand, pride at their exceptional achievement, on the other, approval from adults. Two of the characteristics of this kind of work are, first, that it takes pressure off adults and, second, that it goes beyond the boundaries of generational hierarchy. The children themselves recognise the relevance of their work and consider the shouldering of extra responsibility to be 'honourable' and a transcendence of the 'childhood space of play' which they have been ascribed. They are particularly proud when they experience approval and are treated in a way that disrupts the hierarchical relationship between children and adults:

> Interviewer: What do you imagine your aunt would do without you?
>
> Lucy (12): Oh, she wouldn't know what to do. That would be really difficult for her, it wouldn't look good for her at all. So I think it's better that I do help her.

In taking on voluntary, unpaid work children feel themselves to be part of a community to which they both would like and are able to contribute. It is central to the meaning of such work that children establish within the community their own, independent position which goes beyond any generational hierarchy or dependency.

Developing 'participatory autonomy' and social positioning through work

On the one hand, work represents for children the possibility of becoming independent and acting autonomously. On the other hand, work offers the opportunity to make a significant contribution to the community. The two areas of potential which work offers, 'autonomy' and 'participation', are not, as might be assumed, in opposition to each other, but can be related to one another. In this sense, we can say that children seek a 'participatory autonomy' through their work. The level of participatory autonomy for the children depends on the activity and the significance which the children attribute to the activity.

Unpaid chores in the household as expected by their parents secure the children's position within the community of the family. Still, their own ability to shape and negotiate the kind of activity, its extent and its length, are dependent on the conditions which their parents set them. This places them in the position of minors. This is also true for the paid work which parents expect of their children, although it places in question the construction of an economically non-productive child. But such a transgression of normative prescriptions can only be justified by the parents with reference to 'fun' and the learning benefits which are expected to be gained. A hierarchical relationship is created and established between task-giving adults and the working child, even if – or because – this is intended primarily to serve pedagogical intentions.

The autonomy of the child develops primarily in those areas where it can decide for itself to undertake work which is not demanded of it. Here the children can find an opportunity to take on responsibility by themselves – be it for themselves or for others. Self-selected work which is undertaken for payment offers the child a chance to care independently for his/her needs, without relying on parents or other adults. In this sense the child's autonomous decision relieves the parents. The connection to the community can manifest itself through independent income-generation and determining where the self-earned money will go.

In primarily community tasks that are voluntarily undertaken by the children, where no monetary gratification is in prospect, the question has to be asked as to what motivates the children to engage in such an activity. The autonomous decision to help and through this to make one's own contribution enables the experience of oneself as morally valuable. If this is then also perceived by others, then it contributes to recognition and pride, and beyond that to the establishment of self-confidence.

Shouldering responsibility implies a holistic challenge for children. It means above all that they experience themselves as active subjects who are able to think and to take decisions by themselves and who are able to contribute to the community. As a result we see work as one possibility for children to go beyond the social position they have been given. It is a chance to make known and experience the children's own demands for autonomy and participation.

Notes

1. The research team consisted of Manfred Liebel, Beatrice Hungerland, Anja Liesecke, Anne Wihstutz, Bernd Overwien and Gesine Stühmeier.

2. Glaser and Strauss 1967.

3. For more details see Hungerland, Liebel and Wihstutz 2005.

4. On the theoretical basis for the extension of the concept of work, cf. Schildkrout 1980, p.484; Nieuwenhuys 1994, p.17.

5. Du Bois-Reymond et al. (1994) establish a development in families from an authoritarian command-household to a household based on negotiation. Nevertheless, the generational hierarchy remains in households based on negotiation, since it is the parents who determine the framework and conditions of participation by the children.

6. This and all following names are pseudonyms which the children themselves have chosen.

Part 5

Citizenship and Working Children's Movements and Organisations

Chapter 18

The Stakes of Children's Participation in Africa: The African Movement of Working Children and Youth

Hamidou Coly and Fabrizio Terenzio

Background

Since 1985 Enda Tiers Monde and its partners, the 'Calao African Network' (Reseau Africain Calao, RAC), have been building up a participative approach that facilitates the development and improvement of children's lives in Africa. After nine years of endeavour the 'African Movement of Working Children and Youth' was created on 21 July 1994.

Twenty years later the following points and thoughts have been recorded to be shared with whoever is interested in reading them.

Children's participation is unavoidable

In Africa children constitute a constant and active majority of the population. Culturally they are in a position of 'respect' vis-à-vis the older generation but their demographic importance within a difficult context obliges them to play the part of economic, social and even 'political' actors amid tensions on their continent. Their 'role' or 'protagonism' can be seen as 'good' when children decide to clean the local square or to cultivate an old man's field. On the contrary their role is seen to be 'bad' when they get into trouble or even 'tragic' when they start to use weapons. Nevertheless *children's participation is a basic element in Africa*.

'The unavoidable nature of participation' does not only derive from the United Nations Convention on the Rights of the Child (UNCRC). It originates from the experience of those who are close to children and try to act 'with them' or 'for them'. By considering the repeated failures of their supportive practices they were pushed to advance toward the search for an effective children's participation, that by definition enabled implementation and evaluation of actions concerning them.

The success and sustainability of children's support depends largely on their participation. In some cases it is correct to ask oneself whether it is *the child who has to participate* in adult actions in his support (to act with) or whether it is *the adult who has to support the child in his initiatives* (act by). In the former case the child participates, in the latter the child is the protagonist.

In 1990–91 RAC and Environmental Development Action (ENDA) opted for support of children's protagonism (support to child-led action)!

No child rights without their participation

The 'child rights approach' stems from the UNRC. Therefore it has a precise 'date of birth' but it still needs to be fully developed. An element of confusion is the 'legitimate' vision that many people have of the UNCRC. People consider it as a text of universal law that must become 'national law' and then 'land' inside everybody (or imposed on everyone).

African children do not know the law very well: they are confronted with laws in painful situations such as laws against 'hawking and begging' promulgated during the colonial period (in French-speaking countries). This law puts them into an illegal situation while they are trying to help their family and themselves by undertaking economic activities in urban areas. Thus the 'law' becomes an instrument of repression which they must escape (police raids) or to which they have to submit by paying official or unofficial fines. The latter worsens their economic situation by decreasing their income.

On the other hand they think they have rights (see ENDA 1999, 2001; Liebel 2001c), stemming from 'God' and culture rather than from an international convention. As long as the 'child rights approach' comes down as 'application of law' it will exclude children who might be the most concerned by the UNCRC while most deprived of rights.

By appropriation of rights and by reconstructing them through their own experience African children not only become the 'defenders' of (their own) rights but also the 'architects' of rights with immediate effect on their everyday life.

In July 1994 after domestic girls and street workers marched on Labour Day in Dakar in order to 'show them that we are also working every day!' and solidarity actions in several towns in five countries some delegates who were in Bouaké (Côte d'Ivoire) identified 12 basic rights to build on in order to have a better life. In order to promote them they designed a plan of action. The African Movement of Working Children and Youth (AMWCY-MAEJT was born.

- Right to be taught a trade.
- Right to remain in the village (no exodus).
- Right to work in a safe environment.
- Right to light and limited work.
- Right to rest when sick.
- Right to be respected.

- Right to be listened to.
- Right to health care.
- Right to learn to read and write.
- Right to play.
- Right to self-expression and to form organisations.
- Right to access to equitable legal aid (in case of trouble).

By helping African children take full control of their own rights we are building a coherent and feasible 'child rights approach'. Without their participation we take the lead as 'defenders of rights' and meanwhile relegate children to a rank of 'animals or vegetables in danger' who are obviously unable to defend or build their own rights.

Nowadays this dilemma doesn't exist any more. AMWCY-MAEJT is organised in 400 groups, in 64 towns and in 20 African countries. The 12 rights are commonly used as a common framework for situational analysis and for action planning by working children.

Child participation is greatly welcomed by Africans

'No rights without obligations, no rights without respect.' Starting with a consensus on these two points child participation is greatly welcomed in Africa.

The work of the African Movement of Working Children and Youth (AMWCY) after ten years' existence is a proof of that. Their concrete action in building up rights has always been appreciated: from villages where the WCY undertook many activities to prevent children's 'premature exodus'; in neighbourhoods where they have been communicating with the community, the community-based organisations (CBOs), as well as traditional and religious authorities; in towns where they have talked with mayors; in nations where they have cooperated with government ministers and presidents; to the United Nations General Assembly Special Session (UNGASS); and, lest they are overlooked, trade unions and the media.

The acceptance of their 'social role' comes from rural traditions in which 'each age group must play its part'. In this way, by intervening in everyday life, the WCY re-adopted their 'traditional social role' from which modernity tended to exclude them.

Generally, the African forum in Cairo (UNGASS Process) in May 2001 marked the discovery by the African community that included ministries, civil society, international institutions and all manner of experts of the 'healthy' nature of children's self-expression and participation in a debate that was going to lay down the fundamental guidelines for action building an 'Africa fit for children'.

In April 2003 the African Union invited a delegate from AMWCY-MAEJT to Mauritius for a meeting with its social commission. Some appeared unwilling to accept this 'innovation'; however, the majority of participants, ministries and institutions supported his words.

In September 2003 ECOWAS (Economic Community of West African States), the regional organisation for Western Africa, organised the 'peer review' on child policy. MAEJT and other children participated in the meeting together with ministers and public. It was decided that in each country in the region periodic reviews of childhood policy would bring together government and public organisations including child-led ones.

The children's statement together with the minister's declaration was adopted in December 2003 by the heads of state. The implementation of the 'peer review' is now a decisive matter for the MAEJT, African Global Movement for Children and the African NGO (non-governmental organisation) Coalition for children.

In some countries like Guinea Conakry or Senegal the government is even demanding 'more participation' from AMWCY-MAEJT to increase its contribution to the policy, and thus enhance national policies and their definition and implementation. At other levels (villages, towns, CBOs and NGO coalitions) they already have a voice when they decide to contribute and are sometimes seriously taken into consideration.

The adult role is crucial

Child participation does not mean the advent of a segregated universe where only children are right. Children belong to a world where adults, primarily parents, run into constant difficulties in their 'struggle with poverty'.

Some years ago, a WCY delegate expressed the harshness of everyday life by saying 'You always speak about children in difficult situations, why don't you take care of our parents in difficult situations?' Thus, efforts made to improve their future are closely connected to their parents. The context of 'African children's participation' is very different from the perspective of rich countries.

Adults who facilitate their efforts are often 'urban animators' to whom we refer seldom with regard to participation.

- Statutory institutions do not practise participation but mostly hierarchy. Often they are at the bottom of the scale of salary and power. They receive orders they are compelled to execute every day. How can we imagine they have a participatory attitude towards children to whom, in step with institutional hierarchy, they are inclined to give orders rather than encourage self-expression?

- Often they do not have sufficient guidelines to assist them. They are told 'be participatory!' but they are not told 'how'. It is as if participation was part of their educational or vocational training background. Methodical training programmes on participation are rarely found in institutions working with children because priority is given to 'field action' without having prepared the 'field *for* action'.

- Facilitating participation may seem a thankless task. This is because on the one hand it continually demands standing aside to help children and on the other requires a particular presence. Some make the mistake of interpreting the 'new rules of the game' as a way of distancing themselves from children who will 'decide on their own'. The presence of the facilitator has to be constant even if sometimes it is only physical (and moral) with little right to speak because it is a question of favouring someone else's expression and not our own.

- The African adult knows the role of the 'older brother' very well but this role is different from the support of participation because it implies authority which does not allow the right to express oneself fully in this new context. An older brother who must listen might sometimes make recommendations but can never give orders.

- Satisfaction can and must come from the development of the quality of debates and decisions taken collectively by children and above all from the superior quality of child-led action and its results that was unattainable in the past in the context of 'supportive practices'.

After all, the original role of any educator is to softly disappear as and when the child develops!

The 'technical support group' is a common device used by adults and experienced youth in the AMWCY-MAEJT set up to monitor the development of local associations and their field work. The expertise of accompanying adults and youth is developed through training and evaluation in yearly sessions. The African meeting of AMWCY-MAEJT (a General Assembly takes place every three years) evaluates the impact of technical support and gives new guidelines for its contribution to the movement for the future. In 2003 it was decided that each one of the towns where the movement is organised will be visited at least once, by a team of one adult and one youth for at least one week before the next African meeting that was then planned for early 2006 in Ouagadougou (Burkina Faso).

Let's not demand of children what we are unable to do ourselves… but sometimes they do!

Learning participation is sometimes distressing for adults as much as for children!

For adults the constraints on participation other than those listed above are linked to the slow pace of participatory approaches. It is thus a Damocles' sword, whose effects are felt by the actors of participatory programmes and are always linked to their partners' questions: 'How much action? How many results?'

As for the children, they are also linked to the great responsibility that participation assumes. Once 'taken seriously' by adults they are obliged to be much more serious than in the past, thus losing some privileges of being children such as being carefree and sometimes contradictory. Sometimes, they deplore 'supportive practice' because it was unpleasant to have to take orders but the return was sometimes attractive with some small material incentives and little tyrannies that could be used vis-à-vis the institution. Goods and services are received without having to know neither how nor why it was decided nor where they come from. They are little lies that 'helped us to live'.

By taking responsibility the majority of these practices are excluded; furthermore the responsibility takes up a lot of time and energy!

This is probably why participatory experiences have mainly developed in Africa, Latin America and Asia among children living in the most difficult situations and for whom the reinforcement of rights is not an abstract affair: working children now have the chance to learn how to read and write, have access to healthcare, be trained, be respected, escape from certain forms of repression and 'take time out from their work' in order to express themselves and have fun!

Children sometimes lead adults who express exceptional concepts like 'child rights approach', 'peace building', 'empowerment', 'sustainable development', 'world fit for children' or 'African integration…but have a hard time improving them in their programmes and policies.

Children take these concepts and the values that they carry seriously. They act in solidarity, a brother- and sisterhood within Africa where borders disappear. They realise their rights in a sustainable way, they empower each other, especially the weaker, they organise follow-up of a 'world fit for children' and ask adult governments and the Global Movement for Children to carry on the follow-up[1] of the progress of their programme for the decade. In other words, they take seriously what adults express theoretically but forget in day-to-day practice. One of the things that children mostly reject is adults not respecting their words![2]

However, some 'adult establishments' react by demanding more and more. A thousand conditions are imposed on top of participation: the language they are asked to use in order to express themselves is not their own language but an academic one, meetings they attend will never be equally representative with one adult to one child and equal time to express themselves and an equal right of diversity! Their proposals are not technically appropriate. Their processes need to be 'really democratic' as if the adult ones were. They are asked to manage funds in a way that adults very rarely do. They are denied the right to make mistakes. It is the reluctance, mistrust and the deep-rooted impulse of a slightly apprehensive parent who keeps saying to his child that he must be brave under any circumstance!

There is still a long way to go to integrate children into our processes of thinking and deciding and become integrated into theirs.

'Good development' in question

So why so much effort? Because of a belief, a new slogan and a trend (UNCRC) to which we are trying to adapt?

Everyday problems are not only solved by rights implementation and a good organisation. Poverty still exists there and is faced by children. Their work in itself is a response and contributes to poverty alleviation for them and their families. It also has an impact on the economy.

Since the year 2000 they have initiated a process of developing income-generating activities to increase their movement's sustainability and also to progress in life individually.

Their ultimate goal is to contribute more and better to the growth of their community and country. The children say:

Life has made us learn how to work, we now want to get instruction and good training in order to help ourselves and help our countries to develop. Our right to light and limited work will make it possible to implement the 11 others in order to achieve that goal.

From an 'African development' point of view child participation represents a real opportunity because until now development models that have been adopted have never succeeded in efficiently managing one of the main resources for development: children's energy and creativity!

African children (52 per cent of the overall African population) are statistically evaluated according to inadequate parameters that include random indexes and diagrams that are drawn out of any 'children's (own) knowledge, voice or choice'.

The universal single and inimitably successful model given is 'formal education and ultra competition'. Almost half of the children in Africa do not have the chance to attend and are obviously left behind. Even those who have the chance of going to school feel that 'quality education' is not offered to them...

The 'globalised images' spread through satellites present a 'consumer model' of happiness through so many goods and dollars (or Euros eventually). Expensive studies in foreign countries to earn dollars are the way to somehow be a part of this model (happy world?).

Faced with this image, the great majority of African children are condemned to feel like drop-outs, poor, second or third class and unfulfilled by a scheme totally different and 'deviant' from *African values* which still are present in their 'cultural DNA'.

The good development that we advocate must include all African children and offer them various chances of being educated and empowered at any stage of their development and thus for him and her to build and express their energies, to contribute to the development of a society that she or he will have helped to create through their own culture dreams and aspirations and not the ones of a rich and faraway continent.

The African model must not apply only to its 'elite children'. It must also support the young domestic servant who attends evening classes after a working day in order to improve, to blossom and develop her family and society. African economic development (nowadays expressed by NEPAD, the New Partnership for Africa's Development) will include those who 'have learned how to work' or will not exist.

Building on child inclusion and participation is a real stake for contemporary and future Africa.

Notes

1. A questionnaire was launched by MAEJT and two other regional networks of child-led organisations at the beginning of 2005 to measure whether the 'world is getting fit...for us'.

2. This appears clearly in the answers to their questionnaire whereby they ask adults to 'respect what they have signed'.

Chapter 19

Working with Working Children in India

Nandana Reddy

How our work with children began

It was the summer of 1977. We, a small group of trade unionists, working with the informal, unorganised sector, were flush with the glow of victory. Having been a part of the underground movement during the state of emergency in India, we had successfully contributed to restoring democracy. It was the dawn of a new era. There was optimism and hope with the coming to power of the first opposition government in India and we were involved in nation building of a different kind.

The discourse regarding the developmental path India should follow was, among others, around the Gandhi, Nehru and Lohia models, all indigenous, home-grown prototypes. We would have none of the foreign variety. The world was a different place then. Globalisation was a distant murmur and United Nations (UN) agencies had a positive agenda. Civil society participation took on a new meaning. The power of people's movements had proved significant – we could even bring down an authoritarian state! The new challenge was to protect democracy and make it participatory, ensuring the accountability of the state to its citizens at all times.

To meet this challenge we believed that we needed to strengthen people's movements – be they trade unions, women's movements, struggles of the poor or the homeless – beginning with the most marginalised. The creation of politically motivated social (people's) organisations was a primary objective and we began with working children as they were one of the most vulnerable groups in society.

In our work with the working class we had encountered a large percentage of children in sectors such as street vendors, restaurants, recycling garbage and small-scale industries. We embarked on this path with working children, carrying some of the principles that were integral to our work with the informal sector of labour, and it has led us to a vision of the 'big picture' of participatory democracy suffused with the hues of equality and egalitarianism.

I remember the first public meeting I addressed in the Peenya industrial estate (then one of the largest industrial estates in South Asia), sharing the stage with stalwarts such as Michael Fernandes. Nervous because of my young age and inexperience, I noticed that the first ten rows of our audience were filled with little children, all clutching lunch boxes.

I was concerned and curious, but my colleagues dismissed this with 'Children always come for the *tamasha*.' I was not convinced and went down to talk to these children (9 to 17 years old) after the meeting and found that they were all working in the industrial estate. Four out of every ten had suffered an industrial accident – the loss of an eye, finger or hand. They were all enthusiastic about the formation of a trade union. They wanted *nyaya* or justice and were willing to fight for it.

My trade union colleagues advised me against taking up the issue of child labour, which they felt was sticky ground and a non-issue. They felt that child workers reduced the bargaining power of adult workers (in some cases nearly 40 to 60 per cent of a workforce were children); they were not supposed to be there in the first place and took away jobs that could have been adult jobs. So the argument went! In practice, however, the situation was very different. The jobs that children did were not jobs that adults would do, certainly not adult males. They were the most menial chores – difficult, repetitive, often hazardous and demeaning.

From the perspective of working children, work was a means of survival. Recycling garbage gave instant employment to migrant children. If one was lucky to get a job in a technical or mechanical unit such as motor repair, tool making or garments, you learned a trade/skill. For girls it was an escape from the drudgery of home chores, increased bargaining power at home and the possibility of postponing marriage. It was a backdoor entry into the formal sector; it provided a sense of dignity, self-worth, an identity and a sense of participation.

The children wanted a law that serves them

The children became the most active members of the union. They led rallies, shouted slogans the loudest and attended every meeting, but as a trade union we could do very little for them. The formal sector, governed by legislation banning children below the age of 14 years, was silent on the issue of older children and the informal sector (not covered by legislation) did not provide any protection to child workers – the rationale being that here it was difficult to enforce legislation.

This was slippery ground for collective bargaining and the only recourse we had was to file criminal charges in the case of severe industrial accidents and leverage a settlement for the child. The children were disappointed with the results. Demands to improve working conditions or safety often resulted in their dismissal, a situation they described as 'hitting us in the stomach where it hurts most'. We were helpless. The legal environment provided no visibility for working children. By banning their work in the formal sector and providing no protection in the others, it was virtually ignoring this group of young workers, denying them their rights as children, even their right to survival through work. It was literally sweeping the issue under the carpet and hoping that it would somehow go away.

The children wanted to change this and so did we. We embarked on a parallel project to draft a bill for child labour. The children could not visualise a situation without poverty and approached the problem from the premise that their need to work was a given and would not change. Within this frame they asked for protection from harmful or hazardous work, equal wages for equal work, a medical insurance that was simple, access to education and vocational training and a career development fund that would mature when they turned 18 years instead of a provident fund.

We, on the other hand, viewed legislation as a tool to increase the visibility of child workers, provide them a platform for securing their rights through collective bargaining, and ensure that all initiatives were in their best interest. We also intended that the legislation would differentiate between work and labour, protect work and eliminate labour by providing viable and sustainable alternatives, and in the long term address basic causes. The draft bill integrated the two approaches.

Once the Child Labour – Prohibition, Regulation and Development Draft Bill was prepared, the children were keen to take the next logical step – of presenting this to the government and converting it into a legislation. We requested the chief minister (CM) of Karnataka, Ramakrishna Hegde, to be present at a presentation.

As labour was a concurrent subject, the CM suggested that rather than working for a state legislation, it would be possible to try for a central legislation. With the help of Margaret Alva, the bill was presented to the parliamentary committee and the labour ministers' conference. The broad premise of the draft was accepted and Sri Anjaya, the union labour minister, constituted a committee to draft the government bill consisting of secretaries from the ministries of labour, education and parliamentary affairs and some of us, representatives of CWC (Concerned for Working Children). This result was an improved version of the draft as we had access to more information and resources, including constitutional and legal experts.

By the time the government bill was ready, Sri Sangma was the labour minister. The bill was discussed by the cabinet, mutilated and a very weak version finally passed by a joint session of Parliament. The major problem with the act was that it focused only on prohibition and regulation of child labour. The development component had been excluded and was left to be tackled by an action plan that was not mandatory. Child *labour* and *work* were not clearly defined and the alternatives for children working in hazardous occupations were neither comprehensive nor an improvement on their present situation.

The children developed their own agenda

However, this exercise helped generate a national debate on an issue otherwise neglected and ignored for decades. Many NGOs (non-governmental organisations) dedicated to child labour sprang up all over India and several research studies were conducted. The media began to focus on working children (though not always to their benefit) and numerous interventions were designed and implemented by state and national governments and supported by international agencies. Child workers gained an identity and the issue was placed on the national and international agenda.

The political environment in the late 1970s and early 1980s was conducive to bringing about change. Policy-makers and bureaucrats were more willing to listen. The agenda for India was a 'democratic reconstruction' based on the principles of human and fundamental rights, and people's participation. Though on the child labour front we confronted general ignorance, it did evoke compassion, concern and curiosity. There was also the time and space to give it deep thought, examine situations and consequences and evolve sustainable solutions.

The emergence of a nuanced understanding of work and labour made possible an intelligent debate on the question of child work and child labour. Consequently it was recognised that certain work arenas were also learning arenas and contributed to a child's education and these were actually good for children from all economic and social milieus.

As the Child Labour Act fell short of our expectation and was a disappointment for the children, we decided to practise what we preached, to intervene at a practical level and set up micro models that we could learn from and then upscale. The children decided to form their own union as they felt that their concerns differed from those of adult workers and to avoid conflicting interests. They launched Bhima Sangha in 1989. They also declared 30 April, one day before May Day, as Child Labour Day. They saw the right to organise as a means to alter their situation, improve the quality of their lives, and transform it from one where they were forced to work to one where they did not have to work. They wanted to move from being mere recipients to active participants in determining policies affecting them. They did not see it as just a means to improve working conditions.

Bhima Sangha was taken seriously. Soon they were in a position to negotiate with the state government, improve health-care services for street children, move the location of ration shops to more convenient areas, demand schools and day-care centres and grow forests. Bhima Sangha had arrived; child workers were respected, their organisations taken seriously.

We launched the Toofan Programme in 1995. Since then they have been interacting with local governments using their Makkala Panchayats (children's councils) as a base and through the tripartite task forces that have been set up as link bodies. In several remote villages of South India a peaceful revolution gathered momentum. Children and young persons from extremely marginalised communities living in hierarchical, paternalistic and feudalistic communities were organising themselves, participating in the planning of their own villages. They were gently but firmly breaking down caste and gender barriers. They were identifying their problems and negotiating solutions with their local governments. They began to write their history and actively influence their own destinies.

International challenges

In December 1997 working children representing movements from three continents – Africa, Asia and Latin America – arrived in the small village of Kanyana, Kundapur, on the west coast of South India for the first international meeting of working children. Working children's movements with a long history of struggle in the defence of their rights and for recognition of political and social protagonism came together to share and discuss their concerns and pledge solidarity. This was initiated by the International Working Group on Child Labour, facilitated by CWC and Bhima Sangha and supported by numerous organisations and individuals from around the world.

Children spent two weeks sharing experiences of work, organisation and political action. They presented unified positions on the need to organise politically, to represent themselves and on the right to be consulted by planners at local, national and international levels. It was here that they formed the International Movement of Working Children and began to fight for their right to representation.

However, movements of working children immediately encountered 'organised hostility' at all levels. At the international level this was most apparent at the International Labour Organization (ILO) conference organised by the government of the Netherlands. Eight child delegates from seven movements were invited, placed on an equal footing with adult delegates at the ILO conference.

The success that the children enjoyed in Amsterdam was short-lived. Soon there was organised resistance from the international trade union organisations – the British Trades Union Congress (TUC), the Scandinavian Labour Organisation (SLO), the International, Confederation of Free Trade Unions (ICFTU) and others. Though the International Movement of Working Children had been invited to the next ILO conference in Oslo, Norway, the invitation was withdrawn at the very last minute. The trade unions, who should have been working children's natural allies, were the strongest opponents.

The International Working Group on Child Labour (IWGCL), set up by the Defence for Children International and the International Society for Prevention of Child Abuse and Neglect, was initially mandated to conduct studies in 36 countries and recommend strategies for solving the problems faced by working children. However, the IWGCL gradually began playing a proactive role in international advocacy and influencing policy on child labour and children's rights. In partnership with the International Movement for Working Children it was recognised as a major player and grew to be a counter to the WTO (World Trade Organization). As the world social and political forum for working children it began to upset existing centres of power and threaten power relations.

By 1998 the IWGCL was a major player globally and children's voices were being heard at all policy-making forums. It was becoming more difficult for strategies that were 'anti-children' to be passed. The powers that be were frustrated and after a lot of contrived manipulation the IWGCL was dismantled. Ironically, even the agencies expected to care for children's rights supported this move as they realised that standing by the IWGCL would mean risking their funding bases and international status.

This was followed by very precise strategy of co-option. Trade unions lowered the age for membership to 'youth wings', creating a kind of child labour subgroup. Strong pressure was exerted on developing nations in the form of social sanctions, trade boycotts and labelling. International agencies began to toe the line and the US took control of the International Programme for the Elimination of Child Labour (IPEC) of the ILO. The dismantling of UN agencies was almost complete, further compounded by the introduction of structural adjustment by the WTO.

The consequences of globalisation

The world is now undergoing the third wave of global colonisation, this time by multinational corporations, with economic institutions such as the International Monetary Fund (IMF), WTO and World Bank (WB) growing stronger and pervading every nook and cranny of our public and personal lives. With the dismantling of social structures and contempt for indigenous knowledge and history, the removal of social nets and interference with natural cycles, globalisation is changing the nature of land use and agriculture and sacrificing the rich culture and biodiversity of our planet. The new *mantra* of the present model of globalisation is the wooing of the middle class. Commoditisation and competition to capture a large chunk of the market are key words. Increasing purchasing power through provision of credit is the norm.

With the privatisation of basic services such as education, energy, water, transport and telecommunications and reduction of people's participation in the governance of common goods like forests, land, air, water, fuel, manure and forest produce, increase in urban poverty and the displacement of the poor, children have become the most vulnerable victims of this global war for ultimate resource control. This is a subtle form of genocide.

The WTO, WB, multinational corporations, even the ILO and some national governments have become the institutions of globalisation, propagating a 'development with a human face' to sell their brand of colonisation. This is more dangerous as we do not know what is behind the mask. Now the biggest threat to our children is a model of development that is being thrust on us – violent, dehumanised and out of sync with the natural order and masked with a 'human face'. This is undermining a 'humane model of development' that evolved naturally between humankind and nature, maintained a natural balance and gave people control over their lives. With all the problems this might have entailed, it still maintained a respect and affection for the planet that provides us sustenance and sustained the self-esteem of the individual as a member of a community.

In the past few years we have witnessed several alarming trends in India. Fundamentalist forces have become more widespread with the active spearheading of communal violence and terror among the minority communities in the country. The government is promoting policies and programmes that involve compulsion and punitive action especially in the areas of child labour and education. Ignoring this reality we continue with our 'raid, rescue and rehabilitation' strategy to eliminate child labour, forcibly removing children from their work and putting them into 'educational institutions' that are non-existent or ill-prepared to receive them. On pointing out the plight of such children, we have often heard that 'this is a sacrifice we have to make for development.'

On the whole, the attempt of the government to invest the state with increased power and control succeeded to a fair extent. This has been a very troubled time for social action groups like the Concerned for Working Children (CWC), where the climate is not favourable for freedom of thought and democratic action. We find ourselves battling a new enemy.

The emergence of working children

In the past few years we have seen a trend to modify or blur definitions. There is no distinction between work and labour. In the child labour context, all work is seen as bad. Similarly, all education is good. Participation has come to be understood as only social or cultural and not political participation and so children's participation equals dancing and singing at conferences, not voicing opinions. Now with the commercialisation of education, learning is no more for the sake of knowledge but profit, and civil society organisations are seen as extensions of the state.

Never in the recent past have children been as vulnerable as they are now. This may seem a contradiction, since there are so many global and national initiatives related to child labour and education. However, many of these very programmes are responsible for this present situation. Though these programmes profess to uphold the rights of children, several of them violate them. The rounding up of 'out of school' (working) children and forcing them into formal schools has resulted in illegal confinement, penalties, compulsion and unspeakable trauma for the children involved and their families. The state government claims that they have enrolled 250,000 children into formal schools, but after the first wave of enrolment only 20 per cent have been retained. Working children are seeking employment in more and more invisible occupations. They have developed a fear of all government departments and their 'surveys' and now have a high level of distrust for any initiative that seeks to involve them.

The raid and rescue operations on child workers to comply with trade sanctions; the *forcible enrolment* into schools as a part of the compulsory education intervention; the refusal by ILO to *recognise unions and movements of working children* are illustrative of the attempts of the 'powerful' to silence the 'weak', in this case children.

The environment for a debate on child labour is now clouded by suppression of facts. There is a fear of admitting the existence of child workers. The subject evokes irritation, impatience and discomfort. Global pressure does not allow for the time and space to design sustainable solutions and the norm is 'quick fix' and 'knee jerk' reactions. Child labourers have been swept under the carpet, hidden and rotated in a time warp.

As for child workers, they cannot raise issues related to work or labour. They have no room for collective bargaining and no say in defining the alternatives or rehab package. So they confine themselves to raising only social and developmental concerns which are also community concerns.

What does work mean to children today? It means life, survival, the acquiring of skills, dignity and an identity. However, unlike the past it also means seclusion, isolation, discrimination, exploitation, oppression and annihilation (eradication).

But amazingly, through all this, the children have retained their sense of optimism and faith. They act on issues that confront them and not only know their problems but often the solutions as well. They continue to question the status quo and retain faith in the possibility of change. Above all, they believe that they have a right to participate in developing the solution.

A union of working children

Working children have initiated unions/movements, both regional networks and the International Movement of Working Children (see Swift 2001). They have their own newspapers, community radio/audio news programmes and carry out their own documentation. Bhima Sangha has undertaken campaigns and struggles against alcohol and drug abuse, child marriage, and developed and implemented drought prevention and management strategies. They have acquired the skills and tools to conduct surveys and Participatory Rapid Apraisals. They engage in layered analysis to arrive at definitions and use sophisticated methods to prioritise issues (see Bhima Sangha and Makkala Panchayat 2001; CWC 2002). They even develop five-year plans.

Here children are involved in taking decisions at the level of local government. Their two significant achievements are the creation of a 'political space or forum' to present their views and concerns and the setting up of a process and structure to practise true democracy.

It is often said that the stream of globalisation cannot be stopped. Most people, even those who oppose it, seem to believe that the present model of globalisation is here to stay. However, the Kundapur example shows that it is possible to challenge the very basis of globalisation and centralised, undemocratic decision-making. Such processes can be a strong counter.

In the early days of the Panchayat Toofan Programme in Kundapur, the then president of the Panchayat and the Makkala Mitra, Sir Balanna, had asked the Department of Women and Child Welfare for an Anganwadi (community meeting and care centre for children and mothers living in poverty). The department agreed but not at the suggested location. The president insisted, stating:

> The children and the women have asked for the Anganwadi where it will be most convenient and they are right. It is the children of our panchayat that need it, the place belongs to us and the programme is here to serve the needs of our children. If you are unable to meet their requirements we suggest you close down your other three Anganwadis as well.

Balanna had the courage to say 'no' to programmes that did not respond to the real needs of his people only because of the active and informed participation of children and thereby the whole community. Prior to the involvement of children and their participation in the governance of the Panchayat, he had not understood the needs of the children of his village nor had the courage to question the relevance of schemes thrust on him. Now he is confident that he, the Panchayat, with the help of the adults and children would be able to run the Anganwadis without the support of the department.

These may be small beginnings but, as they say, little streams make an ocean. The present model of globalisation can only be challenged this way, by such people and processes. The children of Kundapura taluk have shown the way and adults have been inspired to take up the challenge to struggle for true decentralisation and participatory democracy.

Though the strengthening of civil society and citizen participation are catchphrases of democratic discourse in India, the nature of that civil society and the object of that participation are today being moulded by a specific interpretation of what it means to be a citizen in India, where civil society organisations are now seen as an extension of the state. The answer to this problem lies in the construction of a new definition of civil society, a highly participatory civil society filled with political content.

The children of Bhima Sangha and the Makkala Panchayat have given 'democracy' and 'civil society participation' new meaning and revitalised their Panchayats. They are proud, eager to contribute to the positive change of their communities and know that they have the ability to do so. These children are firmly rooted in their soil, closely woven into the Indian social and political fabric. They have become powerful agents of change. They are fighting the same battles as those fought by the working class and women's movements. They face the same questions regarding their ability, intentions and integrity. They are struggling for the right of entry to political space. They are making tremendous sacrifices because this struggle means a lot to them.

In order to hear the voice of children, as also with other marginalised groups, we need to struggle for a *humane development model* and not *development with a human face.*

There is a South African saying that 'Until the lions have their own historians, history will be written by the hunters.' What is needed is to enable children to write their own history and reshape society closer to their vision of a better world.

Chapter 20

Dialogue and Empowerment for Change: The Influence of Organisations of Working Children in Southeast Asia on the Social Status of Working Children

Dominique Pierre Plateau

In September 1997 11 working children from Cambodia, Indonesia, the Philippines and Thailand who participated in the Children's Forum and Regional Consultation Against the Most Intolerable Forms of Child Labour organised by Save the Children, ILO–IPEC (International Labour Organization – International Programme for the Elimination of Child Labour), UNICEF (United Nations Children's Fund) and other regional actors in order to produce a Southeast Asian perspective on child labour in the International Child Labour Conference in Oslo (October 1997) proposed that 'Communities, parents, NGOs (non-governmental organisations), and GOs (government organisations) should work in equal partnerships and in consultation with the working children' (RWG-CL 1997).

Over the years that followed, developing and promoting an identity and a role as social actors became one of the main objectives of groups and organisations of working children in the region. The Indonesian working children who participated in the Training of Working Children on the Convention on the Rights of the Child organised by the Education and Information Centre for Child Rights (KKSP) and Child Workers in Asia (CWA) at Medan, Indonesia, from 7 to 11 August 2000, asked for the 'Involvement of children in making plans and making decisions towards problems faced by children interested and the faith of this nation' (KKSP 2000).

This chapter provides insights into the efforts of groups and organisations of working children in Southeast Asia in order to obtain social recognition. It begins by exploring the environment of change that characterises the region in order to describe the effects on the child labour situation and lives of working children as well as surroundings in which international and local organisations strive to promote children's rights. It attempts to demonstrate that in a climate increasingly supportive of social participation, working children, as individuals and organisations, are beginning to develop a sense of identity as social actors in their own right.

The chapter observes that largely through communication efforts and activities, organisations of working children in Southeast Asia have opened a dialogue with adults and other children toward mutual understanding and respect. This, in more than one way, challenges traditional perceptions of children and youth as well as relationships between adults and children. Most importantly this is a process that increases working children's belief in their ability to influence change, strengthen political and social knowledge and awareness of rights and support greater levels of responsibility.

Southeast Asia: a complex and diverse region

Eleven countries make up this region of varied cultures, languages and historical processes. Among them are Indonesia with the fourth highest population of the world (235 million) and East Timor (almost one million), one of the smallest and the poorest with a gross national income per capita of US$500.

For centuries the fortunes of Southeast Asia were determined by centres of power elsewhere. The region found itself at the intersection of Indian and Chinese religious, commercial, cultural and political influences. It saw rivalry between colonial powers and went through years of acquiescence to them. During the 1980s and most of the 1990s Southeast Asia experienced economic growth at a rate unseen in world history before being hit by a severe financial crisis in 1997. The economic recovery that followed has been patchy and slow (Church 2003). Yet the region remains an area of new prosperity, characterised by large disparities of wealth between and within countries where all countries, to one extent or another, are in transition: from command to market economy, from and into conflict, or from poverty to relative wealth. In the aftermath of the attack on the World Trade Center in New York on 11 September 2001 the region is feeling the effects of a global climate that is more uncertain (Church 2003). Some countries like Thailand are beginning to confront new problems such as a deteriorating social security with the institution of the family becoming weaker, rising divorce, crime and accident rates. Child mortality reduction and primary school enrolment were two of the notable achievements in the last decade of the twentieth century. However, major challenges remain that include reducing malnutrition and combating sexual exploitation of children (UNICEF EAPRO 2003).

Issues that affect both the region and child labour

The population of Southeast Asia (in total 560 million of whom 50 per cent are aged less than 20 years) remains rural in majority, working in low-technology agriculture in which child work is necessary for survival. This is particularly true for the many ethnic minorities who have barely been touched by economic development and suffer from considerable discrimination, making their children particularly vulnerable to exploitation. In some countries transition from command to market economy has led to a new form of poverty and national gains in wealth have led to increased but often unacknowledged child labour.

In several countries people are moving from rural areas to cities hoping to share in the new prosperity or as a result of conflicts that disrupt local economies and scatter families. Regional disparities in wealth have fuelled increased migration throughout the region with children among those exploited as illegal migrants. The financial crisis showed just how fragile the new prosperity can be. In Indonesia, which was harder hit than other countries, the number of street children in all urban centres has visibly increased since 1997.

Child labour trends in Southeast Asia

Statistical information on child labour in Southeast Asia is scarce but ILO estimates that in Asia as a whole there are more children working than on any other continent although the proportion working is smaller than in Africa. Six out of the 11 countries that make up the region have ratified ILO Convention 182 against the worst forms of child labour. Domestic work, fishing, mining, rag picking, construction, particularly common among children of migrant families, as well as commercial sex work, are among the most common worst forms of child labour in the region. Agriculture still employs most children although child employment in farming is declining overall while more children are entering urban jobs as a result of rural to urban migration.

Over the past decade there has been a 20 per cent decrease in the number of 10 to 14-year-olds working in the formal sector. This reflects the fact that employers are now more aware of labour law and tend not to employ children. A further trend is that formal sector employers are evading employment costs and labour law by subcontracting production to home workers, including children, in home-based production (UNICEF 2003).

The main concerns of international players in the region are trafficking of women and children and street children. These do not represent the largest number of working children in any national context yet the financial resources available from donors and campaigns of international actors have affected government perceptions of child labour and effectively hijacked the child labour agenda (Ennew and Plateau 2003).

Issues affecting children's rights

In general, Southeast Asian governments are committed to children's welfare. Progress and understanding of related issues is encouraged and facilitated by international actors who are constant elements in almost all countries. Save the Children's interventions, for instance, aim at building national capacities on children's rights in creating child-friendly environments, ensuring equity and inclusion, impact and sustainability. One strength of the region as a whole is the high level of collaboration that exists between international stakeholders which makes planning and joint advocacy possible.

Political changes have been taking place in several countries and this is having a positive effect in the region. In Thailand democracy seems now secure, while in Indonesia the leadership is apparently committed to equal rights for all (Church 2003). Southeast Asia has a wide variety of forms of governance. Organisations like Save the Children have to work with authoritarian regimes, socialist administrations, nations with ongoing internal conflicts, countries recovering from war and others adjusting to economic change. As a result local actors differ from country to country. In some cases, as in the Philippines and Thailand, a well-developed NGO network provides a wealth of partners. In others, such as Vietnam and Laos, local NGOs are a new concept and civil society partners in these countries are quasi-governmental, nationwide organisations such as the Women's Federation or Youth Union.

Groups and organisations of working children in Southeast Asia: role and influence

Most groups and organisations of working children in the region were created in the 1990s for the purpose of providing working and other children with specific services. The oldest, the Child Labour Club (Thailand), was created in 1982 with the aim of providing child workers with opportunities for self-development. Children and young workers aged 13 to 18 years, mostly migrant workers, make up the Club's membership which started with 80 and reached 350 members from 240 factories in Bangkok and its environs in 1996.

In Cambodia the Children's Committee was established on 20 September 1995 by children from different backgrounds such as students, residents of orphanages and pagodas, child workers and residents of NGO centres in order to promote educational awareness, cultural knowledge, as well as environmental awareness and sport. In Indonesia, Tualang Media Anak Merdika (Media of Free Children) started its activities in 1992 with a team of five children to publish a newsletter 'from children for the children'. The Indonesian Committee for Creative Education for Child Labour (KOMPAK) was created at the same time by working children in factories around Jakarta with the aim of implementing a Village School Programme of non-formal education for working children. The Rumah Singgah, also in Indonesia, was established by working children in bus stations who no longer stayed with their parents and lived in the streets. The Rumah Singgah supports children in their working environment and provides non-formal education in the evening.

In Lao PDR (People's Democratic Republic) the Donkoi Children's Development Centre (DCDC) was initiated by Church World Services in 1998 for children of poor backgrounds to participate in income-generating activities such as weaving, mat making, carpentry, rice planting and gardening. About 70 young people aged between 6 and 20 years make up DCDC's membership, planning and implementing activities with the help of an adult volunteer. Some of these children are school drop-outs and former migrant children to Thailand.

In the Philippines Samahan at Ugnayan ng mga Manggagawang Pantahanan ng Pilipinas (SUMAPI) was founded in 1995 with facilitation from the Visayan Forum Foundation in order to rescue abused child domestic workers. SUMAPI now involves over 3000 child domestic workers and former child domestic workers in four major cities of the country.

Several of these organisations are managed by children (for example, CAMP [Child Assistance for Mobilisation and Participation in Cambodia], KOMPAK), others by children and adults together (SUMAPI, DCDC), and others are facilitated by adult organisations such as, for example, the Child Labour Club supported by the Foundation for Child Development (FCD); the DCDC supported by Church World Services; SUMAPI by the Visayan Forum Foundation; and CAMP supported by Save the Children and UNICEF in Cambodia.

However, as time has passed, all groups and organisations developed their own identities and role as social actors. SUMAPI members, together with a network of advocates, have worked for the passing of a law that regulates domestic work and provides for special actions to help child domestic workers. During 1997 in Thailand members of the Child Labour Club submitted a petition that sought the following:

1. We urgently request an increase in the minimum wage, as the cost of living, today, is very high.

2. We appeal to the government and the general public to pay serious attention to the child labour problem.

3. We ask employers to provide clean lodging, wholesome meals and health care for child employees. In the event of an accident, child workers must be able to access medical care and recovery/rehabilitation programmes.

4. We appeal to the government to establish a social security system which provides protection for child workers, in all work places.

5. We request the government to provide educational facilities for rural children up to grade 12.

6. We think there should be more employment opportunities – job creation schemes – for the rural people in their own areas.

7. We ask the government and all agencies concerned to provide social services to child workers i.e. sports, camping, recreational activities.

8. We draw attention to the urgent need for comprehensive inspections of all factories employing children illegally.

9. We ask why society does not promote/provide support-programmes for child workers' self-development schemes; for instance, part-time education or occupational training which facilitates an ongoing education programme that child workers can attend while also going to work.

Indeed, groups and organisations of working children in Southeast Asia have become influential promoters of children's rights. Among the most active actors one finds CAMP that was formed in April 2000 by members of the Children's Committee who, as they reached their eighteenth birthdays, decided to take the Committee's work forward in promoting children's rights using recognition, potential and experience. With help from Save the Children and UNICEF Cambodia they participated in the UN (United Nations) Special Session on Children where they helped promote children's opinions. In the Philippines members of Child Labourers and Advocates for Social Participation (CLASP) 'envision a just society that liberates us from work and child abuse, respects our right: for survival, protection, participation and empowerment; whereby we can live fully and be with our families and other citizens; that promotes the welfare of the children'.

One main aim of groups and organisations of working children comprises developing communication for change beyond conventional child-led advocacy. The mission statement of CLASP, for example, reads:

> We believe all the children have human rights, need to be cared, loved, heard and involved in child activities related to our development. To have a role in the society, and responsibility towards other children; and to have the strength and capacity to unite and promote our welfare. We actively participate in actions and programs concerning our situation, community, government and other institution that protect our rights:
>
> - To take part in child labourers campaign that would increase public awareness, and reach out to other children to protect our rights and goals.
>
> - To appeal to other sector and government to promote our objectives in fighting abuse and exploitation of child labourers, and to provide us a program that would alleviate our lives.
>
> - To coordinate with other groups and institutions that would strengthen the movement against child labour.

CLASP's activities also include promotion of children's rights targeting the government and other institutions and the referral of cases of exploitation and abuse to the relevant authorities.

Interventions by other organisations include public information facilitated by the production of newsletters and other awareness-raising materials, countless radio programmes on children's rights (Radio *Anak* in Indonesia) and representation in adult meetings as well as direct actions. Training on communications is regularly offered to new members such as 'building bridges among children' in the Summer Art Camps held by CLASP. Visits to factories and networking activities frequently occur. Among those recently held was CLASP's association with the Children and Youth as Peace Builders (CAP) which is a global network for peace.

Support from adult organisations

Sustained efforts of groups and organisations of working children in Southeast Asia in developing communication for change and promoting children as social actors who hold rights have made the adult world progressively aware that (working) children are not passive victims but partners in promoting positive change. This recognition is behind the commitment and support of local, regional and international adult organisations to groups and organisations of children while all increasingly tend to work together in partnerships that provide channels and technical support for information dissemination, capacity building and other forms of support including financial support.

Child Workers in Asia (CWA) was established in 1985 as a support group for working children in Asia and the NGOs working with them, and figures among key regional actors. It brings together over 50 groups and organisations working on child labour in 14 countries (South and Southeast Asia) with the vision that 'Asian societies without child labour exploitation where working children have their best interests protected by all social sectors.' CWA facilitates expertise and experience sharing between NGOs and encourages their collaboration in jointly responding to the exploitation of working children in the region. CWA has been a venue for interaction between big and small NGOs since its inception, promoting the rights of working children within the contexts of the UN Convention on the Rights of the Child and the ILO Conventions related to child labour; assisting and facilitating the formation of support groups for working children at country level and seeking new ways of protecting working children. CWA believes 'in the vitality and wisdom of child workers themselves', and that 'the problem of child labour cannot be solved without the participation of children' (CWA 1985).

In 1998 CWA became a founding member of the Regional Working group on Child Labour – South, Southeast, East Asia and the Pacific (RWG-CL) which was an experimental initiative in team work that also involved the International Save the Children Alliance represented by the Save the Children Sweden Regional Office for Southeast Asia, World Vision International, Asia and the Pacific Regional Office and the World Vision Foundation of Thailand, the ILO-IPEC Sub Regional Office for Southeast Asia, UNICEF East Asia and the Pacific Regional Office and the Thailand Office. RWG-CL draws on the diversity of its constituent members to develop projects to strengthen the capacity of organisations in addressing the worst forms of child labour, particularly in promoting the involvement of working children in actions to eliminate the worst forms of child labour and in advocacy for social behaviour change.

Among other regional actors the International Save the Children Alliance is represented in most countries in the region through its national and international members and works in partnership with many local organisations to promote children's rights as well as formation of new child-led organisations such as the Children's Council in Hong Kong that is supported by Save the Children Sweden and Kids Link Fiji, supported by Save the Children Fiji.

Conclusion

Over recent years groups and organisations of working children in the region have accumulated numerous achievements. These achievements provide overall support and encouragement to other projects and organisations, including children's organisations, who promote children's rights in a broader way. The main impact on the situation of children in the region is 'empowerment', a term which is often heard and in Southeast Asian terms, particularly in Thailand and the Philippines, means a process 'of forming a social conscience, and the understanding that children are part of local and global communities' (CWA 2001).

The process instils knowledge (of rights, laws, forms of abuse and exploitation, and so on) and skills (resilience, confidence) that equip working and other children in the pursuit of recognition as social actors and all children as a social class who are looking beyond personal circumstances. In the Philippines it is often added that 'empowerment' does not mean turning children into adults or creating an elite group. Children wish to remain children (CWA 2001).

These groups and organisations of working children in the region have been contributing meaningfully to improving the status of all children in societies where children and youth are traditionally not encouraged to express their views, let alone participate in decision-making processes, where children are maltreated not because they are children, but because they are accorded a lowly status because of their age, gender, size and even birth order (Protacio de Castro in International Save the Children Alliance 2003).

Dialogue and communication make up a culturally acceptable way of bringing about changes in context and culture where adult authority cannot be challenged or when there are few or no local structures for dialogue between adults, policy-makers and children and youth (Protacio de Castro in International Save the Children Alliance 2003).

As children's rights, not least those of working children, are still considered more as privileges by most adults in far too many instances and as the power that adults exercise over children continues to be supported by culturally acceptable practices legitimised by the states (Protacio de Castro in International Save the Children Alliance 2003), the role of groups and organisations of working children as partners in promoting change in order to improve the social status of children in countries in the region remains essential.

Chapter 21

Do the Participation Articles in the Convention on the Rights of the Child Present Us with a Recipe for Children's Citizenship?

Brian Milne

What is intended by 'participation' described by the Convention on the Rights of the Child (CRC)? It nominates a few basic privileges such as rights to form views, enjoy freedom of expression, freedom of thought, conscience and religion and of association and assembly. At face value, Articles 12 to 15 describing those rights appear to offer a great deal toward children assuming an active role in democratic civil society. There are very important counter-balances in Articles 3 (best interests of the child) and 5 (direction and guidance in the exercise of their rights by adults) that can justify any or all of the ostensibly liberating rights being denied or withheld, even imaginably until majority is attained.

However, it is even clearer that the CRC does not go all the way to conveying 'citizenship' since none of the pertinent articles elucidate duties and responsibilities that accompany the rights. Of course, there are ambiguities attached to the idea of duties and responsibilities that have made sociological discourse of the kind expounded by Thomas Marshall (1950, 1964) a much debated notion. Nevertheless, some ideas very deeply entrenched in the concept of citizenship produce an ideal of what makes a person a citizen: we may perhaps call them 'good' and 'bad'. The good citizen is he or she who is morally and socially principled, which is to say obeys and follows the law, conforms to numerous societal norms within the home via neighbourhood to nation, unthinkingly pays taxes and other revenues, is politically responsible by regularly taking part in elections without being overtly oppositional or active at any political extreme and thus, broadly speaking, does not stand out in the crowd without laudable reason. They fulfil duties and responsibilities. People who indulge in contrary qualities are bad citizens, irresponsible individuals who may temporarily or permanently be excluded from full citizenship in some countries; for instance, offenders against the law may be deprived of political rights, access to economic resource, certain benefits or perhaps withdrawal of a driving licence, being barred from their normal profession and so on.

Here we may turn to working children. They often work in spite of laws prohibiting them from so doing. While there may be apposite arguments about children who are forced into work as against those who do so out of choice, the outcome appears very similar. Those children are outside the law; they are not respectable. We can then very easily turn to organised child workers. Whether it can be justifiably identified with a distinct political party or lobby is largely irrelevant since working children's movements almost certainly demand what governments will oppose. However, given that in western nations especially there is general distaste for politicisation of children as a backlash against activities in the 1960s and 1970s, where there is overt political activity they are less 'respectable'. They are simply not meeting exacting standards that justify inclusion because no matter how responsible actions may be in practice, they are considered wrong, thus privileges that bestow citizenship are not granted.

Working children are also outside of the law because they do not pay income taxes, health, social security and other welfare contributions. What they do generate and return into an economy is, needless to say, overlooked because of the generally illicit nature of their income generation.

The CRC entirely overlooks important economic and political rights, going only a single step of several toward integrating children into civil society as bearers of full rights through a few participatory articles. It uses that stride forward very convincingly for the majority of observers. It has been restricted to limited application in very few domains such as children's councils and parliaments, development work using mainly participatory rapid appraisal methods, a few conferences and meetings and a small number of 'respectable' children's movements.

There are two notable flaws. First, while the prescribed participation rights are for all children, in real terms only a small minority have access to activities mentioned and, second, rather than merging adult and child worlds they tend to further segregate them. Indeed this is largely common to the acceptable face of children's 'good' use of CRC participatory rights and the 'bad' face of such projects as working children's movements, political and lobby groups such as environmental and animal rights groups. Since many children's activities often depend on adult patronage or are initiated by adults, they tend to be either soft or play-like facsimiles of 'grown up' counterparts. Many of them are measured against 'ladders' or similar devices which may serve to obscure their real position in civil society. Indeed, I imagine, sometimes genuinely discerning analysis may conclude some to be exploitative since they achieve the purpose of appearing to be forms of participation instigated by and for adults involved mainly for their own benefit.

So we see that children's participation in civil society and path to full citizenship depends on adult assessment of competence and capability, access offered by adults and estimation of the value of the contribution they might make. We thus need to deconstruct the position of children in society and look again at how participation that resembles citizenship can be achieved.

Some clues to how the door to citizenship may be opened are found in philosophical thought that began to describe human beings as bearers of rights. In the middle of the eighteenth century Jean-Jacques Rousseau (1762 and Boyd 1956) expounded a view that socio-economic inequality transformed natural independence and amorality into morally corrupting mutual dependence. That dependence cannot be recovered but the moral integrity of the individual can be achieved within democracy, wherein a form of social contract secures the common good. Moral autonomy is ensured by universal standards that describe the role of each individual in society. Debatably, he included children in his greater picture, but does not really describe individual or collective rights as we understand them today. Universal standards describe what we now think of as good and bad in the way we meet our obligations (duties and responsibilities) within society. In many respects he described the beginnings of how we now see democracy and the ideal setting for our understanding of citizenship; it was also a basic idea of the human being as a bearer of distinct rights.

Less than a century later, John Stuart Mill (1859) declared there an essentially 'weak' autonomy in which adults did not necessarily make wise, correct decisions. His highest value was liberty that gave people the right to choose for themselves. He included women but not children who he assumed too immature to take responsibility for risks involved in making personal decisions. 'Age of consent' divided adulthood from childhood. We regard that 'age of majority' today, the definition having changed over intervening centuries. In reality, his notion of the immature child has scarcely changed since, thus allowing us to 'guide' children according to 'evolving capacities' as Article 5. However, the concept of rights we use today was emerging very plainly. Of course, to fully appreciate the passage of philosophical vision toward the contemporary understanding of society requires at least a brief excursion through Hobbes, Kant, Hume, Locke and on via Marx, Durkheim, Tönnies, Weber and so on. Moreover, we need to bear in mind the fact that from at least the time of Mill through to Durkheim and Weber enormous economic and social change was transforming people's roles in civil society. Notions of human beings as citizens with rights, a place in democracy and far more control over personal destinies became the currency of not only intellectuals but individuals themselves. Those changes also saw an end of a world in which a more conservative and slowly adaptable order was able to receive innovation and gradually transform politically, albeit slowly, in accordance with less pragmatic visions of philosophers. Although an incomplete process today, the momentum for women to achieve equal rights with men began then. Despite that, what Mill thought is largely still valid in principle, albeit the world is far more regulated than in his time, thus choice is not always as free as he believed.

Another *force majeur* brought change, perhaps even distorting the path intellectuals may otherwise have taken the human race down. Industrialisation saw rapidly growing populations in enormous urban industrial centres with high population density and many other changes. Among them was the rate of progress in industrial technology that demanded a more skilled and specialised workforce that needed to be well disciplined and structured. It became a more businesslike world in which capitalism became the dominant ideology. Children began to be removed from industrial employment and taught how to acquiesce with what was expected of them through compulsory education where good behaviour, punctuality and other 'positive' qualities were inculcated alongside enough learning to provide education for future skilled and specialised workers. In chain to these developments a notion of social activism grew with trade unions growing in size and stature but selectively working only for membership to the exclusion of 'outsiders' such as children. Rapid increase in political awareness, through increasing activism until eventually universal franchise for adults was achieved, gave us what we understand to be political citizenship today. Children's employment generally declined as new laws were passed and both length of school days and number of years in compulsory education increased, contributing to defining children as we do today.

To attend school and, moreover, to complete at least the minimum number of years or grades with qualifications has contributed to the image of 'good' citizen. A person who has never attended school is regarded with contempt or pity according to context and whoever has been excluded or simply not achieved minimum qualification tends only to be regarded with derision. Although essentially a capitalist vision, much of what happened was transplanted into almost every modern social system and has greatly influenced and altered even the most tenacious traditional structures.

Thus, we now have a picture of the respectable citizen that does not entirely correspond with the philosophical notion of the human being as a bearer of rights who was emerging approximately 150 years ago. It is also a very Eurocentric impression that assumes a powerful and effective state with sufficient resources for provision of universal compulsory education with social and economic protection of its people. Where weak structures and scarce resources undermine the reality of universal schooling and work is the only available education, beside an economic activity, the image is not consistent with western standards.

Synonymously, we need to bear in mind the development of the welfare state and child protection policy that have defined and redefined childhood several times and moved them further away from autonomy toward confinement within protection. Above all else, best interests and guidance in the exercise of rights by children are defined by adults who are vulnerable to the influence of powerful trends like contemporary child protection attitudes and practices. To challenge those trends by allowing children autonomy, seen by some people as lack of supervision and protection, is to cast both adult caretakers and children out of 'respectable' society. They are not 'good' people.

Thus, where people are marginalised or poor and children are forced to take their own destiny into their own hands they are seen as 'bad' before all else. Marginality and extreme poverty are themselves stigmas that cast those entrapped by them outside of the norm. Thus, even in situations of extreme hardship it is equally difficult to justify the anomaly of allowing children to work. That simply does not conform to qualities that construct the idea of 'good'.

As for the extension of citizenship to children, it would appear that the façade created by participation as it manifests itself 'respectably' is little more than a gesture instead of a real step. In reality, children, irrespective of whether participant in good or bad activities, are no closer to sharing civil society with adults than before and the chance of this improving is small given the general lack of political and societal will to help them achieve that end.

Would full citizenship be the panacea for the child labour 'conundrum'? In itself it would not make their work legitimate but it would certainly reduce the likelihood that a working child be regarded a 'bad' person. It would most certainly dispense with the notion that *because* somebody is a child he or she should not work. However, because of how powerful agencies such as the International Labour Organization (ILO), World Bank, World Trade Organization (WTO) and national bodies such as the US Department of Labor have set goals to eliminate the worst forms of child labour, we might consider inverting that very argument. If such work was also eliminated for adults would we not then achieve the status quo? It is a difficult predicament we are in and could, thus, make it more complex. Could we ever really achieve such ideals anyway? Too many questions remain to be asked before being considered, let alone replied. Nevertheless, since citizenship apparently guarantees choice and opinion in democratic societies then rather than eliminate child labour the choice would need to be offered and adequately discussed before the type of solutions offered at present. Citizenship with all it promises achieves the aims and intentions of the CRC and more. However, since citizenship is itself a much debated notion that carries too many weaknesses, that idealised triumph of the franchise of the mass of humanity over the will of the few is still an experiment that remains to succeed.

If there is a solution then it will be found by those who support the cause for children's inclusion and genuinely believe in breaking down social barriers no less tenacious than racism, sexism, etc. Given the length of time women have been engaged in a similar cause we must equally allow time and patience. Above all else, we must step back from initiation of children's groups that then become segregated from all other adults. We naturally do need to make some allowance for stages of development and so on, but not protect children to the exclusion of their inclusion. The CRC does not, unfortunately, provide much guidance in this task since it is an instrument of law and in no sense a philosophical discourse. We urgently need to revisit philosophical thought and follow its path through to today and present-day philosophers and sociologists who offer a clear view of what citizenship is. We also need to reappraise the legal and moral change that created contemporary childhood. They are intellectual processes that we cannot avoid if we are to construct our arguments well. Of course, intellectual analyses in themselves do not offer enough; more depends on pragmatism. Thus, the solution rests in all of our hands but how to effect that change is a far greater question to which I certainly have no answer.

Part 6

Challenges and Perspectives
for Research and Policy

Chapter 22

Challenges for Social Research and Action with Working Children

Virginia Morrow

The past 15 years have seen a global shift in research into different aspects of working children's lives, and the symposium heard papers that involved children in research and action, using a range of different methods, that have enabled research-ers to gain insight into children's working lives from their points of view. In research and action terms, the standpoint from which children are viewed has shifted radically, from a position that sees children as passive victims whose devel-opment is threatened by their work activities, to a view of children who are actively contributing not only in their productive roles, but also to understandings of these roles through their involvement in research, by co-producing data about their everyday lives and involvement in work. However, the challenge now is to ensure that these methods and the data they produce are accepted, made meaningful and taken seriously by dominant institutions and organisations that have the capacity to bring about improvements in working children's lives.

This chapter draws upon comments made at the end of the conference when I was asked to discuss 'what can we learn from each other?', and is divided around four main themes: methods and standpoints, contexts, North/South reflections, and broader questions about politics and economics.

Methods and standpoints

Methods of research and action with working children in research projects were a key theme of the symposium, and discussions focused on the following areas. First, the importance of being clear and transparent about the methods used in research and participatory projects with working children was emphasised. This included reflecting on how particular methods work or don't work, and what is effective in research and action with working children; the importance of using multi-method approaches, in other words, using different ways of eliciting data from children, including creative methods; and using comparisons, asking for example why some children do not work. Second, definitional issues remain contested around concepts such as 'work' and 'labour', but in addition to this concepts like 'skill', 'competencies' and 'responsibility' were also discussed, and arguably still need to be deconstructed and better understood. In other words, what do these concepts look like from children's viewpoints? Third, models for analysis of data on child work/labour were also described (see Chapter 9 by McKechnie and Hobbs).

Further, there is a clear need to understand the dominant models of childhood held by policy-makers in national government departments (which may be contradictory between departments) and in international organisations (International Labour Organization, ILO) with the view to open a dialogue between researchers, activists and policy-makers on these issues.

Context

A second theme that was emphasised throughout the symposium was the importance of locating children's work experiences in context, and of understanding the centrality of the meaning of work for them. This included the importance of a sense of belonging for children that may arise from their involvement in work, sometimes in extremely disadvantageous circumstances (see chapter 5) and while this sense of belonging may be problematic and 'illusory', it may also afford children a strong sense of identity, even if the situations in which they are working are not ideal or desirable and are extremely dis-empowering. Children often express a sense of pride of ownership of their work. A further point to emphasise is the importance of the quality of social relations in the workplace, in other words, how children are treated in their workplaces in terms of respect, abuse, and so on. Some papers highlighted the importance of locating work identities in the broader context of the multiple identities that children hold (see chapter 16). In other words, their work may be one aspect of their everyday lives and roles they undertake, not a central identifying feature. So rather than seeing themselves as 'child labourers' or child workers, children may see their work as one activity among many, and may not define such activities as 'work' in the formal sense of the word. Within the broad category of 'working children', who are located in sets of power relationships that then render their work invisible and lead to a denial of their rights at work, we need to retain the notion that there is a diversity of childhood experiences of work.

More broadly, some papers highlighted the importance of locating children's work in the historical stage of development of the particular society, in terms of economics and politics, development of education systems, and processes of globalisation.

North–South reflections

From a perspective from the North, children's rights to work in developing countries seem to be very clearly expressed in some of the accounts from the South, and it is very difficult to envisage a 'working children's movement' in northern countries/the UK for this would involve formal acceptance of children's work. Government policies, for example, are very contradictory – tokenistically consulting with children about issues that affect them (such as changes in the law) but failing to consult systematically. This raises questions about children's potential participation, political awareness and consciousness-raising around rights at work. Broadly speaking 'work' seems to be largely an individual matter in the North, perhaps a more collective matter in the South (but we need to be careful about drawing generalisations here).

In the North, child labour in its 'worst' forms declined slowly and gradually through the introduction of compulsory education systems, legislative and factory reforms, but did not disappear. Children still work and in significant numbers. Younger children may work in what have become 'children's jobs'; older children are clearly combining work and education, employed in what could be the jobs of school leavers or adults. Childhood has become increasingly institutionalised, and the school/work divide has become more sharply drawn. Less easily resolvable, and still an issue in many countries in the North, is how to manage the transition to work, how to organise the end of formal schooling, and how children enter the labour market.

It is clear that legislation in many northern countries has not kept pace with the realities of the market and many children are not adequately protected at work. The growth of the service sector in the North has meant that children and young people have become an important source of labour in some countries.

One dilemma of children's involvement in work is that, on the one hand, complacent assumptions about the educational benefits of part-time work while at school, combined with inadequate or unenforceable legislation, may have left children particularly vulnerable to exploitation, but on the other hand, for many young people, part-time work may be a positive experience, as they feel part of a more adult world, and it gives them access to the commodities that signify adult status. Children in the North are significant consumers, and the target of mass marketing by manufacturers of a range of goods; in this sense children are economic actors (see also Levison 2000). If they earn money in order to consume they are at the same time contributing to family income and buying goods that presumably other children expect their parents to purchase.

However, children's work continues to be dismissed as a peripheral, marginal phenomenon, and this makes it difficult to make a convincing case that under-16-year-olds should be included in labour force statistics. Further, the links between children's experiences of work and their future labour market participation, and the reasons why children work and why they don't work, together with employer perspectives, are generally missing from the research.

Health and safety issues for young workers are still inadequately understood – and the long-term health consequences (rather than immediate injury rates) of some forms of work are still unknown.

Dissemination and beyond

Many sessions at the symposium highlighted the importance of raising awareness of the complexities of children's work, and getting the topic taken seriously both academically, and perhaps more importantly at the policy level. This seems to be the crucial challenge – not only to get children's work taken seriously, but to get it taken seriously in a useful way, and involving working children appropriately. From a North perspective, there were questions about the roles that schools and education systems might have in recognising children's work through 'accreditation' systems, but acknowledgement that this could be very problematic given the ways in which schools afford children very little opportunity for autonomy and participation, and could be a further way in which children's perspectives are given a loaded meaning, and their everyday lives are subjected to even greater control and surveillance.

Ultimately the symposium raised many questions about politics and economics, and there was a sense of pessimism particularly from many accounts from the South. One way to do this would be to expand and ground children's participation, working *with* child workers rather than working *for, on,* or *against* child workers. However, this must be done with great caution and an awareness of the limitations of children's participation. If we construct child labour as 'the problem to be solved' and children as the solution to the problem, this raises questions of ethics. As Judith Ennew (2000, p.5) notes:

> It is not fair to expect the powerless to assume responsibility for transforming the hierarchical structures in which their lack of power is inscribed. Indeed, to do this, is to blame them for their situation, and reproduces the same inequalities in political and economic structures, while reinforcing the economic structures that produce and maintain inequalities. In this respect, participation is a kind of conjuring trick.

We also need to be careful too about the idea that children's participation is 'good' for them. It may well be, but this surely shouldn't be the driving goal, which should be working with children to improve services and policies for all children.

There is now extensive, good quality toolkits and resources for research and action with working children – the challenge now is to move the field on. An interchange of experiences could be helpful here: the North could learn from the South about working children's movements and participatory approaches to enhance children's rights at work, and perhaps the South – at least at the level of policy-makers/NGOs (non-governmental organisations)/international NGOs – could draw on experiences from the North about how children combine school and work.

A great deal of research has now been conducted on child labour and working children around the world. Research described in this volume shows the extent to which children's perspectives on their work are now being taken into account, and these studies provide the opportunity to explore the meaning of children's work from their point of view. However, the interpretation of research findings remains adult-directed, and if researchers hold particularly negative views of children's work, then negative accounts and interpretations will dominate the accounts given of children's work. The converse is also the case. There is much scope for developing research in this area, to work with children, employers, parents, and teachers, to move towards seeing children's work experiences and responsibilities more holistically, acknowledge negative and positive aspects, as well as holding a view that children's rights at work should be enhanced. There is also scope for eliciting and utilising children's perspectives on their work, and the issues and problems they face, as the basis for developing better legislative controls that would enhance their rights at work. Theoretically, there is scope for reconceptualising children (and childhood) not as binary opposites to adults (and adulthood), but to expand ideas about inter-dependency and relationships between generations in relation to children's work.

There is potential here not only for further research and exploration, but for children's work contributions to be acknowledged and respected. We also need to find ways to support working children's movements that are valid, plausible, and not open to the criticism that the children involved are being manipulated by their adult facilitators. This is a difficult balancing act while institutions and structures continue to be adult-oriented.

Chapter 23

Some Suggestions for Social Research on Working Children's Initiatives

William E. Myers

Social scientists interested in the development of collective initiatives by children and youth – a fascinating topic with important psychological, sociological, and child development implications – may find it rewarding to investigate the evolution, dynamics and personal and social effects of working children's organizations and movements that have in recent decades surfaced in Africa, Asia and Latin America. In some superficial ways these initiatives recall those of and for working children – most visibly newsboys – formed in the early years of the twentieth century in places as diverse as the USA and Brazil. But in fact they emerge from, inhabit and interact with social and economic environments so different that they must be considered in their own right, almost as a distinct phenomenon. They are important because they raise significant challenges to the ways we are accustomed to think about the nature of childhood, the role of children in society, the criteria of social and economic justice, and the ways in which adults and children can and perhaps should interact in addressing some of the difficult issues of our time. Just to add interest, the issues around working children's organizations boil with controversy, and research into the issues at debate is sure to engender considerable interest.

The organization of working children raises professional interest and excites ideological controversy for various reasons. These reasons have to do with, among other things, conflicting perceptions of both childhood and social justice, as well as with questions of how adults should relate to working children. Such perceptions drive discourses, and even if they are ideologically driven, those discourses make certain assumptions about reality that they posit as facts. For example, depending on the ideological position defended, working children may be characterized as either aware or unaware of dangers inherent in their circumstances. Or their employment may be regarded either as a net economic contribution or as an economically vitiating displacement of higher value adult labor, either others' now or children's own in the future. While ideological positions may be difficult (but not necessarily impossible) to submit to empirical analysis, the assumed facts on which they tend to base at least part of their argument generally are open to testing by modern social science methods. Therefore, social researchers have before them the possibility of changing the terms of ideological debate by empirically illuminating crucial factual claims and assumptions, slender as they may be, that underlie the different positions. Controversies over initiatives taken by working children may be especially amenable to unpacking by research of this type. By way of illustration, I will here indicate three points at which empirical research might be helpful in sorting out controversies now waged in largely ideological terms.

One issue fuelling controversy has to do with the nature of childhood and the cognizance of children about their situation and environment. Those supporting working children's right to organize and their ability to take their own initiatives draw for their argument on a concept of children as competent, aware of their situation and capable of intervening meaningfully in their environment on their own behalf, especially if provided with adequate opportunities and tools. That notion contradicts a different one of working children as relatively naïve, helpless, unaware of their exploitation, and therefore requiring protective intervention from wiser adults who know better than the children what is good for them. Both of these images, although perhaps somewhat simplistic, are consistent with modern understanding of children as at once vulnerable and competent, and as simultaneously able to assume initiatives on their own while also requiring guidance and outside protection. But they have different consequences according to the relative emphasis placed on them.

The idea of working children as competent to represent themselves through their own organizations and initiatives is perceived by many individuals and some important institutions as threatening because it upsets power relationships upon which long conventional national and international policies excluding children from economic participation ultimately depend. Policies prohibiting children from work are based in part on the notion that adults are far more competent than children to decide whether working is appropriate for them. As many have pointed out, this position, whether true or not, is highly convenient for adults because it provides them with an ostensibly respectable reason and decision space for intervening in children's work at their own discretion, disregarding whatever children themselves may think. That social license to overrule children is available to justify either the purest altruism or the most cynical manipulation of children for adult ends, and the cover of social respectability it provides makes it difficult to discriminate between the two. As a host of historical and present-day accounts attest, the adult decision power conferred by this model of childhood has been, and still is, frequently cited to justify even violence against working children, ranging from arbitrarily dismissing them from work (or just choosing not to pay them for it) to extorting payment for allowing them to work, to locking them up in remand homes as petty delinquents.

The question of whether adult arbitrary power to overrule working children is merited or not by child ignorance and helplessness can be tested by investigation into the extent to which children are aware of their situation and competent to make rational decisions on their behalf. Modern social science research tools are adequate to make this determination, as studies by Martin Woodhead (see Chapter 3 in this volume), for example, would suggest. General conclusions on this point, especially regarding the conditions under which children are likely or unlikely to be competent, would require studies of a variety of cases. While skill-intensive, time-consuming and moderately expensive, such research is by no means beyond current individual or institutional capabilities now readily available. Remaining ideological and ethical issues notwithstanding, I am inclined to believe that the heated debate about working children's competence, and by extension their right, to act on their own behalf could largely be put to rest by a good empirical research program. Such a resolution could have enormous national and international policy implications and consequences. While some of those consequences might be predictable and justly regarded as a victory for children's rights and participation space, others almost surely will be unforeseen and perhaps undesirable.

A second ideological issue based in part on empirically testable factual claims has to do with how the work and activism of child workers affects society. More specifically, in what ways and to what extent does it either contribute to or diminish the economy and social justice? A long conventional argument against letting children work and join or establish trade unions holds that their work competes with adults and diminishes adult employment and wages to an extent ultimately greater than the economic contribution made by the child workers. It is also argued that children should not be allowed trade union protection to press their own interests that eventually undermine the wages and employment of adults. More directly, since the International Labour Organization (ILO) Minimum Age Convention No. 138 (and national labor laws based on it) bans the economic participation of children below a specified minimum age, trade unions, the ILO and others insist that children below the legal minimum age for employment cannot be considered legitimate workers, and since they are not workers they cannot legally organize or join trade unions.

The usual counter-argument is that child workers contribute to the economy and society just as do other workers, that they tend to fill work niches that are as likely to support or complement adult employment as to compete with it, that workers are workers regardless of age or legality, and that workers of all ages have common interests and should be able to organize and join other workers in defending them.

The factual claims linked to this argument revolve around whether, when and to what extent children's work competes with or supports that of adults, and whether the organization and collective initiatives of child workers contribute or not to social well-being. These issues are more difficult to define and study than are those regarding the competence of children, but they are not inaccessible. There are major questions about the proper scope of analysis, for example. Should the question of child–adult competition be studied at the level of the firm, the industry, or the nation? Although it is easier to study firms or industries, the volatility of child and adult unskilled labor markets, as well as other factors, probably requires studying national or large sub-national regions. There also are questions about how to discern whether a particular type of children's work is competitive with adults (e.g. when children work in a local business for lower wages than adults but produce the same) or whether it supports adult employment (e.g. when available family labor makes a farm or small business economically viable as a family liveli-hood). Where gender determines work roles, males and females may need to be considered separately. Despite these complications, modern economic and socio-logical research techniques, combined with an increasing availability and quality of employment and income data, make an analysis of employment competition and complementarity possible, even if ambitious.

It needs to be noted that the contributions of working children's organizations often are claimed to include substantial community service projects beyond the defense of their own economic interests. Therefore, their economic and social con-tributions need to be defined to include such activities promoting the good of a wider community. Some observers have suggested that working children's organi-zations may, over the long term, generate economic and community leadership that appears only as the children grow up. Such informal claims about the positive human development effects of participation in working children's organizations are sufficiently widespread to merit studies comparing children involved in working children's organizations with other working children not so organized to determine whether the suggested long-term effects actually occur.

A third issue meriting research attention is the relationship between children and adults in establishing and sustaining working children's organizations. Ideo-logical controversies around this topic have to do with the proper relationship between adults and working children, especially the ways and extent to which adults guide and influence young persons. Virtually all observers agree that most so-called children's organizations and movements are in fact the product of close child–adult cooperation rather than of children acting autonomously, and the operational question is the true nature of that relationship. Champions of working children's organizations claim that involved adults are highly sensitive to chil-dren's needs and rights, and that the relationship is specially tailored to support young persons with increasing skills and capabilities while providing them with ample social space to chart their own course and to make individual and collective decisions on their own. Detractors, on the other hand, insist that adult advisors to working children's organizations actually influence children far more directly than that, form their thinking to adopt the adult's own ideological and political inclina-tions, and manipulate them into roles and activities that promote the adults' own agendas. The few studies along this line tend to be ambiguous – adult influence does appear greater than what some programs suggest, but it does not seem to be as direct, intentional or pervasive as charged by detractors. Clearly, much more remains to be learned about the dynamics of the somewhat special relationship between adults and working children in working children's organizations. Research of this type makes only modest institutional and support demands, but is highly sensitive and requires considerable tact and well-honed skills of indirect questioning and observation.

Because of the controversies engendered by child work issues in general and working children's organizations in particular, much of the documentation available on working children's organizations is of an advocacy nature. Only recently has a more systematic, distanced and hopefully objective research literature on the topic begun to appear, which opens the way for publication of future work in the same vein. However, the issue is pertinent to important child rights and social welfare issues that can be advanced only through careful analysis and consideration and, out of it, the generation of new insights. Those insights are badly needed, and it is to be hoped that new researchers and new studies will soon be providing them. This is an opportunity area that might be especially promising for young researchers looking for new challenges of social and disciplinary significance that have not already been extensively worked by their seniors.

Chapter 24

The Balance Model Reconsidered: Changing Perceptions of Child Employment

Sandy Hobbs and Jim McKechnie

Introduction

The title of this chapter may be a little perplexing to some of our audience. Far from 'reconsidering' it, many of you may not have 'considered' – or even heard of – the Balance Model previously. It seems appropriate, therefore, to begin considering what the model involves and how we came to propose it.

We are British psychologists who have been studying child labour for about a decade and a half. The initial impetus for looking at child labour was intellectual curiosity. Many children work worldwide but, when we looked around at the writings of our fellow psychologists, we found that very few of them seemed to pay any attention to this fact. Children at school, children within families, children and their peers, children at play all seemed worth careful research, but not children at work. We set out to look at the child workers nearest at hand, those in Britain, and looked for ways of telling what impact the work they did might have on their lives.

It soon became clear that most British children work. The relationship between work and school turned out to be a complex one. We also began to realise that although child labour was a topic most British politicians seemed happy to ignore, it did have the potential to become a political issue. This was in part due to the European Union's Directive on the Protection of Children and Young People at Work, about which the British government of the time seemed unenthusiastic. In British law, responsibility for regulating child employment is placed on local authorities. Many local councils seemed to largely ignore their responsibility; others were anxious about their ability to implement the law, given their limited resources. Some of these latter councils sponsored, or collaborated in, our research.

In the mid-1990s, Defence for Children International and the International Society for the Prevention of Child Abuse and Neglect set up an International

Working Group on Child Labour (IWGCL). One of the countries selected as a focus for investigation was Britain. The British sub-committee made contact with us and we wrote a report for them, outlining what we had discovered at that stage. Subsequently, we were largely responsible for the final IWGCL report on Britain. Gradually, the IWGCL made more and more use of our services making us responsible for the regional report on Europe, the country report on the USA and, eventually, we were invited to edit the final global report produced in time for the ILO (International Labour Organization) conference of 1998.

Our experiences when working with the IWGCL were always stimulating and sometimes perplexing. It had been correct for the IWGCL to cover the economies of the 'North' such as the UK and USA as well as countries of the 'South' in Africa, Asia and Latin America. However, we discovered that communication between IWGCL members working in different types of country could be difficult. There were also differences in perspective between academic researchers such as ourselves and activists from NGOs (non-governmental organisations) promoting the cause of child workers. This was despite the fact that from the early stages of our research we had collaborated with a British NGO, the Low Pay Network.

We formed the impression that some of the people we met at IWGCL thought that we were insufficiently fervent in our hostility to abusive child labour. By referring to the possibility that some forms of child employment might have some benefits this may have seemed to them to distract attention from what have become known as the 'intolerable' forms of child labour. In some parts of the world these intolerable forms are so widespread that they naturally demand the attention of campaigners. In Britain, where intolerable forms exist but are much less common, it is easier for researchers such as ourselves to be open to the possibility that for children to work may have both good and bad aspects.

The Balance Model

So far in this chapter, 'work' and 'labour' have been used interchangeably but we discovered that some writers wish to deal with the distinction between good and bad phenomena by employing 'child labour' to refer to what they see as 'bad' and 'child work' for what they see as 'good'. (A relatively recent example of this usage is to be found in the paper by Otis and colleagues (2001). Some of those working for the IWGCL were not happy with this terminology. One problem is that it does not translate easily into other languages. A more serious problem was identified by Ben White and by Clare Feinstein, who both saw the child work/child labour distinction as too crude. In working papers they suggested that we should think in terms of a continuum stretching from the most objectionable and harmful types of work to the beneficial and acceptable forms (see Feinstein 1997; White 1996).

We saw merit in the continuum approach but felt it needed to be taken further. In June 1997, we wrote a working paper for the IWGCL called 'Understanding Children's Work'. At the time we were completing our book, *Child Employment in Britain: A Social and Psychological Analysis*, and included the model there. The following year, when editing the final IWGCL report, it was clear that it should reflect the conceptual debate. Thus, in that report we included both the Continuum and the Balance Models (McKechnie and Hobbs 1998).

The Balance Model shares with the Continuum approach the assumption that, for children, work may have varying degrees of benefits. However, the Continuum Model did not seem to state explicitly that good and bad features could exist side by side in the same work. The Balance Model acknowledges this possibility. Some examples of costs and benefits for a child are listed in Box 24.1.

The examples listed are not exhaustive, nor are they our invention. We included arguments which we had come across in debates about child employment in Britain. Obviously if we had been working in India or Brazil or Tanzania, for example, other positives and negatives might have been uppermost in our minds.

Box 24.1 Costs and benefits of work

Costs of work
Danger to health, safety
Limit to free time
Limit to parent/peer contact
Negative impact on education
Encourage instrumentalism

Benefits of work
Sense of autonomy
Sense of self-reliance
Economic knowledge
Business knowledge
Work experience

What was the intended use of the model? Our main aim was to move away from essentially questions of semantics, such as 'What is work?' and 'What is labour?', and seek a clearer understanding of the complexities of child work. In particular, we suggested that this model was a guide to how research should proceed. The framework is laid out in Box 24.2.

Box 24.2 Framework for research

Input
Questions, assumptions, concepts, hypotheses, evidence

Features to be studied
Context: e.g. economic structure, family
Child: e.g. age, gender
Job: e.g. hours, tasks, physical conditions
Outcomes for child: e.g. health, educational achievement

Outcome
Demonstrate relationship between features studied

However, we did not see the model as applying only to research. We believed that it should underpin the sorts of interactions which are necessary if research is to have any practical application; see Box 24.3.

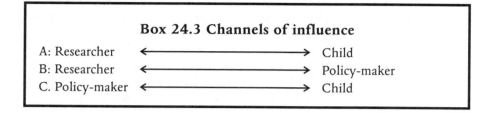

Box 24.3 Channels of influence

A: Researcher   ⟵⟶   Child

B: Researcher   ⟵⟶   Policy-maker

C. Policy-maker   ⟵⟶   Child

Since, as researchers, we have a primary concern for the welfare of children, we see the need for continued three-way dialogues between the children, researchers and policy-makers. We regard 'policy-makers' as including anyone seeking to influence or direct child employment, such as parents, activists and governments. We propose that such communication would be facilitated if all parties dealt in terms of the Balance Model.

We did not make grand claims for the model. It is crude and lacks detail. However, one justification for proposing it was that at the time of writing, discussions of children's work seemed dogged by semantic confusion. What we were offering was 'a platform to develop our knowledge of the impact of children's economic participation' (quoting ourselves, Hobbs and McKechnie 1997, p.139).

We were psychologists researching in Britain and that clearly influenced what we wrote. Nevertheless, the immediate circumstances in which we wrote were the deliberations of the IWGCL and we hoped that the model would appear relevant to people working in contexts different from our own. Was that reasonable?

Relevance

We can understand why someone concerned with extreme cases such as children in armies or bonded labour might look at what we were proposing unfavourably. Is it not an overly academic approach to raise the possibility of 'benefits' when dealing with practices which were self-evidently intolerable? We suggest not. One of the most obvious lessons learned by campaigners on child labour has been that it is not enough merely to stop an unacceptable practice. One must put in place practical alternatives. Child soldiers and bonded labourers are at least fed. To save children from such lifestyles it is necessary to ensure an alternative acceptable to them. However meagre it may be, sustenance is a benefit available to these children and an alternative must be found to replace that benefit. It may be, too, that children in extreme forms of economic activity may benefit in other unsuspected ways, such as from peer relationships. These too might need to be replaced when the children are removed from their work.

One of the most valuable activities sponsored by the IWGCL was the study of the impact of media coverage given to girls working in a clothing factory in

Meknès, Morocco (Zalami *et al.* 1998). British television revealed that they were employed making clothes to be sold by one of the best-known chain stores in Britain. The company succeeded in establishing that it was unaware of conditions in the factory, but the publicity led the factory management to sack the girls. Fatima Badry Zalami followed up the case for the IWGCL. She found that most of the girls she contacted were now much worse off than they had been when they were in the factory, since they were working in less attractive jobs for poorer pay. Zalami and her colleagues concluded:

> The dismissals led to the girls being harmed rather than helped... Alternative approaches...could have been found to protect the welfare of the young girls...without necessarily removing them from their jobs. For example, a tightening up and improving of apprenticeships and the transformation of these into 'work and learn' schemes would have been one possible transitional intervention.

Expressed in terms of the Balance Model, this latter proposal would have involved changing some features of the jobs to increase benefits in comparison to the costs. The Meknès case demonstrates the dangers of crude conceptualisation. The journalist worked on the simple assumption that 'child labour is bad'. However, they created circumstances in which the children in question, whose fate they condemned, had a worse fate when they were excluded. An alternative to the practices observed, with a better balance between costs and benefits to the girls, had not been provided.

A recent paper by the anthropologist Jane Helleiner (2003) makes points which also seem to us to show the need to think in terms of balance when comparing work and its alternatives. She deals with 'child begging' by Roma and other travellers in Ireland. On the face of it, begging might seem a straightforward example of child labour which we would naturally oppose. However, Jane Helleiner points out that the role of the child in the traditional traveller family is a complex one. We shall not go into the detail of that role, except to say that the begging traveller child, by her account, might well have some sense of contributing to the family's economic activities, a 'benefit' which needs to be acknowledged. A more easily understood point is that, whereas the official position of the Irish authorities is that children should be in school rather than begging, many traveller children are subjected to ethnic abuse when they attend school. This is a 'cost' which must be weighed in the balance against anything that these children might gain from attending school.

We chose this example because it refers to a country with an enormously successful, growing economy. Ireland is now one of the richest countries in Europe.

We are sure that activists in developing countries are aware of equivalent complexities and subtleties which arise when dealing with child employment. The point which we wish to stress, however, is that the dilemmas frequently faced can be described in terms of the Balance Model.

Some limitations

Having argued for the relevance of the Balance Model to specific concrete examples, we should now consider some of its limitations, at least as originally formulated.

First we should note that although we explicitly stated that the lists of potential costs and benefits in Box 24.1 were not meant to be definitive, it would be understandable if some readers assumed we were concerned only with psychological and social characteristics. With the exception of the possible dangers to health and safety, all of the examples listed were in the psychosocial domain. However, as can be seen from the way in which we interpreted the Moroccan and Irish cases we have just discussed, costs and benefits should be considered well beyond the narrow lists initially proposed and into the economic sphere too.

A second limitation is that we did not make sufficiently clear that the Balance Model might be applied to children's jobs but also to whatever alternative activities policy-makers might have in mind. Once again, we hope that this is now clear from our interpretations of the two cases just outlined.

Third, it is an obvious limitation of the model that it does not deal with how we are to assess or measure any given variable. To an extent, this is not our weakness but a weakness of much research in the field of child employment. This is an ongoing problem, particularly in the psychosocial field, as is clearly acknowledged in the recent paper on 'Psychosocial impacts of child work' by Martin Woodhead (2004). Woodhead outlines in detail a variety of domains in which work might be shown to have an impact on children, but notes that in most areas appropriate instruments for measuring the impact are not yet available. We note with satisfaction, however, that he clearly advocates the assessment of both positive and negative influences. In this respect his framework is compatible with the Balance Model, as he himself acknowledges.

The image of children's work in developed economies

Ever since the Industrial Revolution there have been voices raised both for and against child employment. (Some examples are outlined in the entry 'Pro-employment arguments' in Hobbs, McKechnie and Lavalette 1999). It seems to us worth pointing out that arguments in favour of children working may be becoming stronger in recent years. When we began our research we came across occasional proposals from proponents of conservatism and neo-liberal economics suggesting many children would benefit both themselves and the community by leaving school early and getting jobs. Such proposals may still be heard. For example, Corey (2004) argues the merits of older children combining schooling with employment, and Blundell (2004) argues that child employment provides a way out of poverty for families in many parts of the world. However, perhaps of more significance is the fact that governmental and other official bodies seem to be arguing the educational merits of work for adolescents. Some of our most recent research has been funded by government agencies which are seeking evidence of learning during employment and exploring the possibility of accrediting work as a part of education. Such proposals are in more measured terms than those who favour children working on ideological grounds. As exponents of the Balance Model we believe these arguments should be taken seriously. However, there is a danger that new government policies allowing teenagers to split their time between school and the workplace and introducing certificates to cover what is supposedly learned on the job will be introduced prematurely. By 'prematurely' we mean before the benefits of teenage work have been properly established and before potential costs have been taken properly into account. When we started our research we faced a government which preferred to ignore the fact that most British children work. Now we may have to work in a rather different political climate in which the government enthusiastically encourages older children to work, without due regard to the realities.

We are in less close contact with the position in the United States but it does appear to be the case that researchers are more willing now to emphasise the positive aspects of work. In their pioneering book of 1986, Greenberger and Steinberg referred in their subtitle to the 'cost' of teenagers working, although of course they did take account of some benefits in their text. Mortimer's recent study (2003) seems to stress the benefits much more strongly, though not ignoring the costs. We cannot be sure whether this is a significant trend, but we find it worth noting that, at the same time as psychologists are finding some advantages in work for teenage Americans, social workers in the United States are arguing that child labour should once again be a central issue of child welfare (Otis *et al.* 2001). Perhaps Otis and his colleagues would regard research such as that of Mortimer (2003) as dealing with children's 'work' rather than children's 'labour'. However, if Otis is correct that 'child labour' is a serious problem in the United States, then that implies that there are limits to how far it is permissible to generalise from Mortimer's results.

Conclusion

We have two points to make in conclusion. Our first is to say that all those concerned with work by children should keep up a dialogue with each other however varied the forms of work and however varied the socio-economic context. We are confident that activists and researchers (and children) still have much to learn from each other. Often communication may be difficult because we have asked different questions and found different answers. However, we suggest that these difficulties may be reduced if different parties adopt a Balance Model. This is our second point. We believe that the model is simple and broad enough to allow everyone to discuss their experiences in terms of the costs and benefits of work and its alternatives, however difficult the benefits may sometimes be to find.

Chapter 25

Exploring Children's Work
Through Pictures

Phil Mizen

There is something peculiarly photogenic about working children. Throughout its history photography has pondered the condition of working children, from the huge photographic survey of child labourers undertaken by the great American documentary photographer Lewis Hine[1] a century ago, through to the digitised picture galleries to be found on web sites like the International Labour Organization's.[2] Less evident has been photography's place in the range of research methods sometimes deployed by researchers to explore children's work and employment. In Hecht's recent ethnography of street children in north-east Brazil (1998; see also Aptekar 1988; Nieuwenhuys 1994), for instance, punctuating the pages of his book are a series of images showing his subjects at work and play, asleep and relaxing, joking, killing empty time, in confrontation with the authorities, etc. Individually these images add further depth to a study already rich in ethnographic detail. In their totality Hecht's photographs of children 'doing' what children often 'do' also contributes a humanising dimension to a group often portrayed in troubling terms.

Photography's capacity to illuminate the lives of working children does not stop here, however. Still photography has, in the words of Prosser (1998, p.1), the potential to 'provide researchers with a different order of data and, more importantly, an alternative to the way we have perceived data in the past.' By employing visually orientated methods as an integral part of the research process, a Visual Sociology of children's work and labour is replete with possibilities (Bolton, Pole and Mizen 2001), particularly when the act of producing images is given over to the research subjects themselves. When directed towards the lives of working children, photography has much to contribute to the emergence of a broader agenda in which the recent theoretical advances that have brought to the fore issues of agency, experience and testimony have not yet been matched at the level of substantive empirical enquiry (Boyden *et al.* 1998).

The photographs discussed here were produced by secondary school aged students (i.e. 11- to 15-year-olds) living in six areas of England and Wales, as part of a qualitative research project[3] examining the employment of children in Britain at the turn of the twenty-first century. By prioritising children's assessments of their work, the research was not so much concerned with what work had to say about the children – in the way that 'adolescent' employment among children in wealthy nations is often used as a marker of psychosocial development – but with what the children had to say about their work (Mizen *et al.* 2001). One way to achieve this was through the use of still photography. By using simple and inexpensive, one-use analogue cameras, around two thirds of the 69 participating children agreed to make 'photo-diaries' of their working lives, producing some 850 photographs. Most of these 'photo-diarists' then went on to reflect upon a self-selected group of their photographs by producing a further written diary. The resulting collection of images and words provides a distinctive and perhaps unique document of a rarely discussed but nonetheless 'majority experience' of modern British childhood.

Emerging from the shadows

As documents *of* children's working lives, the 'photo-diaries' are notable at several levels. At the very least, the images provide a graphic means of confirming what children have told researchers in survey, interview and group discussion for some time now (but which many continue to dismiss or belittle): that school-age employment extends well beyond dog-walking and newspaper deliveries (McKechnie and Hobbs 1997a). Moreover, through their images the children provided previously unavailable sources of detail – its physical structures, settings, fabric, artefacts – of an economy of child employment that we know from other sources of research and information tends to be patterned by (mainly service sector) work in small bars, restaurants, cafés, public houses, clubs and hotels, shops, market stalls, homes and offices, farms, on delivery rounds and home-working.

Visualising the economy of children's employment in this way also allows a fuller understanding of the substance of these children's labours. In what amounts to something like a process of 'triangulation plus', the photographs go beyond simple confirmation and increase our awareness of what these children were employed to do in ways that words collected in interview, group discussion or written diary had never quite conveyed. John's[4] (12, South Wales valley) inclusion of an image of himself seated on a quad bike, for instance, showed us more than a boy proudly demonstrating his command over agricultural machinery. Beyond the figure of John that dominated the foreground, barely visible animals dotted against hills rolling away into the distance conveyed the scale of the family sheep farm on which he worked in ways that had eluded his otherwise meticulous descriptions. Again, only on seeing Jayda's (14, English Midlands inner city) photographs of cardboard boxes crammed with components ready for assembly, full to the brim with assembled units and stacked three high in a hallway, or her close-up shot of a device she had ingeniously improvised to speed assembly, was the scale and repetitive character of her home-working job assembling vent plugs for automotive batteries clearly understood; see Figures 25.1 to 25.3.

Figure 25.1 John on the family farm

Figure 25.2 Boxes of assembled components ready for return to the factory

Figure 25.3 A 'home-made' device for assembling component parts

By making their labour visible through photography the children also revealed that much of their work took place beyond our view. Through their photographs we are given glimpses of those physical spaces within which children's labour was often confined but which for us, whether as customer, patron or researcher, generally remains off limits, 'out back' or simply hidden from view. In one photograph we glimpse a subterranean room piled high with a tangled mass of chairs waiting, the author of this picture later informs us, for him to clean and stack them. Elsewhere the children provide us with images of basement rooms filled with stock, kitchens and food preparation areas in cafés and restaurants, store rooms of supermarkets and grocery stores, photographs of the insides of domestic homes. In a further photograph we view the beer cellar of a public house crowded with metal beer casks, their air lines stretching up and back into the gloom, its significance later confirmed in writing as somewhere, 'I have to take out all the empty barrels as well when I bottle up which is in the same room' (Dick, 14, East Anglia town); see Figure 25.4.

The children also used their photographs to show us places more familiar but this time framed from their vantage points *as workers*; and once again providing further, emphatic confirmation of their status as workers. By using their photographs to quite literally put the viewer in their shoes, the children succeeded in producing a series of distinctive surveys of the ecology of children's work. Revealed in these photographs we see many of those objects which command their attention: cash machines, scales to weigh and measure, display cabinets full of sandwiches, cakes or confectionery, shelving lined with snacks or crockery, sometimes the occasional customer or patron. Writing about her photograph of a small

Figure 25.4 The beer cellar of a public house

white desk shown in close-up and framed from the perspective of the sitter – its surface filled by telephone, booking diary, receipt book, desk organiser and writing equipment – Becky (15, South Wales town) elaborates: 'This is the desk out front where I answer the phone booking people in, also charging for what they have had done. I quite like doing this as it gives me a bit of a break to sit down and relax.'

Photographs like Becky's also offered knowledge about the process of these children's labour. The frequency with which the children presented images of physical plant – the equipment, utensils, implements and tools that their labour regularly set in motion – singled out from the clutter of the workplace and brought to the fore for closer attention, elaborate on the character of their labour; was repeated in image after image. In one photograph we peer into a large plastic refuse receptacle half full of empty drinks bottles; in another we view crates of beverages piled neatly on a stockroom floor waiting to be moved. In other images we see a stainless steel glass washer ready for loading, in close-up three plastic bottles containing cleaning products, a two-tier trolley stacked with confectionery, two bulging vinyl bags packed tightly with newspapers, food residue on plates stacked haphazardly across a stainless steel work surface, a bag of laundry perched on top of a tumble dryer. In a further photograph we see down the spaces between rows of plastic flip-up seats that disappear into the gloom of a large sports auditorium, the foot spaces strewn with a mass of discarded litter. As the photograph's maker, Mark (15, Midlands inner city), explains: 'photo 5/12 shows the seats in which I had to clean and all the rubbish we had to pick up (by hand)'; see Figure 25.5.

Figure 25.5 Picking up rubbish by hand

Smaller numbers of the children gave us fleeting images of themselves quite literally 'at work'. Through these images the children again made their labour concrete, vivid proof that behind the milk bottle or newspaper placed on the doorstep, the clean plate or glass on our dining table in a café or restaurant, the spotless home, or the happy and contented younger child, often lies the exertions of a working child. Included among Susan's (14, East Anglia town) selection we see a photograph of one of her young charges, the pleasure and pains of caring for fractious children clearly expressed in both image and word: 'This picture shows that it isn't all easy, trying to bath a baby isn't easy. It means a lot because I love bathing him. I will never forget bathing him'. In another image, Jamie (14, East Anglia town) provides a vivid image of 'A letter box of a house showing my hand pushing a paper through. I would have to do this every Sunday for 40 odd houses'. Expanding on a photograph of herself standing beside a group of young children in what is clearly the interior of a fast-food restaurant, Fiona (14, East Anglia coastal) elaborates that 'This photo is one of my favourites because I'm taking part in a party. As you can see we've got a lot of children to look after'. The image confirms that this is indeed the case.

Images like these, together with the comments they provoked, revealed that the children had thought carefully about their use of the cameras. Indeed, the children's creative use of photography to capture the detail and explore the content of their work was similarly evident in attempts to decompose aspects of their employment into some of its constituent parts and to use their images to convey process as much as content. In a striking sequence of images, Cassie (13, South Wales valley) provides a clever and revealing cameo of her weekend and holiday job in a small hairdressing salon, where we see her 'giving the desks a quick wipe over', 'towel drying a customer's hair' and 'answering the phone', as well as 'tidying up the shelves and the towels', 'washing hair, for the first time' and 'greeting a customer and taking her coat'; see Figures 25.6 to 25.11.

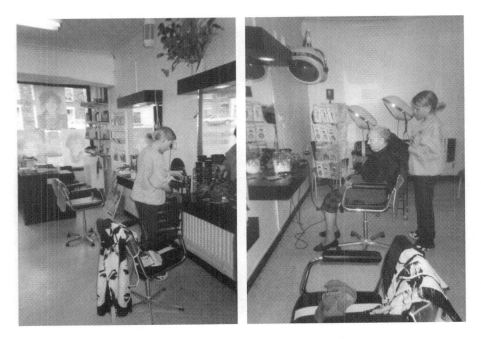

Figure 25.6 Cleaning desks   *Figure 25.7 Drying hair*

Others found equally innovative ways of using their photographs to delve beneath the surface of their working life. In both Anthony and Sarah's selections we find juxtaposed images in which pairs of photographs are used to show objects or locations 'before' and 'after' each of the photographers had got to work upon them. In the case of Anthony (15, East Anglia town), employed at weekends in a small hotel, a first image, 'shows how dirty the carvery [i.e. where cooked meat is sliced directly onto a patron's plate] is when I come to clean it, this particular week it wasn't too bad at all but most weeks it has old bits of food and grease stuck to it'. In the second image we are shown the 'carvery' now literally gleaming: 'This photo shows after I have cleaned the carvery tray it sparkles. It takes up to one hour to do some weeks'. Sarah too provided us with one image of a modern, well-furnished living room but clearly untouched from the evening before, curtains closed, chairs lying haphazardly, clothes and shoes scattered across the floor and a small table with objects sprawled across it. As Sarah (14, East Anglia town) explains, 'This is a picture of the work I am usually required to do each night. The amount of work varies on whether the poeple [sic] have had time to do any or not. The picture is of the lounge'. In a second image the same room has now been clearly transformed, curtains open and neatly tied back, cushions arranged deftly on easy chairs, the table free of clutter and now moved back to the centre of the room: 'This is a picture of the lounge after I have finished the cleaning up. Today I did quite a lot. Normally I would just straighten up but I polished, washed spots off the carpet'; see Figures 25.12 and 25.13.

Figure 25.8 Answering the phone

Figure 25.9 Tidying the towels

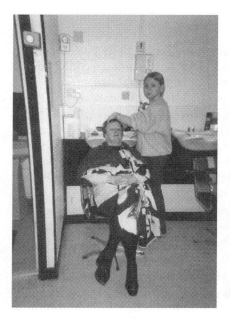

Figure 25.10 Washing hair

Figure 25.11 Greeting a customer

Figure 25.12 Before work

Figure 25.13 After work

Conclusion

These photographs, with their written reflections, thus provide distinctive sources of knowledge concerned with the employment of children. Through this particular Visual Sociology of children's work we are provided with new dimensions to our understanding of the economy of school-age employment in England and Wales – ones, moreover, that words and numbers would most likely struggle to convey. As reflections upon their working lives, the children's photographs give graphic form to their work, its structures and objects, ecology, form and content. Through these photographs we can develop a deeper knowledge of what it means to be a school-age worker. We can get to know better the physicality and confines in which children are set to labour, the equipment and utensils they are required to work with, the tasks that define their working time and the routines that often characterise them. In previously unavailable detail we see, in short, the commonplace banality and mundane order that defines much school-age working in a wealthy nation like the United Kingdom.

Notes

1. Hine donated over 5000 of the photographs taken during his survey of child labour to the US Library of Congress, many of which are available in digitised form at: www.loc.gov/rr/print/.

2. www.ilo.org/public/english/bureau/inf/index.htm.

3. 'Work, Labour and Economic Life in Late Childhood' (L129251035), funded by the Economic and Social Research Council, as part of their programme 'Children 5–16: Growing into the 21st Century'. My thanks also to Chris Pole and Angela Hutton for their collaboration on this project.

4. All names are pseudonyms. All quotations from the children's written diaries are verbatim.

Bibliography

Agarwal, B. (1997) '"Bargaining" and Gender Relations: Within and Beyond the Household.' *Feminist Economics 3*, 1, 1–51.

Alanen, L. (1988) 'Rethinking Childhood.' *Acta Sociologica 31*, 53–67.

Alanen, L. (1992) 'Modern Childhood? Exploring the "Child Question" *Sociology*. Jyväskylä University.

Alanen, L. (1994) 'Gender and Generation: Feminism and the "Child Question".' In J. Qvortrup, M. Bardy, G. Sgritta and H. Wintersberger (eds) *Childhood Matters: Social Theory, Practice and Politics*. Vienna: European Centre.

Alanen, L. (1997) 'Soziologie der Kindheit als Projekt: Perspektiven für die Forschung.' *ZSE – Zeitschrift für Sozialisationsforschung und Erziehungssoziologie 17*, 2, 162–177.

Alaraudanjoki, E. (2000) 'Child Labour: A Multi-disciplinary Review.' In S. Leppänen and J. Kuortti (eds) *Inescapable Horizon: Culture and Context*. Publications of the Research Unit for Contemporary Culture, 64. University of Jyväskylä, Jyväskylä: Gummerus Printing.

Alderson, P. (1998) 'Understanding, Wisdom and Rights: Assessing Children's Competence.' In D.K. Behera (ed) *Children and Childhood in our Contemporary Societies*. Delhi: Kamla-Raj Enterprises.

Aptekar, L. (1988) *Street Children of Cali*. Durhan: Duke University Press.

Ariès, P. (1987) *El niño y la vida familiar en el antiguo régimen*. Madrid: Edit. Taurus.

Balding, J. (1997) *Young People in 1996*. Exeter: Schools Health Education Unit, Exeter University.

Becker, S., Aldridge, J. and Dearden, C. (1998) *Young Carers and Their Families*. Oxford: Blackwell Science.

Becker, S., Dearden, C. and Aldridge, J. (2001) 'Children's Labour of Love? Carers and Care Work.' In P. Mizen, C. Pole and A. Bolton (eds) *Hidden Hands: International Perspectives on Children's Work and Labour*. London: RoutledgeFalmer.

Behr-Heintze, A. and Lipski, J. (2005) *Schulkooperationen. Stand und Perspektiven der Zusammenarbeit zwischen Schulen und ihren Partnern. Ein Forschungsbericht des DJI*. Schwalbach/Ts.: Wochenschau Verlag.

Belsky, J. (1980) 'Child Maltreatment: An Ecological Integration.' *American Psychologist 35*, 320–335.

Benería, L. (1992) 'The Mexican Debt Crisis: Restructuring the Economy and the Household.' In L. Benería and S. Feldman (eds) *Unequal Burden: Economic Crisis, Persistent Poverty, and Women's Work*. Boulder, CO: Westview.

Bequele, A. and Boyden, J. (eds) (1990) *La lucha contra el trabajo infantil*. Geneva: Organización Internacional del Trabajo (English edition: *Combating Child Labour*. Geneva: ILO, 1988).

Bertozzi, R. (2004) 'Bambini e adolescenti stranieri e lavori minorili in Italia.' In Centro nazionale di documentazione e analisi per l'infanzia e l'adolescenza (ed) *Bambini e adolescenti che lavorano, Un panorama dall'Italia all'Europa*. Quaderni del Centro nazionale di documentazione e analisi per l'infanzia e l'adolescenza, Florence: Istituto degli Innocenti.

Bey, M. (2003) 'The Mexican Child: From Work with the Family to Paid Employment.' *Childhood 10*, 287–299.

Bhima Sangha and Makkala Panchayat (2001) *Our Survey Story*. Bangalore: The Concerned for Working Children.

Bieber-Delfosse, G. (2002) *Vom Medienkind zum Kinderstar. Einfluss- und Wirkfaktoren auf Vorstellungen und Prozesse des Erwachsenwerdens.* Opladen: Leske and Budrich.

Black, M. (1997) *Child Domestic Workers: A Handbook for Research and Action.* London: Anti-Slavery International.

Black, M. (2002) *A Handbook on Advocacy, Child Domestic Workers: Finding a Voice.* Horsham: The Printed Word.

Black, M. (2004) *Opening Minds, Opening Up Opportunities: Children's Participation in Action for Working Children.* London: International Save the Children Alliance.

Blanchet, T. (1996) *Lost Innocence, Stolen Childhoods.* Dhaka: University of Dhaka Press.

Blundell, J. (2004) 'Economic truths of child labour.' *The Scotsman,* 23 February.

Boden, S., Pole, C., Pilcher, J. and Edwards, T. (2004) 'New Consumers? The Social and Cultural Significance of Children's Fashion Consumption.' ESRC Cultures of Consumption programme. Working paper 16. (www.consume.bbk.ac.uk)

Bolton, A., Pole, C. and Mizen, P. (2001) 'Picture This: Researching Child Workers.' *Sociology 35,* 2, 501–518.

Bourdieu, P. (1983) 'Ökonomisches Kapital, kulturelles Kapital, soziales Kapital.' In R. Kreckel (ed) *Zur Theorie sozialer Ungleichheiten.* Soziale Welt. Sonderband 2. Göttingen, 183–198.

Bourdillon, M. (2006) *Child Domestic Workers in Zimbabwe.* Harare: Weaver Press.

Boyd, W. (1956) *Émile for Today: The Émile of Jean Jacques Rousseau.* Trans. by William Boyd. London: Heinemann.

Boyden, J. (1990) 'Childhood and the Policy-Makers: A Comparative Perspective on the Globalization of Childhood.' In A. James and A. Prout (eds) *Constructing and Reconstructing Childhood.* London: Falmer.

Boyden, J. (1994) *The Relationship between Education and Childwork.* Florence: ICDC Innocenti Occasional Papers.

Boyden, J. and Ennew, J. (eds) (1997) *Children in Focus: A Manual for Participatory Research with Children.* Stockholm: Rädda Barnen.

Boyden, J., Ling, B. and Myers, W.E. (1998) *What Works for Working Children.* Stockholm: Rädda Barnen.

Brannen, J. (1995) 'Young People and their Contribution to Household Work.' *Sociology 29,* 2, 317–338.

Brannen, J. and O'Brien, J. (1995) 'Childhood and the Sociological Gaze: Paradigms and Paradoxes.' *Sociology 29,* 4.

Bronfenbrenner, U. (1979) *The Ecology of Human Development.* Cambridge, MA: Harvard University Press.

Brown, L.J. and Pollit, E. (1996) 'Malnutrition, Poverty and Intellectual Development.' *Scientific American,* February, 26–31.

Bruner, J.S. and Haste, H. (eds) (1987) *Making Sense: The Child's Construction of the World.* London: Methuen.

Budd, J.W. (2004) *Employment with a Human Face: Balancing Efficiency, Equity, and Voice.* Ithaca, NY: Cornell University Press.

Bühler-Niederberger, D. and Hungerland, B. (2002) 'Children's Social Value: The Sociology of their Assessment Process.' In F. Mouritsen and J. Qvortrup (eds) *Childhood and Children's Culture.* Odense: University Press of Southern Denmark.

Burman, E. (1996) 'Local, Global or Globalized? Child Development and International Child Rights Legislation.' *Childhood 3,* 1, 45–67.

Butterwege, C., Holm, K., Imholz, B., Klundt, M. *et al.* (2003) *Armut und Kindheit. Ein regionaler, nationaler und internationaler Vergleich.* 2nd edition 2004. Wiesbaden: Verlag für Sozialwissenschaften.

Cecchetti, R. (1998) *Children Who Work in Europe: From Exploitation to Participation.* Brussels: European Forum for Child Welfare.

Chandra, V. (2000) *Children's Work in the Family: A Sociological Study of Indian Children in Coventry (UK) and in Lucknow (India).* PhD Thesis submitted in the University of Warwick, UK.

Cheal, D.J. (2003) 'Children's Home Responsibilities: Factors Predicting Children's Household Work.' *Social Behavior and Personality 31*, 8, 789–794.

Christensen, P. and James, A. (2000) *Research with Children: Perspectives and Practices.* London: Falmer.

Church, P. (2003) *A Short History of South-East Asia.* Singapore: John Wiley and Sons (Asia).

Cicchetti, D. and Lynch, M. (1993) 'Toward an Ecological/Transactional Model of Community Violence and Child Maltreatment: Consequences for Children's Development.' *Psychiatry 56*, 96–118.

CLASP 1, June 2001. Bugkos, Manila, Philippines: CLASP.

CLASP 2, April 2002. Bugkos, Manila, Philippines: CLASP.

CLASP 3, August 2003. Bugkos, Manila, Philippines: CLASP.

Cohen, R. (2001) 'Children's Contribution to Household Labour in Three Sociocultural Contexts.' *International Journal of Comparative Sociology, 2,* 4, 353–367.

Colozzi, I. and Giovannini, G. (eds) (2003) *Ragazzi in Europa tra tutela, autonomia e responsabilità.* Milan: Franco Angeli.

Corey, M. (2004) 'Part-Time Education Should not be Seen as Second Best for Young People.' *The Guardian,* 16 March.

Corsaro, W.A. (1997) *The Sociology of Childhood.* Thousand Oaks, London and New Delhi: Pine Forge Press.

Cunningham, H. and Viazzo, P. (1996) *Child Labour in Historical Perspective 1800–1985: Case Studies from Europe, Japan and Columbia.* Florence: Unicef, ICDC.

Cunningham, S. (1999) 'The Problem That Doesn't Exist? Child Labour in Britain 1918–1970.' In M. Lavalette (ed) *A Thing of the Past? Child Labour in Britain in the Nineteenth and Twentieth Centuries.* Liverpool: Liverpool University Press.

Cussiánovich, A. (1997) 'Bambini e adolescenti lavoratori: Una questione sociale fondamentale alla chiusura del XX secolo.' *NATs, Nuovi spazi di crescita 1,* Bologna: EMI.

CWA (1985) *Child Workers in Asia 1,* 1, Jul–Sept.

CWA (2001) *Child Workers in Asia 17,* 2/3, May–Dec.

CWC (2002) *Children and Their Research. A Process Document.* Bangalore: The Concerned for Working Children.

Davies, E. (1972) 'Work Out of School.' *Education,* 10th November, i–iv.

De Berry, J. and Boyden, J. (2000) 'Children in Adversity.' *Forced Migration 9,* 33–36.

De Coninck-Smith, N. (1997) 'The Struggle for the Child's Time – At All Times: School and Children's Work in Town and Country in Denmark from 1900 to the 1960s.' In N. De Coninck-Smith, B. Sandin and E. Schrumpff (eds) *Industrious Children. Work and Childhood in the Nordic Countries 1850–1990.* Odense: Odense University Press, 160–185.

De Leeuw, E., Borgers, N. and Strijbos-Smits, A. (2002) 'Children as Respondents: Developing, Evaluating, and Testing Questionnaires for Children.' Presented at the International Conference on Questionnaire Development Evaluation and Testing Methods, Charleston, South Carolina, November.

De Mause, L. (1974) *The History of Childhood.* New York: The Psychohistory Press.

Delgado, B. (1998) *Historia de la infancia.* Barcelona: Ariel.

Diario das Noticias (2003) 'Um em cada quatro jovens sem o 9o ano' by M.J. Margarido. 10 March.

Dorman, P. (2001) *Child Labour in the Developed Economies.* Geneva: International Labour Office, International Programme on the Elimination of Child Labour.

Du Bois-Reymond, M., Büchner, P., Eccarius, J., Fuhs, B. and Krüger, H.-H. (1994) *Kinderleben. Modernisierung von Kindheit im interkulturellen Vergleich.* Opladen: Leske and Budrich.

Dunn, J. (1988) *The Beginnings of Social Understanding.* Oxford: Blackwell.

Durkin, K. (1995) *Developmental Social Psychology.* Oxford: Blackwell.

Dussel, E. (2000) 'Europa, modernidad y eurocentrismo.' In E. Lander (ed) *La colonialidad del saber: eurocentrismo y ciencias sociales. Perspectivas latinoamericanas.* Buenos Aires: CLACSO; UNESCO, 41–53.

Eckart, C. and Senghaas-Knobloch, E. (2000) 'Fürsorge – Anerkennung – Arbeit.' *Feministische Studien 18*, 3–8.

Edelstein, W. (2001) 'Ansprache bei der Preisverleihung am 29. Mai 2001.' In Stiftung Brandenburger Tor der Bankgesellschaft Berlin (ed) *Jugend übernimmt Verantwortung. Lernziel Verantwortung.* Siftung Brandenburger T or der Bankgesellschaft: Berlin.

Elder, G.H. Jr. and Conger, R.D. (2000) *Children of the Land: Adversity and Success in Rural America.* Chicago: University of Chicago Press.

Elson, D. (1982) 'The Differentiation of Children's Labour in the Capitalist Labour Market.' *Development and Change 13*, 479–497.

Emler, M. and Abrams, D. (1990) 'The Sexual Distribution of Benefits and Burdens in the Household: Adolescent Experiences and Expectations.' ESRC 16–19 Initiative. Occasional Paper, No. 7. London: SSRU.

ENDA (1999) *Les 12 droits du Mouvement Africain des Enfants et Jeunes Travailleurs (MAEJT). Fondement juridiquem, plate-forme revendicative ou instrument du développement?* Dakar: Enda TM Jeunesse Action, JEUDA 104.

ENDA (2001) *Voice of African Children: Work, Strength and Organisation of Working Children and Youth.* Dakar: Enda-Editions, Occasional Papers no. 217.

Ennew, J. (2000) 'How Can We Define Citizenship in Childhood?' *Working Chapter Series 109,* 112. Harvard Centre for Population and Development Studies, Harvard School of Public Health.

Ennew, J. (2002) 'Children's Participation: Experiences and Reflections.' Unpublished.

Ennew, J., Myers, W.E. and Plateau, D.P. (2003) 'The Meaning, Nature and Scope of Child Labour.' Draft paper presented at Colloquium *Combating Abusive Child Labour,* Iowa, July.

Ennew, J. and Plateau, D.P. (2003) 'Child Labour in Southeast Asia: Situation Analysis.' Unpublished.

Erpenbeck, J. (1997) 'Selbstgesteuertes, selbstorganisiertes Lernen.' In *Kompetenzentwicklung, 97. Berufliche Weiterbildung in der Transformation.* Münster, New York, Munich, Berlin: Waxmann, 310–316.

Etherton, M. (2000–2001) 'An Evaluation of Save the Children's Support to Children's and Young People's Participation in the National and International Preparations for UN General Assembly Special Session on Children.' Unpublished.

Farinelli, F. (1999) 'Quando il lavoro è occasione per parlare di intercultura: i bambini cinesi a Roma.' In Centro nazionale di documentazione e analisi per l'infanzia e l'adolescenza (ed) *Pianeta Infanzia, Minori e lavoro in Italia: questioni aperte.* Quaderni del Centro nazionale di documentazione e analisi per l'infanzia e l'adolescenza, Firenze: Istituto degli Innocenti.

Feinstein, C. (1997) 'Understanding the Nature of Child Work.' Paper presented at Conference on Urban Childhood, Trondheim, Norway, 9–12 June.

Finn, D. (1984) 'Leaving School and Growing Up: Work Experience in the Juvenile Labour Market.' In I. Bates, J. Clarke, P. Cohen, D, Finn, R. Moore and P. Willis (eds) *Schooling for the Dole? The New Vocationalism.* Basingstoke: Macmillan.

Flores-Oebanda, C., Roland Romeo, R. and Montanño, V.P. (2001) *The Kasambahay: Child Domestic Work in the Philippines: A Living Experience.* Manila: International Labour Office.

Fontana, R. (1995) *Il lavoro vietato: minori e marginalità nello sviluppo italiano.* Rome: SEAM.

Forastieri, V. (1997) *Children at Work: Health and Safety Risks.* Geneva: ILO.

Former Working Children for Working Children and CWA (2003) *Handbook on Facilitating Working Children's Participation.* Unpublished.

Franco, A. and Jouhette, S. (2002) 'Labour Force Survey. Principal Results 2001. EU and EFTA countries.' *Statistics in Focus. Population and Social conditions* No. 19. http://epp.eurostat.cec.eu.int/portal/page?_pageid=1073,1135281,1073_1135295&_dad =portal&_schema=PORTAL&p_product_code=KS-NK-02-019 (Accessed 9 February 2005).

Frederiksen, L. (1999) 'Child and Youth Employment in Denmark: Comments on Children's Work From Their Own Perspective.' *Childhood 6*, 1, 101–112.

Fuhs, B. (2001) 'Kindliche Verantwortung als biographische Erfahrung.' In I. Behnken and J. Zinnecker (eds) *Kinder. Kindheit. Lebensgeschichte.* Seelze-Velber: Kallmeyerische Verlagsbuchhandlung, 790–805.

Furtner-Kallmünzer, M., Hössl, A., Janke, D., Kellermann, D. and Lipski, J. (2002) *In der Freizeit für das Leben lernen. Eine Studie zu den Interessen von Schulkindern.* München: DJI Verlag Deutsches Jugendinstitut.

Fyfe, A. (1989) *Child Labour.* Cambridge: Polity Press.

Fyfe, A. (2001) 'Child Labour and Education: Revisiting the Policy Debate.' In G.K Lieten and B. White (eds) *Child Labour: Policy Options.* Amsterdam: Aksant.

Gabriel, Y. (1988) *Working Lives in Catering.* London: Routledge.

Galeana Cisneros, R. (1991) *El trabajo infantil y adolescente como instancia socializadora y formadora en, para y por la vida.* Tesis. Departamento de Investigaciones Educativas. IPN. Mexico.

Geissler, B. (2002) 'Die Dienstleistungslücke im Haushalt. Der neue Bedarf nach Dienstleistungen und der Handlungslogik der privaten Arbeit.' In C. Gather, B. Geissler and M.S. Rerrich (eds) *Weltmarkt Privathaushalt. Bezahlte Haushaltsarbeit im globalen Wandel.* Münster: Westfälisches Dampfboot.

Gélis, J. (1985) 'La individualización del niño.' In P. Ariès and G. Duby (eds) *Historia de la vida privada. Del Renacimiento a la Ilustración.* T. 3. Madrid: Taurus, 1989, 311–329.

Giddens, A. (1991) *Modernity and Self-identity. Self and Society in the Late Modern Age.* London: Polity Press; Basil Blackwell.

Gill, G.K. (1998) 'The Strategic Involvement of Children in Housework: An Australian Case of Two-income Families.' *The International Journal of Comparative Sociology 39*, 3, 301–314.

Glaser, B.G. (ed) (1994) *More Grounded Theory Methodology: A Reader.* Mill Valley, CA: Sociology Press.

Glaser, B.G. and Strauss, A.L. (1967) *The Discovery of Grounded Theory: Strategies for Qualitative Research.* London: Weidenfeld and Nicolson.

GMB (1995) *School Children At Work: A Survey of Local Councils on the Implementation of the Bye-Laws on Child Employment.* London: Labour Research Department.

Golini, A., Sgritta, G.B. and Gigantino, M. (eds) (2001) *L'età a rischio. Condizione giovanile e abuso di sostanze in un campione di 35mila diciottenni alla visita di leva.* Bologna: Il Mulino.

Good, C. (2005) 'Trabajando Juntos Como Uno: Conceptos nahuas del Grupo Doméstico y de la Persona.' In *Familia y parentesco en México y Mesoamérica. Unas miradas antropológicas.* Robichaux David. Compilador Universidad Iberoamericana. ENHA. Mexico.

Goodnow, J.J. (1988) 'Children's Household Work: Its Nature and Functions.' *Psychological Bulletin 103*, 1, 5–26.

Goodnow, J.J. and Collins, W.A. (1990) *Development According to Parents.* London: Erlbaum.

Graitcer, P and Lerer, L. (1998) *Child Labour and Health: Quantifying the Global Health Impacts of Child Labour.* Washington: The World Bank.

Green, D. (1998) *Hidden Lives: Voices of Children in Latin America and the Caribbean.* London: Cassell for Rädda Barnen.

Greenberger, E. and Steinberg, L. (1986) *When Teenagers Work: The Psychological and Social Costs of Adolescent Employment.* New York: Basic Books.

Greenfield, P.M. and Cocking, R.R. (eds) (1994) *Cultural Roots of Minority Child Development.* Hillside, NJ: Erlbaum.

Groves, L. (2003) *Good Practice in Working Children's Participation: A Case Study from Brazil.* Unpublished report. London: Save the Children Alliance.

Gunn, S.E. and Ostos, Z. (1992) 'Dilemmas in Tackling Child Labour: The Case of Scavenger Children in the Philippines.' *International Labour Review 131*, 629–646.

Gurevich, A. (1994) *Los orígenes del individualismo europeo.* Barcelona: Crítica, 1997.

Harkness, S. and Super, C. (eds) (1996) *Parents' Cultural Belief Systems.* New York: Guilford Press.

Hart, R. (1992) *Children's Participation: From Tokenism to Citizenship*. Innocenti Essays, No. 4. Florence: UNICEF/ICDC.

Hecht, T. (1998) *At Home in the Street: Street Children in North East Brazil*. Cambridge: Cambridge University Press.

Helleiner, J. (2003) 'The Politics of Traveller "child begging" in Ireland.' *Critique of Anthropology 23*, 17–33.

Hengst, H. (2000) 'Die Arbeit der Kinder und der Umbau der Arbeitsgesellschaft.' In H. Hengst and H. Zeiher (eds) *Die Arbeit der Kinder*. *Weinheim and Munich*, 71–97.

Hengst, H. and Zeiher, H. (eds) (2000) *Die Arbeit der Kinder. Kindheitskonzept und Arbeitsteilung zwischen den Generationen*. Weinheim and Munich: Juventa Verlag.

Hesketh, T., Gamlin, J. and Woodhead, M. (in press) 'Policy in Child Labour: The Importance of Health.' *Archive of Diseases in Childhood*.

Hibbett, A. and Beatson, M. (1995) 'Young People at Work.' *Employment Gazette*, April, 169–177.

Hobbs, S., Lavalette, M. and McKechnie, J. (1992) 'The Emerging Problem of Child Labour.' *Critical Social Policy 12*, 1, 93–105.

Hobbs, S., Lindsay, S. and McKechnie, J. (1996) 'The Extent of Child Employment in Britain.' *British Journal of Education and Work 9*, 1, 5–18.

Hobbs, S and McKechnie, J. (1997) *Child Employment in Britain: A Social and Psychological Analysis*. Edinburgh: The Stationery Office.

Hobbs, S., McKechnie, J. and Lavalette, M. (1999) *Child Labor: A World History Companion*. Santa Barbara, CA: ABC-Clio.

Hockey, J. (1996) 'Motives and Meanings Amongst PhD Supervisors in the Social Sciences.' *British Journal of Sociology of Education 17*, 4, 489–506.

Holloway, S. and Valentine, G. (2000) 'Children's Geographies and the New Social Studies of Childhood.' In S. Holloway and G. Valentine (eds) *Children's Geographies: Playing, Living, Learning*. London: Routledge, 98–117.

Honneth, A. (1992) *Kampf um Anerkennung. Zur moralischen Grammatik sozialer Konflikte*. Frankfurt: Suhrkamp.

Hull, T. (1983) 'Perspectivas y Datos Necesarios para el Estudio del Trabajo de los Niños.' In *Trabajo Infantil, Pobreza y Subdesarrollo*. Geneva: ILO/OIT.

Hungerland, B., Liebel, M., Wihstutz, A. (2005) 'Bedeutungen der Arbeit von Kindern in Deutschland.' *Arbeit–Zeitschrift für Arbeitsforschung, Arbeitsgestaltung und Arbeitspolitik 14*, 2, 77–93.

Hungerland, B., Liebel, M., Liesecke, A. and Wihstutz, A. (2006) 'Paths to participatory autonomy: The meanings of work by children in Germany.' In *Childhood* (in press).

Hungerland, B. and Overwien, B. (eds) (2004) *Kompetenzentwicklung im Wandel. Auf dem Weg zu einer informellen Lernkultur?* Wiesbaden: Verlag für Sozialwissenschaften.

Hungerland, B. and Wihstutz, A. (2003) 'Arbeitende Kinder. Partisanen in der Erwachsenenwelt?' *ZEP – Zeitschrift für internationale Bildungsforschung und Entwicklungspädagogik 26*, 3, 19–24.

ILO (1996) *Child Labour: Targeting the Intolerable*. Geneva: International Labour Office.

ILO (1999) 'Convention Concerning the Prohibition and Inmediate Action for the Elimination of the Worst Forms of Child Labour.' ILO Convention 182. Geneva: International Labour Office.

ILO (2002) *A Future Without Child Labour*. Geneva: International Labour Office.

Ingenhorst, H. (2001) 'Child Labour in the Federal Republic of Germany.' In P. Mizen, C. Pole and A. Bolton (eds) *Hidden Hands. International Perspectives on Children's Work and Labour*. London: RoutledgeFalmer.

International Labour Office, International Programme on the Elimination of Child Labour (2002) *Statistical Information and Monitoring Programme on Child Labour, Every Child Counts. New Global Estimates on Child Labour*. Geneva: ILO-IPEC.

International Save the Children Alliance (2000) *Child-Centred Policies and Programmes for Working Children in Southeast, East Asia and the Pacific Region*. Bangkok: Amarin Printing.

International Save the Children Alliance (2003) *Towards a Strategy to Address Corporal Punishment of Children in Southeast, East Asia and Pacific: Proceedings of the International Save the Children Alliance Regional Workshop on Corporal Punishment of Children, 6–9 October 2003, Bangkok, Thailand.* Bangkok: International Save the Children Alliance.

Invernizzi, A. (1998) 'Il lavoro dei bambini come insieme di legami sociali.' *NATs, Nuovi spazi di crescita 3*, Bologna: EMI.

Invernizzi, A. (2001) *La vie quotidienne des enfants travailleurs. Stratégies de survie et socialisation dans les rues de Lima.* Paris: L'Harmattan.

Invernizzi, A. (2003) 'Street-Working Children and Adolescents in Lima: Work as an Agent of Socialization.' *Childhood 10*, 4, 319–341.

Invernizzi, A. (2005) 'Perspectives on Children's Work in the Algarve (Portugal) and Their Implication for Social Policy.' *Critical Social Policy 25*, 2, 198–222.

Invernizzi, A. (2006) 'Children's Work in Portugal: An Exploration of Children's Motivations, Family Organisation and Views on Socialisation.' *International Journal of Children's Rights*, in press.

Invernizzi, A. and Milne, B. (2002) 'Are Children Entitled to Contribute to International Policy Making? A Critical View of Children's Participation in the International Campaign for the Elimination of Child Labour.' *International Journal of Children Rights 10*, 4, 403–431.

IPEC (2002) *Combating Child Labour: A Handbook for Labour Inspectors.* Geneva, International Labour Office, International Programme for the Elimination of Child Labour.

IPEC (2004) *Helping Hands or Shackled Lives? Understanding Child Domestic Labour and Responses to it.* Geneva: ILO.

IRES (1998) *Il lavoro minorile come causa di esclusione sociale: Clacse rapporto finale Italia, s.e.* Rome: IRES.

ISTAT (2002) *Sistema informativo sul lavoro minorile, Progetto Silm, Relazione Finale, Convenzione Istat e Ministero del lavoro e delle politiche sociali.* Rome: ISTAT.

James, A., Jenks, C. and Prout, A. (1998) *Theorising Childhood.* Cambridge: Polity Press.

James, A. and Prout, J. (eds) (1997) *Constructing and Reconstructing Childhood.* London: Palgrave. 1st edition 1990.

Jamieson, L. and Corr, H. (1990) 'Earning Your Keep: Self-reliance and Family Obligation.' ESRC 16–19 Initiative Occasional Paper No. 30. London: SSRU.

Kakar, S. (1981) *The Inner World: A Psychoanalytic Study of Childhood and Society in India.* New Delhi: Oxford University Press.

Kerckhoff, A.C. (2003) 'From Student to Worker.' In J.T. Mortimer and M.S. Shanahan (eds) *Handbook of the Life Course.* New York: Kluwer Academic/Plenum Publishers, 251–267.

Kirchhöfer, D. (1998) 'Kinderarbeit – ein notwendiger Entwicklungsraum der Heranwachsenden.' *DISKURS, No. 2/98.* Munich: Deutsches Jugendinstitut.

Kirchhöfer, D. (2004a) 'Kinderarbeit in einer sich entgrenzenden Arbeitsgesellschaft.' In B. Hungerland and B. Overwien (eds) *Kompetenzentwicklung im Wandel.* Wiesbaden: Verlag für Sozialwissenschaften, 143–162.

Kirchhöfer, D. (2004b) *Lernkultur-Kompetenzentwicklung. Begriffliche Grundlagen.* Berlin: AG Betriebliche Weiterbildungsforschung.

KKSP Foundation (2000) *General Report of Convention on the Rights of the Child Training (CRC) and Child's Participation and Leadership Development Workshop.* Medan, Indonesia: KKSP Foundation.

Klein, N. (2001) *No Logo.* London: Flamingo.

Knutsson, K.E. (1997) *Children: Noble Causes or Worthy Citizens?* Brookfield, VT: Ashgate Publishing, for UNICEF.

Kudera, W. (1995) 'Zusammenfassung der Ergebnisse.' In Projektgruppe Alltägliche Lebensführung (ed) *Alltägliche Lebensführung. Arrangements zwischen Traditionalität und Modernisierung.* Opladen: Leske and Budrich, 331–370.

Landsdown, G. (1994) 'Children's Rights.' In B. Mayall (ed) *Children's Childhoods: Observed and Experienced.* London: Falmer.

Lavalette, M. (1996) 'Thatcher's Working Children: Contemporary Issues of Child Labour.' In J. Pilcher and S. Wagg (eds) *Thatcher's Children? Politics, Childhood and Society in the 1980s and 1990s.* London: Falmer, 172–200.

LBS-Initiative Junge Familie (2004) *LBS-Kinderbarometer 2003. Stimmungen, Meinungen, Trends von Kindern in NRW.* Münster: LBS-Initiative Junge Familie.

Lee, N. (2003) *Childhood and Society: Growing Up in an Age of Uncertainty.* Buckingham: Open University Press.

Leonard, M. (1999a) 'Childwork in the UK 1970–1998.' In M. Lavalette (ed) *A Thing of the Past? Child Labour in Britain in the 19th and 20th Centuries.* Liverpool: Liverpool University Press.

Leonard, M. (1999b) *Play Fair with Working Children.* Belfast: Save the Children.

Leonard, M. (2002) 'Working on Your Doorstep. Child Newspaper Deliverers in Belfast.' *Childhood 9,* 2, 217–231.

Leonard, M. (2003) 'Children's Attitudes to Parents, Teachers' and Employers' Perceptions of Term-Time Employment.' *Children and Society 17,* 349–360.

Leonard, M. (2004) 'Children's Views on Children's Right to Work: Reflections from Belfast.' *Childhood 11,* 1, 73–89.

Leu, H.R. (1996) 'Selbständige Kinder – ein schwieriges Thema für die Sozialisationsforschung.' In M.-S. Honig, H. Leu and U. Nissen (eds) *Kinder und Kindheit. Soziokulturelle Muster-sozialisationstheoretische Perspektiven.* Weinheim and Munich: Juventa, 174–198.

Levison, D. (2000) 'Children as Economic Agents.' *Feminist Economics 6,* 1, 125–134.

Levison, D., Hoek, J., Lam, D. and Duryea, S. (2003) 'Implications of Intermittent Employment for Child Labor Estimates.' Unpublished.

Liebel, M. (1994) *Protagonismo Infantil. Movimientos de Niños Trabajadores en América Latina.* Managua: Ed. Nueva Nicaragua.

Liebel, M. (2001a) 'Child Labour, Child Work and the International Labour Organisation (ILO).' In M. Liebel, B. Overwien and A. Recknagel (eds) *Working Children's Protagonism.* Frankfurt and London: IKO, 87–102.

Liebel, M. (2001b) *Kindheit und Arbeit. Wege zum besseren Verständnis arbeitender Kinder in verschiedenen Kulturen und Kontinenten.* Frankfurt and London: IKO.

Liebel, M. (2001c) '12 Rights, and Making Their Own Way. The Working Children and Youth of Africa Organise Themselves.' In M. Liebel, B. Overwien and A. Recknagel (eds) *Working Children's Protagonism.* Frankfurt and London: IKO, 197–217.

Liebel, M. (2003) *Infancia y Trabajo.* Lima: Ifejant.

Liebel, M. (2004) *A Will of Their Own. Cross-cultural Perspectives on Working Children.* London and New York: Zed Books.

Liebel, M. (2006a) 'Profit im Klassenzimmer? Zum heimlichen Lehrplan wirtschaftlichen Handelns von Kindern in der Schule.' *Die Deutsche Schule 98,* 1, 11–27.

Liebel, M. (2006b) 'Schülerfirmen – mehr als eine Geschäftsidee? Zwischen Profitorientierung und solidarischer Ökonomie.' *Die Deutsche Schule 98,* 2, 225–240.

Lieten, G.K. and White, B. (2001) 'Children, Work and Education: Perspectives on Policy.' In G.K. Lieten and B. White (eds) *Child Labour: Policy Options.* Amsterdam: Aksant.

Light, H.K., Hertsgaard, D. and Martin, R.E. (1985) 'Farm Children's Work in the Family.' *Adolescence 20,* 78, 425–32.

Lipovetsky, G. (1992) *El crepúsculo del deber. La ética indolora de los nuevos tiempos democráticos.* Barcelona: Anagrama, 2000.

López Limón, M.G. (1998) *El Trabajo Infantil fruto amargo del capital.* Mexico D.F.: Ed. MGLL.

Lucas, R. (1997) 'Youth, Gender and Part-Time Work – Students in the Labour Process.' *Work, Employment and Society 11,* 4, 595–614.

Luthar, S.S. (2003) *Resilience and Vulnerability: Adaptation in the Context of Childhood Adversities.* Cambridge: Cambridge University Press.

MacLennan, E., Fitz, J. and Sullivan, J. (1985) *Working Children.* London: Low Pay Unit, Report No. 2.

Mangoma, J. and Bourdillon, M. (2002) 'The Work of Children in Impoverished Families.' In P. Hebinck and M. Bourdillon (eds) *Rural Livelihoods in South-eastern Zimbabwe.* Harare: Weaver Press, 13–35.

Manke, B., Seery, B.L., Croute, A.C. and McHale, S.M. (1994) 'The Three Corners of Domestic Labour: Mothers' Fathers' and Children's Weekday and Weekend Housework.' *Journal of Marriage and the Family 56,* 657–668.

Mansurov, V. (2001) 'Child Labour in Russia.' In P. Mizen, C. Pole and A. Bolton (eds) *Hidden Hands: International Perspectives on Children's Work and Labour.* London: RoutledgeFalmer.

Marcus, R. and Harper, C. (1996) *Small Hands: Children in the Working World.* London: Save the Children, Working Paper No. 16.

Marshall, T. (1950) *Citizenship and Social Class, and Other Essays.* Cambridge: Cambridge University Press.

Marshall, T. (1964) *Class, Citizenship and Social Development.* Garden City, NY: Doubleday.

Marx, K. (1979) *Das Kapital.* Erster Band. MEW 23. Berlin: Dietz.

Mattioli, F. (1996) *Iqbal Masih non era italiano: percorsi e strategie del lavoro infantile nell'Italia postindustriale.* Rome: SEAM.

Mayall, B. (ed) (1994) *Children's Childhoods: Observed and Experienced.* London: Falmer.

Mayall, B. (1996) *Children, Health and the Social Order.* Buckingham: Open University Press.

Mayall, B. (1998) 'Towards a Sociology of Child Health.' *Sociology of Health and Illness 20,* 3, 269–288.

Mayall, B. (2002) *Towards a Sociology for Childhood. Thinking from Children's Lives.* Buckingham and Philadelphia: Open University Press.

McKechnie, J. and Hobbs, S. (1997a) *Child Employment in the United Kingdom.* London: Stationery Office.

McKechnie, J. and Hobbs, S. (1997b) 'Understanding Children's Work.' Working Paper. Amsterdam: International Working Group on Child Labour.

McKechnie, J. and Hobbs, S. (eds) (1998) *Working Children: Reconsidering the Debates: Report of the International Working Group on Child Labour.* Amsterdam: Defence for Children International.

McKechnie, J. and Hobbs, S. (2001) 'Work and education: Are they compatible for children and adolescents?' In P. Mizen. C. Pole and A. Bolton (eds) *Hidden Hands: International Perspectives on Children's Work and Labour.* London: RoutledgeFalmer.

McKechnie, J., Hobbs, S. and Anderson, S. (2004) *Learning About Work?: The Role of School Students' Part-time Employment.* Glasgow: Careers Scotland.

McKechnie, J., Hobbs, S. and Hill, S. (2002) 'Work and School: Part-time Employment amongst Senior School Students.' A report to Renfrewshire Education and Leisure Services. Paisley: University of Paisley.

McKechnie, J., Hobbs, S. and Lindsay, S. (1998) 'Work and the Older School Student.' In B. Pettit (ed) *Children and Work in the UK: Reassessing the Issues.* London: Child Poverty Action Group.

McKechnie, J., Stack, N. and Hobbs, S. (2001) 'Work by Secondary School Students in Scotland.' *International Journal of Educational Policy, Research and Practices 2,* 287–305.

McMorris, B. and Uggen, C. (2000) 'Alcohol and Employment in the Transition to Adulthood.' *Journal of Health and Social Behavior 41,* 276–294.

Melhuus, M. (1992) *Todos Tenemos Madre. Dios También. Morality, Meaning and Change in a Mexican Context.* Thesis. Department and Museum of Antropology, Faculty of Social Sciences, University of Oslo.

Mensch, B.S., Ibrahim, B.L., Lee, S.M. and El-Gibaly, O. (2000) *Socialization to Gender Roles and Marriage Among Egyptian Adolescents.* Policy, México: MGLL.

Micali, A. (ed) (2002) *Bambini, lavori e lavoretti. Verso un sistema informativo sul lavoro minorile.* Rome: ISTAT and Ministero del lavoro e delle politiche sociali.

Middleton, S., Shropshire, J. and Croden, N. (1998) 'Earning Your Keep? Children's Work and Contributions to Family Budgets.' In B. Pettite (ed) *Children and Work in the UK: Reassessing the Issues.* London: Child Proverty Action Group.

Mignolo, W. (1998) 'Posoccidentalismo: el argumento desde América Latina.' In S. Castro and E. Mendieta (eds) *Teorías sin disciplina. Latinoamericanismo, poscolonialidad y globalización en debate.* México: Miguel Angel Porrúa; University of San Francisco, 31–58.

Mignolo, W. (2000) 'La colonialidad a lo largo y a lo ancho: el hemisferio occidental en el horizonte colonial de la modernidad.' In E. Lander (ed) *La colonialidad del saber: eurocentrismo y ciencias sociales. Perspectivas latinoamericanas.* Buenos Aires: CLACSO; UNESCO, 55–85.

Mill, J.S. (1859) 'On Liberty.' E. Alexander (ed.) (1999) Peterborough: Broadview Press.

Mills, C.W. (1940) 'Situated Actions and Vocabularies of Motive.' *American Sociological Review 5,* 904–913.

Ministerio da Educação (2003) *Cartografia do abandono e insuceso escolares.* Lisboa; www.min-edu.pt/Scripts/ASP/news_det.asp?newsID=187&categoriaID=est (downloaded 26 October 2003).

Ministry of Labour and the Department of Labour and Welfare Development of Thammasat University (2003) *National Plan of Action for the Elimination of the Worst Forms of Child Labour (2004–2009).* Unpublished.

Mizen, P. (1992) 'Learning the Hard Way: The Extent and Significance of Child Labour in Britain.' *British Journal of Education and Work 5,* 3, 5–17.

Mizen, P., Bolton, A. and Pole, C. (1999) 'School Age Workers in Britain: The Paid Employment of Children in Britain.' *Work, Employment and Society 13,* 3, 423–438.

Mizen, P., Pole, C. and Bolton, A. (eds) (2001) *Hidden Hands: International Perspectives on the Work and Labour of Children.* London: RoutledgeFalmer.

MNNATSOP and Ifejant (eds) (1997) *Niños trabajadores y protagonismo de la infancia.* Lima: Ifejant.

Moretti, E. (2004) 'Il lavoro minorile in Italia: un approfondimento a partire dall'indagine ISTAT.' In Centro nazionale di documentazione e analisi per l'infanzia e l'adolescenza (ed) *Bambini e adolescenti che lavorano, Un panorama dall'Italia all'Europa.* Quaderni del Centro nazionale di documentazione e analisi per l'infanzia e l'adolescenza, Florence: Istituto degli Innocenti.

Morice, A. (1983) 'Explotación de los Niños en el Sector no Estructurado: Propuesta de Investigación.' In *Trabajo Infantil, Pobreza y Subdesarrollo.* Geneva: OIT-ILO.

Moro, A.C. (1999) 'Le nuove tipologie di lavoro minorile e la scarsa tutela della personalità in formazione.' In Centro nazionale di documentazione e analisi per l'infanzia e l'adolescenza (ed) *Pianeta Infanzia, Minori e lavoro in Italia: questioni aperte.* Quaderni del Centro nazionale di documentazione e analisi per l'infanzia e l'adolescenza, Florence: Istituto degli Innocenti.

Morrow, V. (1992) *A Sociological Study of the Economic Roles of Children, with Particular Reference to Birmingham and Cambridgeshire.* Unpublished PhD thesis, Faculty of Social and Political Sciences, University of Cambridge.

Morrow, V. (1994) 'Responsible Children? Aspects of Children's Work and Employment Outside School in Contemporary UK.' In B. Mayall (ed) *Children's Childhoods: Observed and Experienced.* London: Falmer, 114–127.

Morrow, V. (1996) 'Rethinking Childhood Dependency: Children's Contribution to the Domestic Economy.' *The Sociological Review 44,* 58–77.

Mortimer, J.T. (2003) *Working and Growing Up in America.* Cambridge, MA: Harvard University Press.

Mortimer, J.T., Efron Pimentel, E., Ryu, S., Nash, K. and Lee, C. (1996) 'Part-time Work and Occupational Value Formation in Adolescence.' *Social Forces 74,* 1405–1418.

Mortimer, J.T. and Finch, M.D. (eds) (1996) *Adolescents Work and the Family: An Intergenerational Developmental Analysis.* Thousand Oaks, CA: Sage.

Mortimer, J.T., Harley, C. and Staff, J. (2002) 'The Quality of Work and Youth Mental Health.' *Work and Occupations 29,* 166–197.

Mortimer, J.T. and Johnson, M.K. (1998) 'Adolescent Part-time Work and Educational Achievement.' In K. Borman and B. Schneider (eds) *The Adolescent Years: Social Influences and Educational Challenges.* Chicago: National Society for the Study of Education, 183–206.

Mortimer, J.T., and Krueger, H. (2000) 'Pathways from School to Work in Germany and the United States.' In M. Hallinan (ed) *Handbook of the Sociology of Education.* New York: Kluwer Academic/Plenum Publishers.

Mortimer, J.T. and Staff, J. (2004) 'Early Work as a Source of Developmental Discontinuity during the Transition to Adulthood.' *Development and Psychopathology 16,* 1047–1070.

Mortimer, J.T., Staff, J. and Oesterle, S. (2003) 'Adolescent Work and the Early Socioeconomic Career.' In J.T. Mortimer and M.J. Shanahan (eds) *Handbook of the Life Course.* New York: Kluwer Academic/Plenum Publishers, 437–459.

Mulder, N. (2003) *Southeast Asian Images Towards Civil Society?* Thailand: Silkworm Books.

Mulhare, E. (2003) 'Respetar y confiar: ideología de género versus comportamiento en una sociedad post nahua.' In D. Robichaux (ed) *El matrimonio en Mesoamérica ayer y hoy. Unas mirada antropológicas.* Robichaux David. Mexico City: Compilador Universidad Iberoamericana.

Myers, W.E. (ed) (1991) *Protecting Working Children.* London: Zed Books.

Myers, W.E. (2001) 'Valuing Diverse Approaches to Child Labour.' In G.K. Lieten and B. White (eds) *Child Labour: Policy Options.* Amsterdam: Aksant.

Nasman, E. (1994) 'Individualisation and Institutionalisation of Childhood in Today's Europe.' In J. Qvortrup, M. Bardy, G. Sgritta and H. Winterberger (eds) *Childhood Matters: Social Theory, Practice and Politics.* Aldershot: Avebury.

National Coalition for Children's Participation (2002) *Building a Child-Friendly Nation.* Manila Philippines: VJ Graphic Arts, Inc.

National Research Council, Institute of Medicine. Committee on the Health and Safety Implications of Child Labor (1998) *Protecting Youth at Work: Health, Safety, and Development of Working Children and Adolescents in the United States.* Washington, DC: National Academy Press.

Newman, K.S. (1999) *No Shame in My Game.* New York: Knopf and Russell Sage Foundation.

Nieuwenhuys, O. (1994) *Children's Lifeworlds: Gender, Welfare and Labour in the Developing World.* London: Routledge and New Delhi: Social Science.

Nieuwenhuys, O. (1995) 'The Domestic Economy and the Exploitation of Children's Work: The Case of Kerala.' *The International Journal of Children's Right 3,* 213–225.

Nieuwenhuys, O. (1996) 'The Paradox of Child Labour and Anthropology.' *Annual Review of Anthropology 25,* 237–251.

Nieuwenhuys, O. (1998) 'Global Childhood and the Politics of Contempt.' *Alternatives 23,* 267–289.

O'Donnell, O., van Doorslaer, E. and Rosati, F. (2002) *Child Labour and Health: Evidence and Research Issues.* Florence: ILO/UNICEF/World Bank Understanding Children's Work Project.

O'Donnell, C. and White, L. (1998) *Invisible Hands: Child Employment in North Tyneside.* London: Low Pay Unit.

O'Kane, C. (2000) 'Street and Working Children's Participation in Programming for their Rights: Conflicts Arising from Diverse Perspectives and Directions for Convergence.' Unpublished.

O'Kane, C. (2002) 'Key Reflections and Learning from Children's Participation and Children's Organisations on South and Central Asia: Moving Towards Partnerships with Adults.' Unpublished.

Oakley, A. (1994) 'Women and Children First and Last: Parallels and Differences between Children's and Women's Studies.' In B. Mayall (ed) *Children's Childhoods Observed and Experienced.* London: Falmer.

Oakley, A. (1996) 'Gender Matters: Man the Hunters.' In H. Roberts and D. Sachdev (eds) *Young People Attitudes.* Illford: Barnardos.

OECD (1996) 'Growing Into Work: Youth and the Labour Market Over the 1980s and 1990s.' *Economic Outlook.* Paris: Organisation for Economic Co-operation and Development.

OIT (2000) *El Trabajo Infantil.* Mexico, D.F.: Ed. Alfaomega.

OIT and UNICEF (1996) *El Trabajo Infantil en México.* Xalapa: Ed. Universidad Veracruzana, Mexico.

Oldman, G. (1994) 'Childhood as a Mode of Production.' In B. Mayall (ed) *Children's Childhoods: Observed and Experienced.* London: Falmer.

Otis, J., Paszor, E.M. and McFadeen, E.J. (2001) 'Child Labor: A Forgotten Focus for Child Welfare.' *Child Welfare 80*, 611–622.

Pancera, C. (1987) 'Educare nel lavoro, educare al lavoro.' In E. Becchi (ed) *Storia dell'educazione.* Florence: La Nuova Italia.

Paone, G. and Teselli, T.A. (2000) *Lavoro e lavori minorili. L'inchiesta CGIL in Italia.* Rome: Ediesse.

Pérez, I. (1994) *Tlalcuapan. Tierra donde Abundan las Víboras: Memoria de Generaciones.* Ed. SEPE, SEP, USET. Mexico, D.F..

Pfigu, T. (2003) *'Invisible Workers': A Study of Child Domestic Work in Zimbabwe.* Unpublished MSc dissertation, Department of Sociology, University of Zimbabwe.

Pflug, B. (1995) *An Overview of Child Domestic Workers in Asia.* Geneva: ILO.

Pole, C., Mizen, P. and Bolton, A. (1999) 'Realising Children's Agency in Research: Partners and Participants?' *International Journal of Social Research Methodology, Theory and Practice 2*, 1, 33–54.

Pond, C. and Searle, C. (1991) *The Hidden Army: Children at Work in the 1990s.* London: Low Pay Unit.

Price, R.H., Choi, J.N. and Vinokur, A.D. (2002) 'Links in the Chain of Adversity Following Job Loss: How Financial Strain and Loss of Personal Control Lead to Depression, Impaired Functioning, and Poor Health.' *Journal of Occupational Health Psychology 7*, 4, 302–312.

Prosser, J. (1998) 'Introduction.' In J. Prosser (ed) *Image-based Research: A Sourcebook For Qualitative Researchers.* London: RoutledgeFalmer.

Prout, A. (2004) *The Future of Childhood: Towards the Interdisciplinary Study of Childhood.* London. RoutledgeFalmer.

Prout, A. and James, A. (1997) 'Introduction.' In A. James and A. Prout (eds) *Constructing and Reconstructing Childhood.* London: Falmer. 2nd edition.

Punch, S. (2001) 'Household division of labour: Generation, gender, age, birth order and sibling composition.' *Work, Employment and Society 15*, 4, 803–823.

Punch, S. (2003) 'Childhoods in the Majority World: Miniature Adults or Tribal Children?' *Sociology 37*, 2, 277–295.

Quijano, A. (2000) 'Colonialidad del poder, eurocentrismo y América Latina.' In E. Lander (ed) *La colonialidad del saber: eurocentrismo y ciencias sociales. Perspectivas latinoamericanas.* Buenos Aires: CLACSO; UNESCO, 201–246.

Qvortrup, J. (1985) 'Placing Children in the Division of Labour.' In P. Close and R. Collins (eds) *Family and Economy in Modern Society.* London: Macmillan Press.

Qvortrup, J. (1987) 'Introduction.' *International Journal of Sociology 17*, 3, Special Issue 'The Sociology of Childhood.'

Qvortrup, J. (1994) 'Childhood Matters: An Introduction.' In J. Qvortrup, M. Bardy, G. Sgritta and H. Winterberger (eds) *Childhood Matters: Social Theory, Practice and Politics.* Aldershot: Avebury, 1–24.

Qvortrup, J. (1997) 'Childhood and Social Macrostructures.' Paper presented to ESRC Seminar, *Conceptualising Childhood – Perspectives on Research.* ESRC Children 5–16: Growing Into the 21st Century Programme, University of Keele, UK.

Qvortrup, J. (1999) 'Childhood and Societal Macrostructures: Childhood Exclusion by Default.' Department of Contemporary Cultural Studies, University of Odense: Working Paper No. 9.

Qvortrup, J. (2000) 'Kolonisiert und verkannt: Schularbeit.' In H. Hengst and H. Zeiher (eds) *Die Arbeit der Kinder.* Weinheim and Munich: Juventa.

Qvortrup, J. (2001) 'School-work, Paid Work and the Changing Obligations of Childhood.' In P. Mizen, C. Pole and A. Bolton (eds) *Hidden Hands: International Perspectives on Children's Work and Labour.* London: RoutledgeFalmer, 91–107.

Rädda Barnen (1997) *Trabajo Infantil en Centroamérica: El Salvador, Guatemala y Nicaragua.* San Salvador: Ed. Rädda Barnen.

Rerrich, M.S. (2002) 'Von der Utopie der partnerschaftlichen Gleichverteilung Zur Realität der Globalisierung von Hausarbeit.' In C. Gather, B. Geissler and M.S. Rerrich (eds) *Weltmarkt Privathaushalt. Bezahlte Haushaltsarbeit im globalen Wandel.* Münster: Westfälisches Dampfboot, 16–29.

Reunión Tripartita Oficiosa de Nivel Ministerial (1996) *El trabajo Infantil: que hacer: Actas de la Reunión Tripartita de la Reunión Tripartita Oficiosa de Nivel Ministerial.* Geneva: OIT-ILO.

Reynolds, P. (1991) *Dance Civet Cat: Child Labour in the Zambezi Valley.* London: Zed Books and Athens OH: Ohio University Press.

Richter, A. (2000) *Wie erleben und bewältigen Kinder Armut? Eine qualitative Studie über Belastungen aus Unterversorgungslagen und ihre Bewältigung aus subjektiver Sicht von Grundschulkindern einer ländlichen Region.* Aachen: Shaker Verlag.

Ridge, T. (2002) *Childhood Poverty and Social Exclusion from a Child's Perspective.* London: The Policy Press.

Riquer, F.F. (ed) (1998) *La niña de hoy es la mujer de mañana. Estado de la discusión sobre la niñez mexicana.* Mexico: Ed. GIMTRAP, DIF. UNICEF, Vol. 3.

Robichaux, D. (1996) *Problemas Metodológicos en el Estudio del Grupo Doméstico en México.* Mexico: Ed. UIA.

Rodgers, G. and Standing, G. (1983) 'Funciones Económicas de los Niños Problemas de Análisis.' In *Trabajo Infantil, Pobreza y Subdesarrollo.* Geneva: OIT-ILO.

Rommelspacher, B. (1992) *Mitmenschlichkeit und Unterwerfung. Zur Ambivalenz der weiblichen Moral.* Frankfurt and New York: Campus.

RWG-CL (1997) *Children's Forum and Regional Consultation Against the Most Intolerable Forms of Child Labour/Targeting the Invisible and the Neglected Ones.* Bangkok, Thailand: Regional Working Group on Child Labour.

RWG-CL (2001) *Working Children's Participation in Actions Against the Worst Forms of Child Labour in Asia.* Bangkok, Thailand: Regional Working Group on Child Labour.

RWG-CL (2003) *Learning to Work Together: A Handbook for Managers on Facilitating Children's Participants in Actions to Address Child Labour.* Bangkok, Thailand: Regional Working Group on Child Labour.

Saini, D.S. (1994) 'Children of a Lesser God, Child Labour Law and Compulsory Primary Education.' *Social Action 44*, July–September, 1–13.

Save the Children (1998) *Voice of Disadvantaged Children in Vietnam.* London: International Save the Children Alliance.

Schaffer, R.H. (1996) *Social Development.* Oxford: Blackwell.

Schibotto, G. (1990) *Niños Trabajadores. Construyendo una identidad.* Lima: Ed. IPEC.

Schildkrout, E. (1980) 'Children's Work Reconsidered.' *International Social Science Journal XXXII*, 3, 479–489.

Schlemmer, B. (ed) (2000) *The Exploited Child.* London and New York: Zed Books.

Schlemmer, B. and Gérard, E. (2004) 'Le rapport à l'école dans les milieux populaires de Fès.' Paper delivered at the *Le droit à l'éducation – Quelles effectivités au Sud et au Nord' conference, organised by AFEC, FASAF, IIEDH, IRD and GRETAF in Ouagadougou, 8–12 March 2004.*

Schoenhals, M., Tienda, M. and Schneider, B. (1998) 'The Educational and Personal Consequences of Adolescent Employment.' *Social Forces 77*, 723–762.

Schröter, W. (2004) *Visionen für die Arbeitswelten in der Informationsgesellschaft.* Forum Soziale Technikgestaltung. www.bloch-akademie.de

Shanahan, M.J. and Flaherty, B.P. (2001) 'Dynamic Patterns of Time Use in Adolescence.' *Child Development 72*, 385–401.

Shanahan, M.J. and Mortimer, J.T. (1996) 'Understanding the positive consequences of psychological stress.' In B. Markovsky, M. Lovaglia and R. Simons (eds) *Advances in Group Process 13*, 189–209.

Shorter, E. (1975) *The Making of the Modern Family.* New York: Basic Books.

SIETI (2001) *Caracterização social dos agregados familares portugueses con menores em idade escolar.* Lisbon: ILO/SIETI/DETEFP.

Sigel, I., McGillicuddy-DeLisi, A.V. and Goodnow, J.J. (1985/1992) *Parental Belief Systems.* Hillsdale, NJ: Erlbaum.

SIMPOC (2002) 'Standard Household-Based Child Labour Survey Instruments.' Geneva: IPEC, International Labour Office. Unpublished.

Solberg, A. (1997) 'Negotiating Childhood: Changing Constructions of Age for Norwegian Children.' In A. James and A. Prout (eds) *Constructing and Reconstructing Childhood,* 2nd edition. London: Falmer, 126–144 (1st edition 1990).

Stack, N. (2004) *The Benefits and Costs of Part-time Employment for Full-time School Students: A Psychological Investigation.* PhD thesis, University of Paisley, UK.

Staff, J. and Mortimer, J.T. (2005) 'Educational and Work Strategies from Adolescence to Early Adulthood: Consequences for Educational Attainment.' Unpublished.

Stegmann, K. (2003) *Child Health and the Worst Forms of Child Labour.* London: Anti-Slavery International, Working Document.

Steinberg, L. and Cauffman, E. (1995) 'The Impact of Employment on Adolescent Development.' *Annals of Child Development 11,* 131–166.

Strassman, D. (1993) 'Not a Free Market: The Rhetoric of Disciplinary Authority in Economics.' In M. Ferber and J. Nelson (eds) *Beyond Economic Man: Feminist Theory and Economics.* Chicago: University of Chicago Press.

Strathern, M. (1988) *The Gender of the Gift: Problems with Women and Problems with Society in Melanesia.* Berkeley: University of California Press.

Straus, M.A. (1962) 'Work Roles and Financial Responsibility in the Socialisation of Farm, Fringe and Town Boys.' *Rural Sociology 27,* 257–274.

Strauss, A. (1993) *Continual Permutations of Action.* New York: Walter de Gruyter.

Strauss, A. and Corbin, J. (1990) *Basics of Qualitative Research: Grounded Theory Procedures and Techniques.* London: Sage Publications.

Swift, A. (2001) 'India – Tale of Two Working Children's Unions.' In M. Liebel, B. Overwien and A. Recknagel (eds) *Working Children's Protagonism.* Frankfurt and London: IKO, 181–196.

Taggart, J. (2003) *Como los niños aztecas aprenden ser adultos: inculcando el respeto hoy en día en una comunidad mexicana.* Mexico City: Ponencia Valdivia.

Tagliaventi, M.T. (1999a) 'Per un alfabeto comune.' In Centro nazionale di documentazione e analisi per l'infanzia e l'adolescenza (ed) *Pianeta Infanzia, Minori e lavoro in Italia: questioni aperte.* Quaderni del Centro nazionale di documentazione e analisi per l'infanzia e l'adolescenza, Florence: Istituto degli Innocenti.

Tagliaventi, M.T. (1999b) *Preadolescenti che lavorano: le connessioni con i percorsi formativi.* Tesi di dottorato in Sociologia e politiche sociali, IX ciclo, Università di Bologna.

Tagliaventi, M.T. (2002) *Lavoro minorile e percorsi formativi in una società industriale avanzata.* Perugina: Morlacchi.

Tagliaventi, M.T. (2004) 'Questioni aperte sul lavoro minorile in Europa alle soglie del 2000.' In Centro nazionale di documentazione e analisi per l'infanzia e l'adolescenza (ed) *Bambini e adolescenti che lavorano, Un panorama dall'Italia all'Europa.* Quaderni del Centro nazionale di documentazione e analisi per l'infanzia e l'adolescenza, Florence: Istituto degli Innocenti.

Thrall, C.A. (1978) 'Who Does What? Role Stereotyping, Children's Work and Continuity Between Generations in the Household Division of Labour.' *Human Relations 31* (March).

Tolfree, D. (1998) *Old Enough to Work, Old Enough to Have a Say: Approaches to Supporting Working Children.* Stockholm: Rädda Barnen.

TUC (1997) *Working Classes: A TUC Report on School Age Labour in England and Wales.* London: Trades Unions Congress.

US Department of Labor (2002) *The Department of Labor's 2001 Find on the Worst Forms of Child Labor.* Washington: US Department of Labor.

UNICEF (1997) *State of the World's Children.* New York: Oxford University Press.

UNICEF (1999) *Standing Up for Ourselves: A Study on the Concepts and Practices of Young People's Rights to Participation.* Manila: UNICEF.

UNICEF and EAPRO (2003) *Towards a Region Fit for Children: An Atlas for the Sixth East Asia and Pacific Ministerial Consultation.* Bangkok: Keen Publishing.

UNICEF Innocenti Centre (1999) *Innocenti Digest 5: Child Domestic Work.* Florence: UNICEF.

Van Bueren, G. (1998) 'Children's Rights: Balancing Traditional Values and Cultural Plurality.' In G. Douglas and L. Sebba (eds) *Children's Rights and Traditional Values.* Aldershot: Ashgate.

Van der Waal, C.S. (1996) 'Rural Children and Residential Instability in the Northern Province of South Africa.' *Social Dynamics 22,* 1, 31–53.

Vasant, F. (1991) 'Prevailing Conditions of Girl Child.' In J.A. Williams (ed) *Anatomy of Girl Child.* Madras: Asian Youth Centre.

Vollmer, G. (2005) *Unternehmen machen Schule. Mit Lernpartnerschaften zu wirtschaftsorientierten Bildungsregionen.* Bonn: Idee and Produkt Verlag.

Volpi, R. (2001) *I bambini inventati.* Florence: La Nuova Italia.

Voß, G.G. (1998) 'Die Entgrenzung von Arbeit und Arbeitskraft. Ein subjektorientierte Interpretation des Wandels der Arbeit.' *Mitteilungen aus der Arbeitsmarkt- und Berufsforschung 31,* 3, 473–487.

Waksler, F. (1986) 'Studying Children: Phenomenological Insights.' *Human Studies 8,* 171–182.

Wallerstein, E. (1999) 'La cultura como campo de batalla ideológico del sistema mundo moderno.' In S. Castro-Gómez, O. Guardiola-Rivera and C. Millán de Benavides (eds) *Pensar (en) los intersticios. Teoría y práctica de la crítica poscolonial.* Bogotá: Instituto Pensar, 163–187.

Waring, M. (1988) *Counting for Nothing: What Men Value and What Women Are Worth.* Wellington, New Zealand: Bridget Williams Books.

Warren, J.R., Lepore, P.C. and Mare, R.D. (2000) 'Employment During High School: Consequences for Students' Grades in Academic Courses.' *American Educational Research Journal 37,* 943–969.

Weber, M. (1922) *Economy and Society,* 3 volumes (G. Roth and C. Wittich (eds) 1978, Berkeley: University of California Press).

Webster's New World Dictionary, Second College Edition (1976) Cleveland, OH: William Collins, World Publishing Company.

White, B. (1996) 'Globalisation and the Child Labour Problem.' *Journal of International Development 8,* 6, 829–839.

White, B. and Indrasari, T. (1998) *Child Workers in Indonesia.* Bandung: Akatiga.

White, L.K. and Brinkerhoff, D.B. (1981) 'Children's Work in the Family: Its Significance and Meaning.' *Journal of Marriage and Family 43,* 789–798.

Wihstutz, A. (2004) 'Arbeit ein Lernfeld für Kinder.' In B. Hungerland and B. Overwien (eds) *Kompetenzentwicklung im Wandel.* Wiesbaden: Verlag für Sozialwissenschaften, 111–128.

Wintersberger, H. (2000) 'Kinder als ProduzentInnen und KonsumentInnen. Zur Wahrnehmung der ökonomischen Bedeutung von Kinderaktivitäten.' In H. Hengst and H. Zeiher (eds) *Die Arbeit der Kinder.* Weinheim and Munich: Juventa.

Wintersberger, H. (2005) 'Work, Welfare and Generational Order: Towards a Political Economy of Childhood.' In J. Qvortrup (ed) *Studies in Modern Childhood.* Basingstoke: Palgrave, 201–220.

Woodhead, M. (1997) 'Psychology and the Cultural Construction of Children's Needs.' In A. James and A. Prout (eds) *Constructing and Reconstructing Childhood.* London: Falmer, 63–84.

Woodhead, M. (1998) *Children's Perspectives on their Working Lives.* Stockholm: Radda Barnen.

Woodhead, M. (1999a) 'Combating Child Labour: Listen to What the Children Say.' *Childhood 6,* 1, 27–49.

Woodhead, M. (1999b) *Is There a Place for Work in Child Development?* Stockholm: Radda Barnen.

Woodhead, M. (1999c) 'Reconstructing Development Psychology – Some First Steps.' *Children and Society 13,* 3–19.

Woodhead, M. (2001) 'The Value of Work and School: A Study of Working Children's Perspectives.' In G.K. Lieten and B. White (eds) *Child Labour: Policy options.* Amsterdam: Aksant.

Woodhead, M. (2004) 'Psychosocial Impacts of Child Work: A Framework for Research, Monitoring and Intervention.' *International Journal of Children's Rights 12*, 4, 321–377.

Woodhead, M., Burr, R. and Montgomery, H.K. (2003) 'Adversities and Resilience.' In H.K. Montgomery, R. Burr and M. Woodhead (eds) *Changing Childhoods: Local and Global.* Chichester: John Wiley and Sons Ltd and The Open University.

Zalami, F.B, Reddy, N., Lynch, M.A. and Feinstein, C. (1998) *Forgotten on the Pyjama Trail.* Amsterdam: International Working Group on Child Labour.

Zeiher, H. (2004) 'Hausarbeit – ein soziales Lernfeld für Kinder.' In B. Hungerland and B. Overwien (eds) *Kompetenzentwicklung im Wandel.* Wiesbaden: Verlag für Sozialwissenschaften, 129–141.

Zelizer, V.A. (1994) *Pricing the Priceless Child. The Changing Social Value of Children.* Second edition. Princeton, NJ: Princeton University Press.

Zelizer, V.A. (2002) 'Kids and Commerce.' *Childhood 9*, 4, 375–396.

Zelizer, V.A. (2005) 'The Priceless Child Revisited.' In J. Qvortrup (ed) *Studies in Modern Childhood.* Basingstoke: Palgrave.

The Contributors

Michael Bourdillon, Professor Emeritus of the Department of Sociology, University of Zimbabwe, Harare, Zimbabwe.

Vinod Chandra, Assistant Professor of Sociology, Department of Humanities and Social Sciences, Indian Institute of Technology, Khargpur, India.

Hamidou Coly, Street worker and collaborator of the African Movement of Working Children and Youth, Senegal and Benin.

Sandy Hobbs, Senior Lecturer in Psychology, University of Paisley, Scotland, UK.

Beatrice Hungerland, Professor for Childhood Studies at the University of Applied Sciences Magdeburg-Stendal, Germany.

Antonella Invernizzi, Lecturer in Applied Social Studies, University of Wales, Swansea, UK.

Dieter Kirchhöfer, Associate Professor of Education at University of Potsdam, Germany.

Madeleine Leonard, Senior Lecturer in School of Sociology and Social Policy, Queen's University, Belfast, UK.

Deborah Levison, Associate Professor of Population Analysis and Policy, Hubert H. Humphrey Institute of Public Affairs, University of Minnesota, Minneapolis, USA.

Manfred Liebel, Professor Emeritus of Sociology at Technical University of Berlin and member of the International Academy at Free University of Berlin, Germany.

Jim McKechnie, Senior Lecturer in Psychology, University of Paisley, Scotland, UK.

Brian Milne, Consultant researcher and trainer in children's rights, Swansea, UK.

Phil Mizen, Lecturer at Department of Social Policy and Social Work, University of Warwick, Coventry, UK.

Virginia Morrow, Lecturer in Education at the Institute of Education and course organiser for a new Master in Childhood Studies, University of London, UK.

Jeylan T. Mortimer, Director of Life Course Center, NIMH-NRSA Training Program, Mental Health and Adjustment in the Life Course, University of Minnesota, Minneapolis, USA.

William E. Myers, International child rights expert, University of California, Davis, USA.

Zandra Pedraza-Gómez, Professor at Faculdad de Ciencias Sociales CESO, Departamento Antropologia, Universidad de los Andes, Colombia.

Dominique Pierre Plateau, Coordinator of Save The Children Sweden, Southeast Asia and Secretariat of the Regional Working Group on Child Labour Bangkok, Thailand.

Christopher Pole, Lecturer at Department of Sociology, University of Leicester, UK.

Nandana Reddy, Director of Development CWC, The Concerned for Working Children, Bangalore, India.

Martha Areli Ramírez Sánchez, Lecturer at Department of Social Sciences and Politics, Universidad Iberoamericana, Mexico City, Mexico.

Bernard Schlemmer, Director of Institute de Recherche pour le Développement, Bondy near Paris, France.

Maria Teresa Tagliaventi, Research Assistant at Istituto degli Innocenti, Centro nazionale di documentazione e analisi per l'infanzia e l'adolescenza, Florence, Italy.

Fabrizio Terenzio, Regional Coordinator of Youth Action Team, ENDA, Senegal.

Anne Wihstutz, Lecturer at Martin-Luther University of Halle-Wittenberg, Department of Education, Germany.

Martin Woodhead, Professor of Childhood Studies at Centre for Childhood, Development and Learning (CHDL), School of Education, The Open University, Milton Keynes, UK.

Subject Index

adult–child competition for work 221–2

adult work, child work as preparation for 99–107

affluent societies, children's work in 123–32

African Movement of Working Children and Youth (AMWCY) 179–85

'agency perspective' 68

American children 117–22

AMWCY *see* African Movement of Working Children and Youth

attitudes towards child work 9, 30, 99–100, 119, 167

autonomy gained by working children 148, 172–5

Balance Model 226–8
- limitations of 230
- relevance of 228–9

beauty competitions 124–5

begging of traveller children in Ireland 229

benefits and costs of work, Balance Model 227

Berlin project 168–75

Berlin Senate, one-euro jobs 48–50, 51–2

Bhima Sangha, Indian children's union 190, 191, 194, 195

Brazil
- ethnographic study of children 233
- and intermittent child work 18–19

Britain
- attitudes to working children 99–100
- changing perceptions of child employment 226

British children
- 'photo-diaries' of 233–44
- subjective experiences of employment 151–60
- work as preparation for adulthood 99–107

CAMP *see* Child Assistance for Mobilisation and Participation in Cambodia

child–parent relationships, inter-dependence of 68

Child Assistance for Mobilisation and Participation in Cambodia (CAMP) 201, 202

child begging by traveller children 229

Child Employment in Britain: A Social and Psychological Analysis (Hobbs and McKechnie) 226

child labour
- debates on 67–8
- difficulties in analysing 161–2
- effects of media coverage 228–9
- harmful effects of 31–8
- historical perspectives 43–4
- legislation 148–9
- necessity of in low-income families 26–7
- negative connotations of 11
- petition, Thailand 201
- studies 109–10
- trends in Southeast Asia 199
- vs. child work debate 226–7
- worst forms of, defining 32
- *see also* child work; employment

Child Labourers and Advocates for Social Participation (CLASP) 202

child rights 202
- African children 180–1
- Southeast Asia 199–200
- *see also* United Nations Convention on the Rights of the Child

child work
- for economic survival 40, 139–40, 143, 188, 198–9
- functions of 40–1
- as part of everyday life 31
- public attitudes towards 167
- *see also* child labour; employment

Child Workers in Asia (CWA) 197, 203

childhood
- agency perspective 68
- cultural perception of 23–30
- definitions of 28–9, 89–90, 207, 208

Children and Young Persons Act (1933) 99

children as active social agents 34, 68

children's citizenship 205–9

children's organisations 200–3, 219–23

children's participation
- adult role in 182–4
- in Africa 179–85
- and increased self-determination 136–7
- UNCRC articles 205–9

children's perspectives 19–20, 40, 75, 150, 188, 216–17

Author Index